EMOTIONAL AGILITY

EMOTIONAL AGILITY

Get Unstuck, Embrace Change,

and Thrive in Work and Life

SUSAN DAVID, PhD

AVERY | an imprint of Penguin Random House | New York

AVERY

an imprint of Penguin Random House LLC
375 Hudson Street
New York, New York 10014

Most Avery books are available at special quantity discounts for bulk purchase for sales promotions, premiums, fund-raising, and educational needs. Special books or book excerpts also can be created to fit specific needs. For details, write SpecialMarkets@penguinrandomhouse.com.

Library of Congress Cataloging-in-Publication Data
Names: David, Susan A., author.
Title: Emotional agility : get unstuck, embrace change, and thrive in work
    and life / Susan David, PhD.
Description: New York : Avery, [2016]
Identifiers: LCCN 2016009037 | ISBN 9781592409495 (hardback)
Subjects: LCSH: Adjustment (Psychology) | Emotions. | Resilience (Personality trait) |
    Self-realization. | BISAC: PSYCHOLOGY / Applied Psychology.
Classification: LCC BF335 .D38 2016 | DDC 155.2/4—dc23 LC record available at
    https://lccn.loc.gov/2016009037

Printed in the United States of America
        7   9   10   8

Book design by Gretchen Achilles

Names and identifying characteristics have been changed, and in some cases composites created, in order to protect the privacy of individuals involved.

To the love of my life, Anthony,

&

to my darlings, Noah and Sophie,

who know how to dance each and every day

► CONTENTS

EMOTIONAL
AGILITY

HOOKED

SHOWING UP

STEPPING OUT

WALKING YOUR WHY

MOVING ON

THRIVING

CHAPTER 1

RIGIDITY TO AGILITY

Years ago, in the *Downton Abbey* era, a well-regarded captain stood on the bridge of a British battleship, watching the sun set across the sea. As the story goes, the captain was about to head below for dinner when a lookout suddenly announced, "Light, sir. Dead ahead two miles."

The captain turned back toward the helm.

"Is it steady or moving?" he asked, these being the days before radar.

"Steady, Captain."

"Then signal that ship," the captain ordered gruffly. "Tell them, 'You are on a collision course. Alter course twenty degrees.'"

The answer, from the source of the light, came back moments later: "Advisable *you* change *your* course twenty degrees."

The captain was insulted. Not only was his authority being challenged, but also it was being done in front of a junior seaman!

"Send another message," he snarled. "'We are HMS *Defiant*, a thirty-five-thousand-ton battleship of the dreadnaught class. Change course twenty degrees.'"

"Brilliant, sir," came the reply. "I'm Seaman O'Reilly of the second class. Change *your* course immediately."

Apoplectic and red in the face, the captain shouted, "We are the flagship of Admiral Sir William Atkinson-Willes! CHANGE YOUR COURSE TWENTY DEGREES!"

There was a moment of silence before Seaman O'Reilly replied, "We are a lighthouse, sir."

As we travel through our lives, we humans have few ways of knowing which course to take or what lies ahead. We don't have lighthouses to keep us away from rocky relationships. We don't have lookouts on the bow or radar on the tower, watching for submerged threats that could sink our career plans. Instead, we have our emotions—sensations like fear, anxiety, joy, and exhilaration—a neurochemical system that evolved to help us navigate life's complex currents.

Emotions, from blinding rage to wide-eyed love, are the body's immediate physical responses to important signals from the outside world. When our senses pick up information—signs of danger, hints of romantic interest, cues that we're being accepted or excluded by our peers—we physically adjust to these incoming messages. Our hearts beat faster or slower, our muscles tighten or relax, our mental focus locks onto the threat or eases into the warmth of trusted companionship.

These physical "embodied" responses keep our inner state and our outward behavior in sync with the situation at hand, and can help us not only survive but also flourish. As with Seaman O'Reilly's lighthouse, our natural guidance system, which developed through evolutionary trial and error over millions of years, is a great deal more useful when we don't try to fight it.

But that's not always easy to do, because our emotions are not always reliable. In some situations, they help us cut through pretenses and posturing, working as a kind of internal radar to give us the most accurate and insightful read into what's really going on in a situation. Who hasn't experienced those gut feelings that tell us "This guy's lying," or "Something's bugging my friend even though she says she's fine"?

But in other situations, emotions dredge up old business, confusing our perception of what's happening in the moment with painful past experiences. These powerful sensations can take over completely, clouding our judgment and steering us right onto the rocks. In these cases, you might "lose it" and, say, throw a drink in the lying guy's face.

Of course, most adults rarely surrender control to their emotions with inappropriate public displays that take years to live down. More likely, you'll trip yourself up in a less theatrical but more insidious fashion. Many people, much of the time, operate on emotional autopilot, reacting to situations without true awareness or even real volition. Others are acutely aware that they expend too much energy trying to contain or suppress their emotions, treating them at best like unruly children and at worst as threats to their well-being. Still others feel their emotions are stopping them from achieving the kind of life they want, especially when it comes to those feelings that we find troublesome, such as anger, shame, and anxiety. In time, our responses to signals from the real world can become increasingly faint and unnatural, leading us off course instead of protecting our best interests.

I am a psychologist and an executive coach who has studied emotions and how we interact with them for more than two decades. When I ask some of my clients how long they've been trying to get in touch with, fix, or cope with their particularly challenging emotions or the situations that give rise to them, they'll often say five, or ten, or even twenty years. Sometimes the answer is, "Ever since I was a little kid."

To which the obvious response is, "So, would you say that what you're doing is working?"

With this book, my goal is to help you become more aware of your emotions, learn to accept and make peace with them, and then flourish by increasing your emotional agility. The tools and techniques I've brought together won't make you a perfect person who never says the wrong thing or never gets wracked by feelings of shame, guilt, anger, anxiety, or insecurity. Striving to be perfect—or always perfectly happy—will only set you up for frustration and failure. Instead, I hope to help you come to terms with even your most difficult emotions, enhance your ability to enjoy your relationships, achieve your goals, and live your life to the fullest.

But that's just the "emotional" part of emotional agility. The "agility" part addresses your thinking and behavior processes as well—those habits of mind and body that can also prevent you from flourishing, especially when, like the captain of the battleship *Defiant*, you react in the same old obstinate way to new or different situations.

Rigid reactions may come from buying into the old, self-defeating story you've told yourself a million times: "I am *such* a loser," or "I always say the wrong thing," or "I always fold when it's time to fight for what *I* deserve." Rigidity may come from the perfectly normal habit of taking mental shortcuts and accepting presumptions and rules of thumb that may have served you once—in childhood, in a first marriage, at an earlier point in your career—but aren't serving you now: "People can't be trusted." "I'm going to get hurt."

A growing body of research shows that emotional rigidity—getting hooked by thoughts, feelings, and behaviors that don't serve us—is associated with a range of psychological ills, including depression and anxiety. Meanwhile, emotional agility—being flexible with your thoughts and feelings so that you can respond optimally to everyday situations—is key to well-being and success.

And yet emotional agility is not about controlling your thoughts or forcing yourself into thinking more positively. Because research also shows that trying to get people to change their thoughts from, say, the negative ("I'm going to screw up this presentation") to the positive ("You'll see—I'll ace it"), usually doesn't work, and can actually be counterproductive.

Emotional agility *is* about loosening up, calming down, and living with more intention. It's about choosing how you'll respond to your emotional warning system. It supports the approach described by Viktor Frankl, the psychiatrist who survived a Nazi death camp and went on to write *Man's Search for Meaning,* on leading a more meaningful life, a life in which our human potential can be fulfilled: "Between stimulus and response there is a space," he wrote. "In that space is our power to choose our response. In our response lies our growth and our freedom."

By opening up that space between how you feel and what you do about those feelings, emotional agility has been shown to help people with any number of troubles: negative self-image, heartbreak, pain, anxiety, depression, procrastination, tough transitions, etc. But emotional agility isn't beneficial just for people struggling with personal difficulties. It also draws on diverse disciplines in psychology that explore the characteristics of successful, thriving people, including those like Frankl, who survived great hardship and went on to do great things.

Emotionally agile people are dynamic. They demonstrate flexibility in dealing with our fast-changing, complex world. They are able to tolerate high levels of stress and to endure setbacks, while remaining engaged, open, and receptive. They understand that life isn't always easy, but they continue to act according to their most cherished values and pursue their big, long-term goals. They still experience feelings of anger, sadness, and so on—who doesn't?—but they face these with curiosity, self-compassion, and acceptance. And rather than letting these feelings derail them, emotionally agile people effectively turn themselves—warts and all—toward their loftiest ambitions.

My interest in emotional agility and this kind of resilience began in apartheid-era South Africa, where I grew up. When I was a child during this violent period of forced segregation, most South Africans had a better chance of being raped than of learning how to read. Government forces removed people from their homes and tortured them; police shot citizens who were simply walking to church. Black and white children were kept separate across all domains of society—schools, restaurants, restrooms, movie theaters. And even though I am white and therefore didn't suffer in the deeply personal ways that black South Africans did, my friends and I were not immune to the social violence around us. A friend was gang-raped. My uncle was murdered. As a result, I became deeply interested at a young age in understanding how people deal (or don't deal) with the chaos and cruelty going on around them.

Then, when I was sixteen, my father, who was just forty-two at the time, was diagnosed with terminal cancer and told that he had only months to live. The experience was traumatic and isolating for me: I didn't have many adults to confide in, and none of my peers had gone through anything similar.

Thankfully, I had a very caring English teacher who encouraged her students to keep journals. We could write about anything we wanted, but we had to hand in our journals each afternoon so she could respond. At some point, I began journaling about my father's illness and, ultimately, his death. My teacher wrote sincere reflections on my entries and asked questions about how I was feeling. The journaling became a main source of support for me, and I soon recognized that it was helping me to describe, make sense of, and process my experiences. It didn't make me grieve any less, but it allowed me to move through the trauma. It also showed me the power of facing into, rather than trying to avoid, difficult emotions, and it put me on the career path I have followed ever since.

Fortunately, apartheid is a thing of the past in South Africa, and while modern life is hardly free of grief and horror, most of you reading this book live without the threat of institutionalized violence and oppression. And yet, even in the relative peace and prosperity of the United States, where I have resided for more than a decade, so many people still struggle to cope and live their best lives. Just about everyone I know is stressed-out and overloaded with the demands of career, family, health, finances, and a slew of other personal pressures along with large societal forces such as an unsettled economy, rapid cultural change, and a never-ending onslaught of disruptive technologies that distract us at every turn.

Meanwhile, multitasking—today's go-to response to being overworked and overwhelmed—brings us no relief. One recent study found the effect of multitasking on people's performance was actually comparable to driving drunk. Other studies show that low-grade daily stress (from the lunch box that needs to be filled at the last minute, the cell phone battery that dies right as you need to get on a critical conference call, the train that's always running late, the looming pile of bills) can prematurely age brain cells by as much as a decade.

My clients tell me all the time that the demands of modern life make them feel caught, hooked, and flipping like fish on a line. They want to do something bigger with their lives, like explore the world, get married, finish a project, succeed at work, start a business, get healthy, and develop strong relationships with their children and other family members. But their day-to-day actions don't move them anywhere closer to (and in fact are often completely misaligned with) these desires. Even as they struggle to find and embrace what's right for themselves, they are trapped not only by their actual circumstances but also by their own self-defeating thoughts and behaviors. Moreover, my clients who are parents worry incessantly about how this stress and overload affects their children. If there was ever a time to become more emotionally agile, it is now. When the ground is constantly shifting under us, we need to be nimble to keep from falling on our faces.

RIGID OR AGILE?

When I was five years old, I decided to run away from home. I was upset with my parents for some reason—I can't remember why—but I do remember thinking that running away was the only reasonable thing to do. I carefully packed a small bag, took a jar of peanut butter and some bread from the pantry, put on my prized red-and-white ladybug clogs, and set off in search of freedom.

We lived near a busy road in Johannesburg, and my parents had long drummed into me that I was never, under any circumstances, to cross the street by myself. As I approached the corner, I realized that continuing forward into the big wide world was not an option. Crossing the street was an absolute, unquestionable no-no. So I did what any obedient five-year-old runaway who was not allowed to step into the street would do: I walked around the block. Again, and again, and again. When I finally made it home after my oh-so-dramatic breakaway adventure, I had been circling the same block, walking past my own front gate, for hours.

We all do this in one way or another. We walk (or run) around the blocks of our lives over and over, obeying rules that are written, implied, or simply imagined, getting hooked by ways of being and doing that don't serve us. I often say that we act like wind-up toys, repeatedly bumping into the same walls, never realizing there may be an open door just to our left or our right.

Even when we acknowledge that we're hooked and could use some help, the people we turn to—family, friends, kindly bosses, therapists—aren't always helpful. They have their own issues, limitations, and preoccupations.

Meanwhile, our consumer culture promotes the idea that we can control and fix most of the things bothering us, and that we should toss or replace the things we can't: Unhappy in a relationship? Find another. Not productive enough? There's an app for that. When we don't like what's going on in our inner world, we apply the same mindset. We go shopping, we get a new therapist, or we resolve to fix our own unhappiness and dissatisfaction and simply "think positive."

Unfortunately, none of this works very well. Trying to correct troubling thoughts and feelings leads us to obsess unproductively on them. Trying to smother them can lead to a range of ills from busywork to any number of self-soothing addictions. And trying to change them from negative to positive is an almost surefire way to feel worse.

Many people turn to self-help books or courses to deal with their emotions, but a lot of these programs get self-help completely wrong.

Those that tout positive thinking are particularly off base. Trying to impose happy thoughts is extremely difficult, if not impossible, because few people can just turn off negative thoughts and replace them with more pleasant ones. Also, this advice fails to consider an essential truth: Your so-called negative emotions are often actually working in your favor.

In fact, negativity is normal. This is a fundamental fact. We are wired to feel negative at times. It's simply a part of the human condition. Too much stress on being positive is just one more way our culture figuratively overmedicates the normal fluctuations of our emotions, just the way society often literally overmedicates rambunctious children and women with mood swings.

Over the past twenty years of consulting, coaching, and research, I've tested and refined the principles of emotional agility to help numerous clients achieve big things in their lives. These clients have included mothers feeling trapped in corners, struggling to keep things together while juggling family and work; United Nations ambassadors battling to bring immunization to children in hostile countries; leaders of complex multinational corporations; and people who simply feel that life has more to offer.

Not long ago I published some of my findings from this work in an article that appeared in *Harvard Business Review*. In it, I described how almost every one of my clients—not to mention I myself—tend to get hooked by rigid, negative patterns. I then laid out a model for developing greater emotional agility to unhook from these patterns and make successful, lasting changes. The article stayed on the magazine's Most Popular list for months and within a short time was downloaded by nearly a quarter of a million people—the same number as *HBR*'s total print circulation. It was heralded by *HBR* as a "Management Idea of the Year" and was picked up by numerous publications, including the *Wall Street Journal, Forbes,* and *Fast Company.* Editors described emotional agility as the "next emotional intelligence," a big idea that changes the way our society thinks about emotions. I bring this up not to toot my own horn, but because the reaction to this article made me realize the idea had struck a nerve. Millions of people, it seems, are searching for a better path.

This book contains a greatly expanded and amplified version of the research and advice I offered in the *HBR* article. But before we get into the nitty-gritty, let me give you a survey of the big picture so that you can see where we're going.

Emotional agility is a process that allows you to be in the moment, changing or maintaining your behaviors to live in ways that align with your intentions and values. The process isn't about ignoring difficult emotions and thoughts. It's about holding those emotions and thoughts loosely, facing them courageously and compassionately, and then moving past them to make big things happen in your life.

The process of gaining emotional agility unfolds in four essential movements:

SHOWING UP

Woody Allen once said that 80 percent of success is simply showing up. In the context of this book, "showing up" means facing into your thoughts, emotions, and behaviors willingly, with curiosity and kindness. Some of these thoughts and emotions are valid and appropriate to the moment. Others are old bits stuck in your psyche like that Beyoncé song you've been trying to get out of your head for weeks.

In either case, whether they are accurate reflections of reality or harmful distortions, these thoughts and emotions are a part of who we are, and we can learn to work with them and move on.

STEPPING OUT

The next element, after facing into your thoughts and emotions, is detaching from and observing them to see them for what they are—just thoughts, just emotions. By doing this we create Frankl's open, nonjudgmental space between our feelings and how we respond to them. We can also identify difficult feelings as we're experiencing them and find more appropriate ways of reacting. Detached observation keeps our transient mental experiences from controlling us.

The broader view we gain by stepping out means learning to see yourself as the chessboard, filled with possibilities, rather than as any one piece on the board, confined to certain preordained moves.

WALKING YOUR WHY

After you've uncluttered and calmed your mental processes and then created the space we need between the thoughts and the thinker, you can begin to focus more on what we're really all about: our core values, our most important goals. Recognizing, accepting, and then distancing ourselves from the scary, or painful, or disruptive emotional stuff gives us the ability to engage more of the "take the long view" part of us, which integrates thinking and feeling with long-term values and aspirations, and can help us find new and better ways of getting there.

You make thousands of decisions every day. Should you go to the gym after work or skip it in favor of happy hour? Should you take the call from the friend who hurt your feelings or send him to voice mail? I call these small decision moments *choice points*. Your core values provide the compass that keeps you moving in the right direction.

MOVING ON

THE TINY TWEAKS PRINCIPLE

Traditional self-help tends to see change in terms of lofty goals and total transformation, but research actually supports the opposite view: that small, deliberate tweaks infused with your values can make a huge difference in your life. This is especially true when we tweak the routine and habitual parts of life, which, through daily repetition, then afford tremendous leverage for change.

THE TEETER-TOTTER PRINCIPLE

A world-class gymnast makes difficult moves look effortless through her agility and the well-developed muscles of her torso—her core. When something throws her off-balance, her core helps her correct. But to compete at the highest level, she has to keep pushing beyond her comfort zone to attempt increasingly difficult moves. We, too, need to find the perfect balance between challenge and competence so we're neither complacent nor overwhelmed but are instead excited, enthusiastic, and invigorated by challenges.

The businesswoman Sarah Blakely, the founder of Spanx shapewear and at one time the world's youngest self-made female billionaire, describes how at the dinner table each evening her father would say, "So, tell me how you failed today." The question wasn't designed to demoralize her. Instead, her father meant to encourage his children to push the limits; it was okay—even admirable—to stumble when trying something new and difficult.

The ultimate goal of emotional agility is to keep a sense of challenge and growth alive and well throughout your life.

I hope this book serves as a road map for real behavioral change—a new way of acting that will help you live the life you want and help you to reincorporate your most troubling feelings as a source of energy, creativity, and insight.

Let's get started.

INTERNAL CHATTERBOX + TECHNICOLOR THOUGHT BLENDING + EMOTIONAL PUNCH = **HOOKED**

CHAPTER 2

HOOKED

A Hollywood script lives or dies by its "hook," the simple premise that captures the audience's interest, sets the story in motion, and drives the action forward. A hook necessarily involves conflict, and seeing how the conflict gets resolved is why, once we're hooked into a movie, we stay engaged and keep watching.

As a psychologist, I find that the books and movies that hook me most are the ones in which the conflict—or at least a big part of it—exists within the hero's own nature. A struggling actor doesn't understand women until, desperate for a job, he pretends to be a woman in real life (*Tootsie*). An ingénue fears commitment (*Runaway Bride*). Or, in one of the truly great hooks of all time—a skilled assassin gets bonked on the head, wakes up in the middle of a guns-blazing intrigue, and has no idea who he is or what he wants (*The Bourne Identity*).

We may not drive convertibles past palm trees or take meetings with movie stars, but each of us, in our own way, is a Hollywood screenwriter. That's because every minute of every day we're writing the scripts that get screened at the Cineplex inside our heads. Only in our own life stories, getting hooked doesn't imply the excitement of being on the edge of your seat. It means being caught by a self-defeating emotion, thought, or behavior.

The human mind is a meaning-making machine, and a big part of being human involves laboring to make sense of the billions of bits of sensory information bombarding us every day. Our way of making sense is to organize all the sights and sounds and experiences and relationships swirling around us into a cohesive narrative: *This is me, Susan, waking up. I am in a bed. The small mammal jumping on me is my son, Noah. I used to live in Johannesburg, but now I live in Massachusetts. I have to get up today and prepare for a meeting. That's what I do. I'm a psychologist, and I meet with people to try to help them.*

The narratives serve a purpose: We tell ourselves these stories to organize our experiences and keep ourselves sane.

The trouble is, we all get things wrong. People without a realistically consistent story, or a story completely divorced from reality, may be labeled "psychotic." But while most of us may never hear voices or have delusions of grandeur, in scripting our own stories we all take liberties with the truth. Sometimes we don't even realize we're doing it.

We then accept these persuasive self-accounts without question, as if they were the truth, the whole truth, and nothing but the truth. These are stories that, regardless of their veracity, may have been scribbled on our mental chalkboards in third grade, or even before we could walk or talk. We crawl into these fables and let a sentence or a paragraph, which may have originated thirty or forty years ago and never been objectively tested and verified, represent the totality of our lives. There are about as many of these confused scenarios as there are people:

"My parents got divorced right after I came along, so I'm responsible for my mother's alcoholism."

"I was the introvert in a family of social butterflies, which is why nobody loves me."

Ad infinitum.

We create these stories every day on a smaller scale too. I know I've done it. Here's an example: A few years ago, a colleague casually informed me in a voice mail that he was going to borrow—another word would be "steal"—a concept of mine to use as the title of his forthcoming book. He hoped I "wouldn't mind," he said, not asking permission but calmly stating a fact.

Hello—of course I minded! He was using *my* concept, one I'd planned to use myself. I cursed the day I'd mentioned it to him in an unguarded moment at a conference. But what could I do? Professionals can't go screaming at each other.

I buried my anger and did what most anyone would do: I called my spouse to vent. But my husband, Anthony, is a physician, and upon answering the phone he said, "Suzy, I can't talk. I have a patient in the operating room, waiting for an emergency procedure." So here I was, "wronged" for a second time, and in this case by my own husband!

The logic of the situation—saving his patient's life, in fact, mattered more than talking to me right then—did nothing to calm my rising anger. How could my husband treat me this way—the one time I really need him? That thought quickly morphed into "He's never really there for me." My anger swelled, as did my plan to ignore his callback when it came. I was hooked.

That's right. Instead of having a conversation with my colleague in which I expressed calmly, but in no uncertain terms, my disapproval of his actions and tried to figure out a satisfactory resolution,

I spent two days in a snit, giving my guiltless husband the silent treatment because he was "never there for me"!

Brilliant, yes?

It isn't just that these dubious, not-always-accurate stories we tell ourselves leave us conflicted or waste our time or result in some chilly days around the house. The bigger issue is the conflict between the world these stories describe and the world we want to live in, the world where we could truly thrive.

During the average day, most of us speak around sixteen thousand words. But our thoughts—our internal voices—produce thousands more. This voice of consciousness is a silent but tireless chatterbox, secretly barraging us with observations, comments, and analyses without pause. Moreover, this ceaseless voice is what literature professors call an *unreliable narrator*—think Humbert Humbert in *Lolita,* or Amy Dunne in *Gone Girl.* As with these two characters, whose accounts of events can't be entirely trusted, our own internal narrator may be biased, confused, or even engaged in willful self-justification or deception. Even worse, it will *not shut up.* You may be able to stop yourself from sharing every thought that pops into your head, but stopping yourself from having those thoughts in the first place? Good luck.

While we often accept the statements bubbling up from within this river of incessant chatter as being factual, most are actually a complex mixture of evaluations and judgments, intensified by our emotions. Some of these thoughts are positive and helpful; others are negative and unhelpful. In either case, our inner voice is rarely neutral or dispassionate.

For example, right now I'm sitting at my desk, writing this book, and progressing rather slowly. "I'm sitting at my desk." That's a simple thought grounded in fact. So is "I'm writing a book." So is "I'm a slow writer."

Okay. So far, so good. But from here, it's all too easy for my factual observations to slip over into the realm of opinion. The story I tell myself could easily develop a hook, leaving me hung up on a dodgy, unexamined idea, flailing like a bass that's about to be some fisherman's dinner.

"I'm *too* slow at writing" is the self-critical evaluation that can all too quickly follow "I'm a slow writer." Another, "I'm slower than most other writers," turns the fact-based thought into a comparison. "I'm falling behind" adds an element of anxiety. And then the damning judgment to sum it all up: "I've been kidding myself about how much I can write before this deadline. Why can't I be honest with myself? I'm done for." Which is a long way from my fact-based starting point: I am sitting at my desk, slowly writing a book.

To experience just how effortlessly people can slide from fact to opinion to judgment and anxiety, try this brain-bouncing exercise. Think about each of these prompts, one at a time:

Your cell phone
Your house
Your job
Your in-laws
Your waistline

When you free-associate, some of your thoughts may be factual. "I had dinner with my in-laws last week," or "I have a project due on Monday." But then see how quickly those pesky opinions, evaluations, comparisons, and worries enter in:

My cell phone . . . needs an upgrade.
My house . . . is always a mess.
My job . . . is Stress Central.

My in-laws . . . spoil the kids.

My waistline . . . gotta get back on that diet.

In workshops, I sometimes ask people to anonymously list difficult situations and the thoughts and emotions that tag along with them. Here are some unhelpful "self stories" that one group of high-flying executives recently came up with and the situations that inspired them:

Someone else succeeds: "I'm not good enough. Why wasn't it me?"

Working full-time: "My life's a failure. Everything around me is a mess, and my family resents me for missing out on all of the fun we could be having together."

Performing a difficult task: "Why the hell is this taking so long? If I had any talent, I'd be able to do it faster."

A missed promotion: "I'm an idiot, and a wuss. I let myself get cheated."

Being asked to do something new: "I'm terrified. This is never going to work."

A social engagement: "I'm going to freeze up and everyone's going to think I was raised in a cave."

Receiving negative feedback: "I'm going to get fired."

Meeting up with old friends: "I'm a loser. They're all living way more exciting lives than I am. And making more money!"

Trying to lose weight: "I'm a disgusting pig. I should just give up. Everyone in the room looks better than me."

And here's a clue to why this progression from neutral thought to fish on a line is so easy:

Mary had a little _____.

"Lamb," right? Not too tough. The word popped into your head automatically.

What makes getting hooked almost inevitable is that so many of our responses are just as reflexive.

The hook is usually a situation you encounter in your day-to-day life. It might be a tough conversation with your boss, an interaction with a relative that you've been dreading, an upcoming presentation, a discussion with your significant other about money, a child's disappointing report card, or maybe just ordinary rush-hour traffic.

Then there is your autopilot response to that situation. You might say something sarcastic, or shut down and avoid your feelings, or procrastinate, or walk away, or brood, or pitch a screaming fit.

When you automatically respond in whatever unhelpful way you do, you're hooked. The result is just as predictable as the word "lamb" that popped into your head after "Mary had a little . . ." The bait hook is dangling right there in front of you, and you snap at it without a moment's hesitation.

Getting yourself hooked begins when you accept thoughts as facts.

I'm no good at this. I always screw it up.

Often, you then start avoiding situations that evoke those thoughts.

I'm not even going to try.

Or you may endlessly replay the thought.

The last time I tried it was so humiliating.

Sometimes, perhaps following the well-meaning advice of a friend or a family member, you attempt to will these thoughts away.

I shouldn't have thoughts like this. It's counterproductive.

Or, soldiering on, you force yourself to do what you dread, even when it's the hook itself, not anything you genuinely value, that's driving the action.

I've got to try. I've got to learn to like this, even if it kills me.

All this internal chatter is not only misleading; it's exhausting.

It's sapping important mental resources you could put to much better use.

Adding to the "hooking" power of our thoughts is the fact that so many of our mental habits are actually hardwired to merge with our emotions and produce a turbocharged response.

Suppose for a moment you're taking a class to learn a new intergalactic language. In that language one of the figures above is called "bouba," and the other is called "kiki." On a pop quiz, the teacher asks which is which. Chances are you'd pick the shape on the left as "kiki," and the one on the right as "bouba."

The creators of this experiment, V. S. Ramachandran and Edward Hubbard, found that 98 percent of people saw it that way. Even two-year-olds who hadn't yet learned language patterns and didn't speak English made the same choice. From Ramachandran's campus at the University of California, San Diego, to the stone walls of Jerusalem, to the isolated shores of Swahili-speaking Lake Tanganyika in central Africa, this is a universal preference woven into the brain: Regardless of language, culture, or alphabet, within seconds of being shown the nonsense symbols, the human hearing centers identify the word "kiki" as having a sharp inflection, and the word "bouba" as being softer and more rounded.

This association of a certain shape with a certain sound is thought to take place in part because the angular gyrus, the brain region in which this judgment occurs, sits at the crossroads of our touch, hearing, and vision centers. It engages in sensory blending, integrating sounds, feelings, images, symbols, and gestures, and might even account for our ability to think in metaphors. "That's a loud shirt," we say, or "That's sharp cheese," even though the tacky Hawaiian shirt makes no noise and the hunk of cheddar you're enjoying won't slice off your finger anytime soon. (Patients with damage to the angular gyrus might be able to speak perfect English but not to grasp metaphors. This is also true of lower primates, who have an angular gyrus about one-eighth the size of ours.)

Our capacity for sensory blending doesn't just help poets and writers come up with engaging turns of phrase. It also, unfortunately, sets up all of us to get and stay hooked. That's because we don't experience our thoughts with a flat, Mr. Spock–like neutrality: "I just had the thought that I am being undermined by a rival. How interesting."

Instead, thoughts come fully accessorized with visual images, symbols, idiosyncratic interpretations, judgments, inferences, abstractions, and actions. This gives our mental life a vibrant intensity, but it can also take away our objectivity and leave us at the mercy of intrusive ideas—whether they're true or not, and whether they are helpful or not.

In court, judges tend to allow juries to see autopsy photos but rarely crime scene photos. That's because chaotic, violent, bloody images pack an emotional wallop that judges often fear will overwhelm the jury's hoped-for logical, neutral deliberations. Autopsy photos are taken in bright light on a steel table—all very clinical. But crime scene photos can include little details that humanize the victim—her child's picture on the blood-splattered dresser, the untied shoelace of his well-worn running shoes—or that dramatize the victim's suffering. Such emotionally evocative images could "impassion" jurors and push them toward a retaliatory mindset: "The victim was just like me. The defendant has a pretty good alibi, but somebody has to pay for this outrage!"

The vivid, Technicolor nature of our cognitive processing, blended with and ramped up by emotion, is an evolutionary adaptation that served us well when snakes and lions and hostile neighboring tribes were out to get us. Under threat from an enemy or a predator, your average hunter-gatherer couldn't afford to waste time with Spock-like abstraction—"I am under threat. How should I evaluate my options?"

The kind of responses our ancient ancestors needed to stay alive required that they feel danger viscerally, grasping the meaning in a way that led automatically to a predictable response driven by the endocrine system's fuel-injection process: the freeze-or-fight-or-flight response.

When I was in my twenties and living with my mother for a year, a friend and her boyfriend were raped and beaten in their apartment by a gang of criminals who broke into their home and lay in wait for them to return from a dinner date. Horrific crimes like this were, as I've mentioned, all too common in Johannesburg. After it happened, I was on edge more than ever.

One night I got completely lost driving home from someplace and ended up in a very dangerous neighborhood. As I made my way home, I started to worry that I was being followed. But by the time I got home, I couldn't see anyone. I went indoors, planning to return to my car to collect my luggage. About thirty minutes later, as I emerged from the house and walked toward the car, things seemed safe and fine. Then I heard a guttural sound. I looked up. Two men were coming toward me, guns in hands. My emotions were so heightened by my recent hours of fear, coupled with the memory of my friends' attack, that without a second's delay I started screaming. Loud, colorful, and aggressive profanities tumbled out of my mouth (I'm not a prude, but believe me, they were way too vile to repeat here). The men, caught off guard, stared at me in their own fright. (I can only imagine what was going through their minds, seeing this crazy woman on the loose!) Then they scrambled into the bushes where they'd come from and disappeared down the road. To this day I am grateful to my brain's sensory blending: See, remember, feel, hear, and react—all at once.

This incredible blending facility, however, also predisposes us to getting hooked. In today's world, thankfully, most of our problems, even most of our threats, are vague and long-term: It isn't *"Aaaah! A snake!"* It's "Is my job secure?" or "Am I going to hit retirement with enough savings set aside?" or "Is my daughter so hung up on that no-good Petersen kid that her grades are starting to slip?" But because of the emotions associated, our thoughts, even the mildest "slice of life" scenarios projected in our heads—a couple getting older, a high school girl in love—become triggers that can evoke an autopilot response of high anxiety, dread, and the feeling of immediate threat.

Here's how a random thought can turn into a persistent hook:
Internal Chatterbox + Technicolor Thought
Blending + Emotional Punch = Hooked

1. It starts when we listen to our **Internal Chatterbox** . . .
   I haven't spent any mother-daughter time with Jane for a few days. I'm just not around enough. I need to be with her more.

But how do I manage that with everything I've got going on at work? I just can't keep up. Michelle Smith seems to have the time to create special moments with *her* daughter. She's such a good mother. She really has her priorities straight. What's wrong with me? I've got it all wrong.

2. Thanks to **Technicolor Thought Blending,** the chatter mixes with memories, visual images, and symbols . . .

   Just look at my little girl. She's growing up so fast. I can almost smell the snack my mother used to make for me when I got home from school. I should bake treats for Jane. I can already see her, graduated from high school and leaving home—with that no-good Ricky Petersen!—and hating me. Why is this client emailing me about work on a Saturday? I'm going to give that jerk a piece of my mind right now. And NO, JANE. I CAN'T TAKE YOU SHOPPING. WHAT PART OF "I HAVE TO WORK" DO YOU NOT UNDERSTAND?

3. Add the **Emotional Punch** . . .

   I can't believe I just snapped like that at my beloved child. I feel so guilty. I'm going to die alone because my daughter hates me. I used to love my job, but now I hate it; it's robbing me of my family time. I'm a rotten, miserable failure. My life is a waste.

An emotional punch is just one of the many "special effects" that give such enormous power to the scripts we write to make sense of our lives, even when the plot is pure fiction. The poet John Milton summed it up in the seventeenth century: "The mind is its own place, and in itself can make a heaven of hell, a hell of heaven." And yet, in the world of punchy aphorisms there's also "If wishes were wings, then pigs would fly." Meaning that, yes, the mind creates its own universe; but no, we can't solve our problems through affirmations and positive thinking alone. And the fact is, New Agey solutions that put smiley-face stickers over our problems can make those problems worse. So the question for us going forward is: Who's in charge—the thinker or the thought?

Then again, part of our problem might be simply the way our thoughts are processed.

THINKING FAST AND SLOW

In 1929, the Belgian painter René Magritte poked the art world in the eye with a canvas called *The Treachery of Images*. You've probably seen it: A tobacco pipe floats above the legend *Cici n'est pas une pipe.* Translation: "This is not a pipe."

At first you might think the artist was simply being, well, a surrealist, provoking his audience with the absurd. But in fact his assessment is an important cautionary tale about how we process information and how the way our minds race ahead and cut corners can sometimes cause us to jump to false conclusions, or get stuck in harmful cognitive ruts.

What we're looking at when we observe *The Treachery of Images* is pigmented oil brushed onto canvas in a way that makes us think of a pipe. But Magritte is absolutely right: It's *not* a pipe. It's a two-dimensional representation of our idea of a pipe. And the only way you could smoke it would be to rip up the canvas and stick the pieces into a real pipe. In his own way, Magritte was saying that the image is not the thing, or, as the philosopher Alfred Korzybski put it, "The map is not the territory."

Humans love to create mental categories and then fit objects, experiences, and even people into them. If something doesn't fit in a category, it goes into the category of "things that don't fit." Categories can be useful, such as when you classify stocks as high risk or low risk, which makes it easier to pick investments that might suit your financial objectives.

But when we become too comfortable with—and habituated to—rigid, preexisting categories, we're using what psychologists term *premature cognitive commitment,* which is a habitual, inflexible response to ideas, things, and people, even ourselves. These quick and easy categories, and the snap judgments they lead to, are often called *heuristics,* but "rules of thumb" works just as well. Heuristics range from reasonable prohibitions—"I don't eat mezes from outdoor cafés in Istanbul in August"—to pernicious blinders like racial or class prejudice and to self-limiting fun stealers like "I don't dance."

As with the tendency of our thoughts to blend with our emotions, the tendency to fit what we see into boxes for easy sorting—and then to make quick, gut decisions about them—evolved for a reason. Life is just a hell of a lot easier when you don't have to analyze *every* choice (as at those trendy restaurants where the waiter keeps asking you ever more exquisitely detailed questions about your preferences until you want to scream, "Just bring me the damn salad! Dump mayonnaise on it! I don't care!"). We would all be stuck in paralysis through analysis without our own personal rules of thumb, which allow us to get through the routine stuff without expending a lot of mental energy.

Heuristics kick in the moment we meet someone and immediately begin to determine whether we want to get to know her better or steer clear. And as it turns out, we are very good at instinctively sizing up people. The evaluations we make in these scant few seconds, based on very little evidence, are usually pretty accurate. And, as studies have shown, a subject's first impressions of an unknown person often prove consistent with personality assessments made by the person's friends and family.

Millennia ago, being able to size up strangers on the spot helped humans form bonds of trust that reached beyond blood relatives. That, in turn, led to the development of villages and towns and societies (i.e., civilization).

If human beings lacked the predictive ability of heuristics ("strong handshake, nice smile—seems like a nice guy") and needed to consciously process every facial expression, conversation, and piece of information anew, we'd have no time for actually living life.

Unfortunately, though, our snap impressions can be wrong. They can be based on unfair and inaccurate stereotypes or manipulated by con artists. And once established, they can be tough to reconsider and change. When we make quick judgments, we often overvalue the information that is readily available and undervalue subtleties that might take a while to dig out.

In *Thinking Fast and Slow,* the psychologist Daniel Kahneman described the human mind as operating in two basic modes of thought. *System 1* thoughts are typically fast, automatic, effortless, associative, and implicit, which means they are not available to immediate introspection. They often carry a lot of emotional weight and are ruled by habit and, as a result, are very good at getting us hooked.

System 2 thoughts are slower and more deliberative. They require much more effort and a deeper level of attention. They are also more flexible and amenable to rules that we consciously establish. It is these System 2 operations that allow us to create the space between stimulus and response that Victor Frankl spoke of, the space that provides for the full expression of our humanity and allows us to thrive.

I remember once watching Bill O'Reilly talking with David

Letterman. The conservative pundit posed some question and then began to badger the comedian, saying, "It's an easy question!"

Letterman responded, "It's not easy for me because I'm thoughtful."

Dave got a big round of applause.

As mentioned, quick, intuitive System 1 thinking can sometimes be powerful and accurate. Dr. Gerd Gigerenzer, the director of the Max Planck Institute for Human Development, in Berlin, and one of the scientists whose work was discussed in Malcolm Gladwell's bestseller *Blink,* is a social psychologist known for his work on intuitive thinking. He describes these kinds of gut responses as something of a mystery, even to the person feeling them. All we know is that they rely on simple cues in the environment, while filtering out other information that our conditioning or life experience (or obliviousness or habit) tells us is not necessary.

Some intuitive responses arise from practice and skill. There's the chess master who can glance at someone else's game in progress and rattle off the next dozen moves, or the coronary care nurse who can spot a heart attack a mile away, or the firefighter who knows when it's time to evacuate—now!

But System 1 gut responses have a dark side. When heuristics begin to dominate the way we process information and behave, we wind up applying our rules of thumb in inappropriate ways, which makes us less able to detect unusual distinctions or new opportunities. We lack agility.

The average moviegoer, immersed in watching a film, can miss details and errors in story or scene continuity, such as when an actor is holding a coffee cup in a close-up but not in a wide shot two seconds later. In the lab, researchers have had participants watch short videos that contain deliberate continuity errors. During a filmed scene of conversation in which the camera switches back and forth from one speaker to the other, for example, one of the character's clothing keeps changing. Or a character stands up to answer the phone, the camera angle changes, and in the next shot the character is being played by an entirely different actor. On average, two-thirds of participants watching don't notice these errors, even when the main character is the one who's replaced.

The same researchers behind those experiments did another study in which an experimenter stopped individual students on a campus to ask directions. While each student and the researcher conversed, two other members of the research team walked between them carrying a wooden door. In a sleight-of-hand move worthy of Penn and Teller, the team members used the opportunity to switch places, so that when the visual barrier (the door) was removed, the original seeker of directions had been replaced by a different person. Astoundingly, half the students in the experiment failed to notice the switch and wrapped up the conversation as if nothing had happened.

A tragic, real-life example of this phenomenon took place in Boston, in the predawn hours of a January day in 1995, as a police officer named Kenny Conley was pursuing a shooting suspect up and over a chain-link fence. Officer Conley was so focused on catching the bad guy that he failed to notice something else happening at the scene: Other cops were savagely beating another man they assumed was a suspect—but who was, in fact, an undercover officer. Later, in court, Conley testified that he ran right past the place where the brutal assault of his colleague took place but, with his tunnel vision directed on his own task, he didn't even notice it.

The lesson: Once our minds slip into default mode, it takes a great deal of flexibility to override this state. This is why specialists are often the last ones to notice commonsense solutions to simple problems, a limitation economist Thorstein Veblen called the "trained incapacity" of experts. Inflated confidence leads old hands to ignore contextual information, and the more familiar an expert is with a particular kind of problem, the more likely he is to pull a prefabricated solution out of his memory bank rather than respond to the specific case at hand.

In another study, psychology professionals were asked to watch an interview conducted with a person they were told was either a job applicant or a psychiatric patient. The clinicians were instructed to apply their expertise and evaluate the interviewee. When they believed the interviewee was applying for a job, the professionals characterized him as normal and fairly well adjusted; when told that he was a patient, however, they described this same person as distressed and impaired. Instead of paying close attention to the actual person in front of them, the clinicians relied on the superficial cues that, through longtime experience, allowed them to make diagnoses "in their sleep." Truth be told, they might as well have been asleep.

In general, experts—or people who are highly regarded in any field—are often hooked on their own self-importance. But sometimes status or accomplishment in one realm has no relevance in another. A group of stockbrokers I once met at a conference all agreed surgeons were notoriously bad investors because they would listen to investment advice only from other surgeons. (The irony is that the stockbrokers, in their consensus of the surgeons' poor investment prowess, were also using a very blunt rule of thumb.) And CEOs on corporate team-building retreats out in the wild often assume that they should be in charge, failing to consider that the young guy just out of the army who works in the mail room might be better equipped to lead an exercise that involves climbing rocks and dangling from ropes.

People who are hooked into a particular way of thinking or behaving are not really paying attention to the world as it is. They are insensitive to context—whatever the context. Rather, they're seeing the world as they've organized it into categories that may or may not have any bearing on the situation at hand.

People frequently die in fires or crash landings because they try to escape through the same door they used when they entered. In their panic, they rely on an established pattern instead of thinking of another way out. In the same manner, our suffering, our disengagement, our relationship challenges, and our other life difficulties are almost never solved by thinking in the same old, automatic way. Being emotionally agile involves being sensitive to context and responding to the world as it is right now.

We certainly don't want to put an end to the thoughts and emotions coursing through us, because that would mean the end of *us.* But once again, the question is, "Who's in charge—the thinker or the thought?" Are we managing our own lives according to our own values and what is important to us, or are we simply being carried along by the tide?

When we are not in charge of our own lives, when we're not acting according to our own thoughtful volition and with the full range of options that a perceptive intelligence can conjure, that's when we get hooked.

THE FOUR MOST COMMON HOOKS

HOOK #1: THOUGHT-BLAMING

"I thought I'd embarrass myself, so I didn't mingle at the party."

"I thought she was being aloof, so I stopped sharing information on the project."

"I thought he was going to start in on our finances, so I walked out of the room."

"I thought I would sound stupid, so I didn't say it."

"I thought she should make the first move, so I didn't call."

In each of these examples, the speaker blames his or her thoughts for his or her actions—or inactions. When you start thought-blaming, there's not enough space between stimulus and response, in Frankl's terms, for you to exercise real choice. Thoughts in isolation do not cause behavior. Old stories don't cause behavior. We cause our behavior.

HOOK #2: MONKEY-MINDEDNESS

"Monkey mind" is a term from meditation used to describe that incessant internal chatterbox that can leap from one topic to the next like a monkey swinging from tree to tree. Maybe you have a fight with your significant other (though it could just as easily be your parent, child, friend, or coworker), and he stomps out the house. As you ride the train to the office, you find your mind buzzing: "Tonight I'm going to tell him just how frustrated I feel when he criticizes my parents." This anticipatory thought turns into a mock conversation in your head as you plan for the interaction. He might say something else nasty about your parents, so you'll respond with a comment about his loser brother. You forecast what you think he might say and plan your responses. By the time you get to work, you're completely worn out from the intense argument you've had—inside your own head.

When we're in monkey-mind mode, it's easy to start "awfulizing"— imagining worst-case scenarios or making too much of a minor problem. It's a huge sap of our energy and a complete waste of time. Even more than that, when you're spinning these imaginary dramas in your head, you aren't living in the moment. You're not noticing the flowers in the park or the interesting faces on the train. And you're not giving your brain the neutral space it needs for creative solutions—maybe even the solution to whatever it was you were fighting about in the first place.

Monkey mind is obsessed with the push of the past ("I just can't forgive what he did") and the pull of the future ("I can't wait to quit and give my manager a piece of my mind"). It's also often filled with bossy, judgmental inner language, words like "must" and "can't" and "should" ("I must lose weight," "I can't fail," "I shouldn't feel this way"). Monkey mind takes you out of the moment and out of what is best for your life.

HOOK #3: OLD, OUTGROWN IDEAS

Kevin desperately wanted to be in a serious relationship. On the surface he was fun and frivolous. But deep down he was closed and distrustful, and kept women at arm's length. Predictably, all his relationships fizzled. Kevin told me his father had been an abusive alcoholic who would mock and beat him for his shortcomings, sometimes in front of his friends. As a child, Kevin learned not to show sadness or share vulnerabilities because his father would use them against him. The lesson was, if even the people you're closest to will turn on you, it's better to remain detached from your feelings, and from everyone around you. Kevin's behavior was completely functional when he was a small child; it protected him emotionally, and it kept him safe physically. But that was then.

Twenty years down the road, Kevin's distrust was constricting him like a too-small pair of shoes. He behaved as if he were still living his childhood trauma each day. What he needed was the emotional agility to adapt to the very different, much more positive circumstances of his adult life. His old uncomfortable thought process simply didn't serve him anymore.

One of my coaching clients, Tina, had recently been passed over for a promotion to CEO of a large financial services company. At the start of her career, she had worked as a trader in New York in a hard-hitting and male-dominated environment. On the trading floor, she learned that talking about her personal life was taboo, and she needed to show that she was just as strong as the rough-and-tumble guys around her. This worked for her on the trading floor, and she loved her job, but when she moved to a new organization, she realized that people didn't want to follow an automaton. She needed to show some emotion and authenticity but struggled with allowing herself to get close to anyone. Like Kevin, she was living out an expired story. What got her this far wasn't going to take her any further. She needed the agility to adapt to changing circumstances.

HOOK #4: WRONGHEADED RIGHTEOUSNESS

They say in a court of law you never get justice; if you're lucky, you just get the best deal possible. In so many other areas of life, we hang on too long to the idea of justice, or of vindication, or of having it proved beyond a shadow of a doubt that we are *right*. Anyone who has been in a romantic relationship for more than a few months knows the moment in an argument, especially with a loved one, when you realize . . . *ahh* . . . the troubled waters have calmed, some kind of understanding—a truce, perhaps—has been reached, and the best thing you could do now would be to shut your mouth, let it go, turn off the light, and go to sleep. Then something compels you to say just one more thing to demonstrate that, in fact, you were right and your spouse was wrong—and all hell breaks loose again.

That same need to have the rightness of your cause validated, or your unjust treatment confirmed, can steal years from your life when you let it persist. In many families, and in many parts of the world, feuds have endured for so long, no one can actually remember the original misunderstanding. Ironically, this merely prolongs the injustice, because you're depriving yourself of other good things that you value, such as the warm connection of family or friends. I love the phrase we use in South Africa to describe this type of self-defeating phenomenon: "cutting off your nose to spite your face."

The ancient Greek master of paradox, Heraclitus, said that you can never step into the same river twice, meaning that the world is constantly changing and thus always presenting us with new opportunities and situations. To make the most of it, we must continually break down old categories and formulate new ones. The freshest and most interesting solutions often come when we embrace "the beginner's mind," approaching novel experiences with fresh eyes. This is a cornerstone of emotional agility.

A generation or two ago, society was pretty set on what constituted "male activities" and "female activities." Now, you could get punched in the nose for assuming such a rigid distinction. Similarly, some of us tend to pigeonhole ourselves, failing to recognize our own worth as an individual, seeing ourselves narrowly and exclusively as a rich person, or a fat person, or a geek, or a jock. We learned a long time ago that the self-categorization of "Mr. Johnson's wife" was a limiting and losing proposition. But so is "CEO," or "man among men," or "smartest kid in the class," or even "Super Bowl quarterback." Things change. We need flexibility to ensure that we can change too.

Emotional agility means being aware and accepting of all your emotions, even learning from the most difficult ones. It also means getting beyond conditioned or preprogrammed cognitive and emotional responses (your hooks) to live in the moment with a clear reading of present circumstances, respond appropriately, and then act in alignment with your deepest values.

In the chapters that follow, I'm going to show you how to become an emotionally agile person who lives life to the fullest.

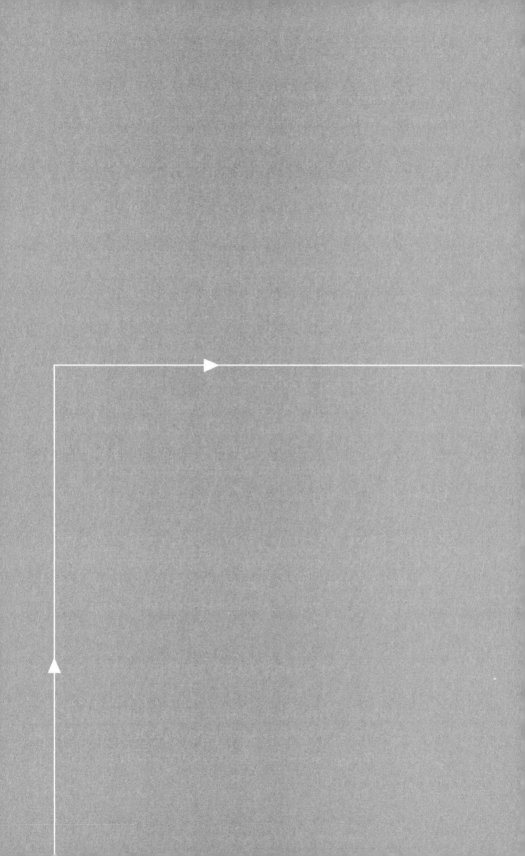

BOTTLING?

BROODING?

CHAPTER 3

TRYING TO UNHOOK

The count will vary depending on which expert you ask, but for our purposes, let's say there are seven basic emotions: joy, anger, sadness, fear, surprise, contempt, and disgust. As we've already seen, all these emotions are still with us because they've helped us survive through millions of years of evolution. And yet five of them—anger, sadness, fear, contempt, and disgust—are clearly on the not-so-comfortable end of the affective spectrum. ("Surprise" can go either way.)

What does it mean that most of our emotions reflect the dark side of human experience? If so many of our emotions are troubling, and yet helpful enough to make the cut of natural selection, doesn't that mean that even the dark and difficult feelings have a purpose? Is that why we shouldn't try to avoid them but rather should accept them as a useful—though sometimes uncomfortable—part of our lives?

Yes.

Precisely.

But learning to accept and live with *all* our emotions is by no means what most of us do. Most of us use default behaviors that we hope can deflect or disguise our negative feelings so we won't have to face them. Others settle deeply into these feelings and struggle to get beyond them. Or we attempt to cope with difficult times and difficult emotions through cynicism, irony, or gallows humor, refusing to admit that anything is worth taking seriously. (But as Nietzsche said, loosely translated, "A joke is an epitaph for an emotion.") Still others try to ignore their feelings and, like that more contemporary philosopher Taylor Swift said, "Shake it off." When we try to "unhook" simply by killing off our feelings, the real victim is our own well-being.

To see where your responses fit within the spectrum of these less-than-effective solutions, try these scenarios on for size:

1. Your boss makes a change that upsets you. You are most likely to . . .

   A. Ignore your frustration and anger. It'll go away eventually, and you have other stuff to deal with.
   B. Think long and hard about what you'd like to say to your boss, rehearsing the "I'll say . . ." and "he'll say . . ." lines over and over in your mind.
   C. Spend some time thinking about why the change upsets you, make a plan to talk this through with your boss, and then get back to work.

2. Your three-year-old leaves his toys on the floor. You come home from a tough day at work, trip over them, and yell at him. Afterward, you are most likely to . . .

A. Brush away your frustration, telling yourself, "It's fine—I just had a long day."

B. Chastise yourself all evening for yelling at your son, wonder why you always respond this way, and conclude you are the world's worst parent.

C. Sit down with your spouse to discuss your day, realizing your reaction to your son came from your frustration with your boss. Give your son a hug and an apology and put him to bed.

3. You're going through a painful romantic breakup. You . . .

A. Go out drinking with friends to distract yourself. You might even meet some new people. That will help numb the pain.

B. Sit at home alone wondering what you could have done differently. Why are you so bad at relationships?

C. Feel upset for a while. Write about the experience or talk to your friends, and learn from it.

If you answered A on most of these questions, you are a bottler. Bottlers try to unhook by pushing emotions to the side and getting on with things. They're likely to shove away unwanted feelings because those feelings are uncomfortable or distracting, or because they think that being anything less than bright and chipper is a sign of weakness, or a surefire way to alienate those around them.

If you're a bottler who hates work, you might try to rationalize away your negative feelings by telling yourself, "At least I've got a job." If you're unhappy in your relationship, you might immerse yourself in a project that just *has* to get done. If you're losing yourself in the busyness of caring for others, you might push your sadness or stress aside by reminding yourself that your "time will come." If you're leading team members who are deeply anxious about budget cuts and proposed restructuring, you might tiptoe around those subjects for fear of opening up an emotional can of worms.

Even with the important caveat that people don't always behave according to the gender norms found in research, it usually comes as no surprise to my clients when I tell them that men are more likely to bottle than women are.

When I first began studying psychology in the 1990s, there seemed to be a cottage industry producing books that explored gender differences in emotional style. *Men Are from Mars, Women Are from Venus,* written by relationship counselor John Gray, sold ten million copies. Another hugely successful book from that era, *You Just Don't Understand,* by linguist Deborah Tannen, explores the different ways men and women use language to communicate, or more precisely, to *not* communicate.

Today, you can see a parody of these stereotypical communication styles in the online comedy clip "It's Not About the Nail." In this video, a young woman appears on the screen, lamenting her frustrations to her boyfriend. "There's all this pressure, you know?" she says. "I can feel it in my head. And it's relentless. And I don't know if it's ever going to stop."

The camera pans to the left, and we see a nail sticking out of her forehead.

Her boyfriend tells her matter-of-factly, "You do have a nail in your head."

"It's not about the nail!" she cries. "Stop trying to fix it. You always do this. You always try to fix things when all I need you to do is listen."

He sighs and tries again: "That sounds really hard. I'm sorry."

"It is. Thank you," she says. She leans in to kiss him and the nail slams farther into her forehead.

"Ow!"

The video is funny because it holds a nugget of cultural truth: Men are usually seen as task-focused fixers, and women as more emotional beings. And the blond boyfriend in the video displays classic bottling behavior—tie it up, push it forward, move on. Action, action, action! His girlfriend does, after all, have a nail in her head, and it behooves him to point this out and find a solution.

The problem with bottling is that ignoring troubling emotions doesn't get at the root of whatever is causing them. (Yes, the nail is causing the pain, but how did the nail get in her head in the first place?) The deeper issues remain.

More than once, I've met bottlers who find themselves, years later, in the same miserable job, relationship, or circumstance. They've been so focused on pushing forward and being a good doobie that they haven't been in touch with a real emotion in years, which precludes any sort of real change or growth.

Another aspect of bottling behavior is trying to think positively, to push the negative thoughts out of your head. Unfortunately, trying *not* to do something takes a surprising amount of mental bandwidth. And research shows that attempting to minimize or ignore thoughts and emotions only serves to amplify them.

In a ridiculously simple but very famous study led by the late social psychologist Daniel Wegner, subjects were told to avoid thinking about white bears. They failed miserably. Even later, in fact, when the ban was lifted, they thought about white bears much *more* than a control group that hadn't started out under the "no thoughts about white bears" sanction. Any dieter who has dreamed of chocolate cake and french fries understands the counterproductive nature of "just don't think about it" and other avoidance strategies.

This is the irony of bottling. It feels like it gives us control, but it actually denies us control. First, it's your emotions that are calling the shots. Second, the suppressed emotions inevitably surface in unintended ways, a process that psychologists call *emotional leakage.* Perhaps you're angry with your brother. You try to suppress it. Then, after a glass of wine at Thanksgiving dinner, a snarky comment slips out of your mouth. Now you have a major family drama on your hands. Or you ignore your disappointment over a failed promotion at work, and then a few days later find yourself bawling like a baby while watching *Armageddon* for the tenth time. This is the risky business of bottling.

Bottling is usually done with the best intentions, and to the practical person it does feel productive. "Think positive," "forge forward," and "get on with it," we tell ourselves. And poof, just like that, the unwanted emotions seem to vanish. But really they've just gone underground—ready to pop back up at any time, and usually with surprising and inappropriate intensity ginned up by the containment pressure they've been under.

It's no surprise either that bottling can have a negative effect on relationships. "We just had a massive fight, and he heads off to work as if nothing had happened," says the beleaguered wife of the bottler. "He just doesn't care!"

In one study, researchers found that bottling increases *other* people's blood pressure, even if those people don't know that the bottler is bottling. Wait until the divorce lawyers get hold of that research! "Your Honor, my client's husband is going to give her a heart attack because he refuses to express his feelings."

SPIRALING IN ANGST

If your choice was B for most of the three scenarios I presented a few pages back, you're a brooder. And just as bottlers are more likely to be men, brooders are more likely to be women.

When hooked by uncomfortable feelings, brooders stew in their misery, endlessly stirring the pot around, and around, and around. Brooders can't let go, and they struggle to compartmentalize as they obsess over a hurt, a perceived failure, a shortcoming, or an anxiety.

Brooding is a cousin of worry. Both are intensely self-focused, and both involve trying to inhabit a moment that's not now. But while worry looks forward, brooding looks back—an even more pointless exercise. Brooders lose perspective as molehills become mountains and slights become capital crimes.

But brooders are ahead of bottlers in one respect: In their attempt to solve their problems, brooders are at least "feeling their feelings"— meaning, aware of their emotions. While brooders may not be in danger of emotional leakage, though, they might drown in a flood. When you brood, your emotions don't gain strength by being pressurized in a bottle, but they do gain strength. With brooders, emotions become more powerful in the same way a hurricane does, circling and circling and picking up more energy with each pass.

The psychologist Brad Bushman did a study in which he asked students to pour their hearts into a piece of writing. Then he had "another student" offer a withering critique. In fact, the other student was Bushman, and the criticism was the same to everyone: "This is one of the worst essays I have read."

The feedback had the desired effect: It made the participants really, really angry. Then Bushman asked the subjects to spend some time hitting a punching bag. He instructed one group to think about their anger (that is, to brood) while they smacked the bag. He even offered them a fake photo of the "critical student" to give a little extra juice to their jabs and uppercuts. He encouraged a second group to distract themselves (that is, to bottle) by thinking about improving their physical fitness while they punched. He had a third, control group sit quietly for a few minutes while he pretended to repair his computer.

After the punching session, each participant was given an air horn and invited to blast the people next to them—a measure of aggressive behavior. All three groups were still angry, but the control group showed the least amount of aggression, blasting the horn the least often. The bottlers displayed more aggression (and more horn blasting) than the control group. But those in the brooding group were the angriest of all, and they were most aggressive in blasting their neighbors with horrendous, earsplitting noise.

Like bottlers, brooders usually have the best of intentions. Ruminating on troubling feelings offers a comforting illusion of conscientious effort. We *want* to deal with our unhappiness or to learn how to cope with a difficult situation, so we think it through—then think, and think, and think some more. At the end, we are no closer to resolving the issue at the core of our distress.

Brooding also makes you more likely to blame yourself with questions such as "Why do I always react like this?" and "Why can't I handle this better?" Like bottling, it takes up massive amounts of intellectual energy. It's exhausting and unproductive.

Brooding isn't always a solo activity. When you go out with a friend and have a big, fat moan about how your widowed father is mismanaging his finances, you're doing what's called co-brooding. When you find yourself complaining to an office mate for the umpteenth time about your boss's tone, you're doing the same. We might think that these venting sessions will make us feel better, but given that there's no forward movement or resolution, the end result is you're likely to feel even more annoyed at your father, or so infuriated by your boss you can't concentrate.

Remember how we talked about bottlers' effect on the people who love them? Brooders are similarly hard to deal with because they tend to dump their real, heavy emotions on others. They want to talk it out with those close to them, but at some point, even their nearest and dearest get empathy fatigue—tiring of a brooder's constant need to talk about fears, worries, and struggles. Moreover, the brooder's self-focus leaves no room for anyone else's needs, so listeners often ultimately walk away, leaving the brooder feeling both frustrated and alone.

And then, of course, brooders can slip into the trap of misery-about-misery anxieties, in which they worry about all their worrying.

In psychology, just as there is System 1 and System 2 thinking, there are also *Type 1* and *Type 2* thoughts. Type 1 thoughts are the normal human anxieties that come up as you tackle life's everyday obstacles: the big project at work, the crazy schedule, last night's fight, parenting concerns. Type 1 thoughts are straightforward: "I'm worried about X" or "I'm sad about Y."

Type 2 thoughts happen when you enter the mental house of mirrors and start to layer in unhelpful thoughts *about* the thoughts. "I worry that I worry so much" or "I'm stressed about being stressed." To our troubling emotions we add guilt for having them. "Not only am I worried about X or sad about Y, but also I have no right to be." We're angry at our anger, worried about our worry, unhappy about our unhappiness.

It's like quicksand. The harder you struggle with your emotions, the deeper you sink.

Whatever we may think we're accomplishing by bottling or brooding, neither strategy serves our health or our happiness. It's much like taking an aspirin for a headache: The medicine relieves your pain for a few hours, but if the source of the headache is a lack of sleep, a knot in your neck, or a horrendous cold, that headache will return with full force as soon as the analgesic wears off.

Bottling and brooding are short-term emotional aspirin we reach for with the best of intentions. But when we don't go directly to the source, we miss the ability to really deal once and for all with what's causing our distress.

If I held a stack of books away from my body, with my arms straight out in front of me, I'd be okay for a few minutes. But after two minutes . . . three minutes . . . ten minutes, my arms would begin to shake. This is what happens when we bottle. Trying to keep things at a stiff arm's length can be exhausting. So exhausting, in fact, that we often drop the load.

But when I hold the books tight to my body, hugging them as if to crush them, my arm muscles will also begin to shake. In this position, my arms and hands are clenched—closed and unable to do anything else. This is what happens to us when we brood.

In both cases, we lose our ability to be fully engaged with the world around us: to hug our children, to be present with a colleague, to create something new, or to simply enjoy the smell of the newly mowed grass. Openness and enthusiasm are replaced by rules, confining stories from the past, and invidious judgments, and our ability to solve problems and make decisions actually declines. These rigid postures stop us from being agile when we need to deal with life's stressors.

The occasional brood or bottle, or even a flip back and forth between the two now and then, won't kill you (this is a book on agility, after all). Indeed, sometimes these coping strategies may be the best course of action. For instance, if your beloved unceremoniously dumps you the night before your bar exam, it behooves you to shove your distress aside so you can concentrate on the task at hand. (If this has actually happened to you, by the way, you have my sincere sympathy.)

It's when these strategies are used as default coping methods, as they often are, that they become counterproductive and actually embed the hooks deeper and deeper.

We learn to brood or bottle early in life, and if you have children, it's worth pausing for a moment to think about the content of your conversations with them.

The unwritten rule book about emotions (and how men and women should respond to them) contains what psychologists call *display rules*. "Big boys don't cry" and "We don't do anger here. Go to your room and come out when you've got a smile on your face" are examples of the imposition of display rules. I'll never forget the day we buried my father. Well-meaning family and friends told my twelve-year-old brother that he shouldn't cry because he needed to focus on looking after our mother, my sister, and me.

We learn these rules from our caregivers and, in turn, we often unintentionally pass them down to our own children. For example, we're much more likely to ask boys about tasks ("What did you do at school today?" "How was the game?" "Did you win?"), whereas we tend to ask girls about emotions ("How did you feel?" "Did you have fun?"). Children quickly internalize these rules, which, as we'll see in Chapter 10, don't always serve them.

HOOKED ON HAPPINESS

Brooding and bottling aren't the only unproductive ways people cope with life's stresses. Another common strategy is the belief, in one form or another, that all will be well if we can just "keep on smiling."

Despite what it says in the Hollywood script, Forrest Gump did not actually invent the smiley face. But after fifty years and hundreds of millions of "Have a Nice Day" buttons, T-shirts, and coffee mugs, that bright yellow circle with the schematic grin and black-dot eyes is as iconic as the red, white, and blue. (And why not? After all, the "pursuit of happiness" is front and center in America's Declaration of Independence.)

In the digital age, the smiley face has morphed into the emoticons and emojis that pop up everywhere. (Side note: I've just discovered that if I try to go old-school and type a colon followed by a right parenthesis, my computer changes it to a ☺ whether I want it or not.) And with each advance—or some might say, regression—in our consumer culture, in which marketers hustle to fulfill desires we didn't even know we had, the blissed-out state of Mr. Smiley becomes ever more the Holy Grail, the organizing principle of our existence.

Wait. Isn't happiness why we're here? Isn't happiness good for us?

Well, that depends.

A while back, two researchers at the University of California, Berkeley, LeeAnne Harker and Dacher Keltner, searched the records of Mills College, a nearby private women's school, and inspected the yearbook photos from 1958 and 1960. As nearly every happiness researcher will tell you, genuine and false smiles activate different muscle groups, so the two scientists examined the look on each student's face to see whether her zygomaticus major or orbicularis oculi muscle was at work. When we give an authentic, teeth-baring, bright smile that produces crow's-feet, both muscles are at work. But the orbicularis oculi cannot be contracted voluntarily, so if we put on a fake happy face, this tiny muscle, which is located near the eyes, stays still. This gave Harker and Keltner a pretty good idea of how genuinely positive each student was feeling at the time her photograph was taken.

Thirty years later, the students who'd exhibited the sunniest and most genuine yearbook smiles in that fraction of a second as the shutter clicked were doing much better than those who had offered smiles that were a little less real. The genuine smilers had more satisfying marriages, greater feelings of well-being, and were more content. *Click.*

Given a choice, we'd probably prefer to be slaphappy all the time, and there *are* advantages to that pleasurable state. More "positive" emotion is linked with a lower risk of various psychological illnesses, including depression, anxiety, and borderline personality disorder.

Positive emotions also drive us to success, help us make better decisions, reduce the risk of disease, and allow us to live longer. In some cases, they even help broaden how we think and act by directing our attention to new information and opportunities. They help build vital social, physical, and cognitive resources that lead to positive outcomes and affiliations.

With all this, you might presume happiness ranks right up there with food and sunshine in its contribution to human well-being. But as our increasingly obese, melanoma-afflicted society has come to understand, it is possible to have too much of a good thing. And research shows it's possible not only to be too happy but also to experience the wrong types of happiness, and to go about trying to find happiness at the wrong time and in the wrong ways.

I'm not saying it's better to go around in a funk all the time. But I hope to get you to keep the pursuit of happiness in perspective and to see your "negative" emotions in a new and more accepting light. In fact, I strongly submit that describing them as "negative" only perpetuates the myth that these useful—albeit sometimes challenging—feelings are, you know, negative. If I can persuade you otherwise, I'll be happy (but not too happy).

When we're overly cheerful, we tend to neglect important threats and dangers. It's not too big a stretch to suggest that being excessively happy could kill you. You might engage in riskier behaviors like drinking too much ("A fifth round on me!"), binge eating ("Mmm, more cake!"), skipping birth control ("What could possibly go wrong?"), and using drugs ("Let's party!"). An excess of free-wheeling giddiness and a relative absence of more sober emotions can even be a marker for mania, a dangerous symptom of psychological illness.

People with high happiness levels sometimes exhibit behavior that is actually more rigid. That's because mood affects the way our brains process information. When life is good, and we feel great, and when the environment is safe and familiar, we tend not to think long and hard about anything too challenging—which helps explain why highly positive people can be less creative than those with a more moderate level of positive emotion.

Not to stereotype the happy among us, but when we're in an "everything is awesome!" mood, we're far more likely to jump to conclusions and resort to stereotypes. The happy more often place disproportionate emphasis on early information and disregard or minimize later details. This typically takes the form of the halo effect, in which, for example, we automatically assume that the cute guy we've just met at the party is kind, just because he wears cool clothes and tells funny jokes. Or we decide that the bespectacled, middle-aged man with a briefcase is more intelligent or reliable, say, than the twenty-two-year-old blonde wearing hot-pink Juicy Couture shorts.

Our so-called negative emotions encourage slower, more systematic cognitive processing. We rely less on quick conclusions and pay more attention to subtle details that matter. (Okay, the guy is hot, and he seems into you, but why is he hiding his wedding-ring hand behind his back?) Isn't it interesting that the most famous fictional detectives are notably grumpy? And that the most carefree kid in high school is rarely valedictorian?

"Negative" moods summon a more attentive, accommodating thinking style that leads you to really examine facts in a fresh and creative way. It's when we're in a bit of a funk that we focus and dig down. People in negative moods tend to be less gullible and more skeptical, while happy folks may accept easy answers and trust false smiles. (Is that show of pearly whites below the pencil-thin mustache just the zygomaticus major, or is the orbicularis oculi also involved?) Who wants to question surface truth when everything is going so well? So the happy person goes ahead and signs on the dotted line.

The paradox of happiness is that deliberately striving for it is fundamentally incompatible with the nature of happiness itself. Real happiness comes through activities you engage in for their own sake rather than for some extrinsic reason, even when the reason is something as seemingly benevolent as the desire to be happy.

Striving for happiness establishes an expectation, which confirms the saying that expectations are resentments waiting to happen. That's why holidays and family events are often disappointing, if not downright depressing. Our expectations are so high that it's almost inevitable we'll be let down.

In one study, participants were given a fake newspaper article that praised the advantages of happiness, while a control group read an article that made no mention of happiness. Both groups then watched randomly assigned film clips that were either happy or sad. The participants who had been induced to value happiness by reading the article came away from viewing the "happy film" feeling less happy than those in the control group who had watched the same film. Placing too high a value on happiness increased their expectations for how things "should be," and thus set them up for disappointment.

In another study, participants were asked to listen to Stravinsky's *Rite of Spring*, a piece of music so discordant and jarring that it caused a riot at its 1913 debut. Some participants were told to "try to make yourself feel as happy as possible" while they listened to the music. Afterward, they evaluated themselves as being less happy compared with a control group that was not chasing Mr. Smiley.

The aggressive pursuit of happiness is also isolating. In yet another study, the higher the participants ranked happiness on their lists of objectives or goals, the more they described themselves as lonely on daily self-evaluations.

Happiness also comes in a variety of cultural variations that open up the possibility of being happy in the wrong way. In North America, happiness tends to be defined in terms of personal accomplishment (including pleasure); whereas in East Asia, happiness is associated with social harmony. Chinese Americans prefer contentment, while Americans with European backgrounds prefer excitement. Japanese culture is built around loyalty, with its connection to guilt, whereas American culture embodies more socially disengaged emotions such as pride or anger. To be happy within a given culture depends more than a little on how in sync your feelings are with that culture's definition of happiness.

In short, chasing after happiness can be just as self-defeating as the bottling and brooding we talked about earlier. All these coping mechanisms arise from discomfort with "negative" emotions and our unwillingness to endure anything even remotely associated with the dark side.

GOOD NEWS ABOUT BAD MOODS

While it's rarely fun to be in a bad mood, and it's certainly not healthy to constantly stew in negative emotions, here's what experiences of sadness, anger, guilt, or fear can do:

Help us form arguments. We're more likely to use concrete and tangible information, be more attuned to the situation at hand, and be less prone to making judgment errors and distortions, all of which lends an aura of expertise and authority that can make us more persuasive as writers and speakers.

Improve memory. One study found that shoppers remembered significantly more information about the interior of a store on cold, gloomy days when they were not feeling so exuberant than they did on sunny and warm days when life felt like a breeze. Research also shows that when we're in a not-so-good mood, we're less likely to inadvertently corrupt our memories by incorporating later, misleading information.

Encourage perseverance. After all, when you already feel great, why push yourself? On academic tests, an individual in a more somber mood will try to answer more questions—and get more of them right—than he or she will when feeling cheerful. It might actually be a good idea, then, for your college-bound son or daughter to be in a slight funk when it's time to take the SAT. (And given the typical state of most seventeen-year-olds, you're probably already in good shape on that aspect of test preparation.)

Make us more polite and attentive. People in less exuberant moments are more cautious and considered, and more likely to engage in nonconscious social mimicry (in which we mirror another person's gestures and speech without knowing it), a behavior that increases social bonding. When we're feeling great, we're much more assertive, which often means we're focused more on me, me, me and might ignore what others have to offer or are going through.

Encourage generosity. Those in negative moods pay more attention to fairness, and are more apt to reject unfair offers.

Make us less prone to confirmation bias. In a study of people with strong political opinions, those who were angry chose to read more articles that disagreed with their positions, instead of practicing confirmation bias, the common tendency to seek out information that supports what we already believe to be true. After exploring these contrary views, they were more willing to change their minds. It seems that anger produces a "nail the opposition" mentality that encourages us to explore what the other guy has to say in order to tear it apart, ironically leaving the door open to being persuaded.

THE UPSIDE OF ANGER (AND OTHER CHALLENGING EMOTIONS)

Pretending to be happier than we are is a losing proposition, and pushing ourselves to be more "genuinely" happy is definitely self-defeating, partly because it raises impossible expectations and partly because our own false smiles and eagerness to grab all the gusto deprive us of the benefits of "negative" emotions.

It's usually when we get knocked down a few pegs that more of the subtle, sometimes painful but potentially important underlying details in life come to the fore. Not surprisingly, great writers from the Greek tragedians to the romantic poets to the authors of those huge nineteenth-century Russian novels have found much that was instructive and valuable on the dark side of the human emotional scale. It was our old friend John Milton who, in "Il Penseroso," exclaimed, "Hail divinest Melancholy."

Our raw feelings can be the messengers we need to teach us things about ourselves and can prompt insights into important life directions. I saw this when a client came to me with an "anger problem." The two of us worked together to examine his feelings and sort them out. He realized that maybe he didn't have an anger problem so much as he had a wife who was placing nearly impossible demands on him. By accepting and understanding his difficult emotions, rather than trying to suppress or fix them, he began to improve his marriage, not by remaking himself into milquetoast, but by learning to set better boundaries for what was acceptable behavior.

In addition to anger (a.k.a. wrath), envy is one of the other "seven deadly sins." In truth, envy can be a strong motivator—even stronger than admiration—in driving us toward self-improvement. One study showed that students who expressed benign envy toward a more successful student showed greater motivation than those who expressed admiration. The envious participants ramped up their schoolwork and performed better on various verbal tasks.

Other "bad" emotions are useful for different reasons. Embarrassment and guilt can serve important social functions in fostering appeasement and furthering cooperation. Sadness is a signal to ourselves that something is wrong—often that we are looking for a better way to be here and participate. And outward expressions of sadness signal to others that we could use some help. Suppress the sadness under a veil of false cheer and you deny yourself the directional guidance, and maybe also the helping hand.

As you may recall, when we ran through the list of common, everyday scenarios of being "hooked," there was always an option C. That approach is neither bottling nor brooding but rather being present and having an open heart to all your emotions in a curious and accepting manner.

That's where we're going to turn next, to show you the methods that actually work to get you "off the hook" and into a healthier and, yes, happier, way of living.

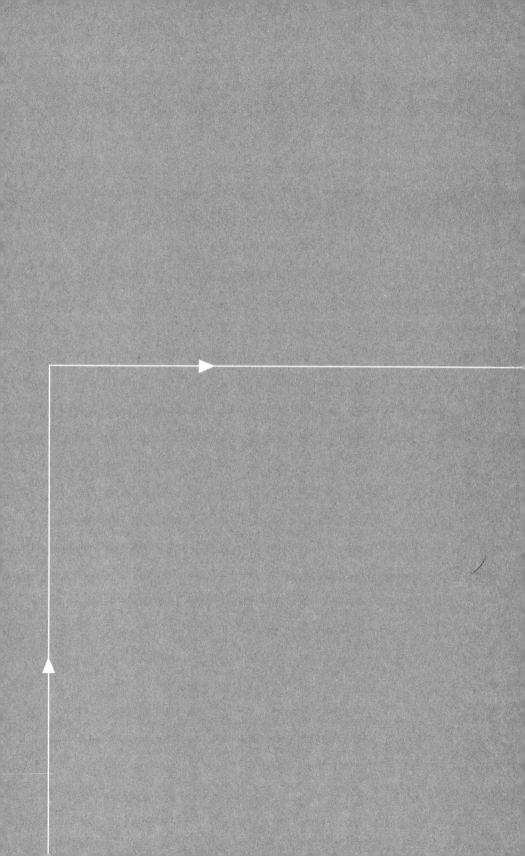

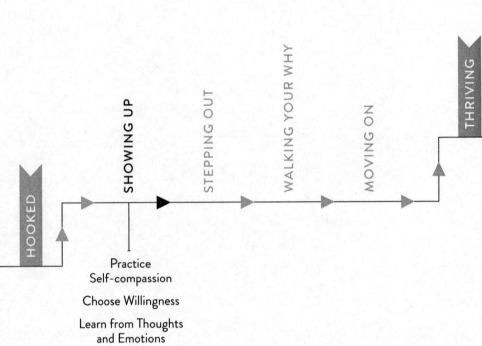

HOOKED

SHOWING UP

Practice
Self-compassion

Choose Willingness

Learn from Thoughts
and Emotions

STEPPING OUT

WALKING YOUR WHY

MOVING ON

THRIVING

CHAPTER 4

SHOWING UP

In 1975, a young filmmaker was struggling to write a script for a sprawling space adventure, and he couldn't quite get the story off the ground. Then he rediscovered a book he'd read in college: Joseph Campbell's *The Hero with a Thousand Faces*. In that 1949 classic, Campbell explored the idea, first developed by the psychologist Carl Jung, that all humans share certain universal but unconscious mental models for relationships and important life experiences. From the birth of civilization, according to Campbell and Jung, humans have embedded these models in myths. These ancient stories address timeless topics like families, fear, success, and failure, and they share certain elements, called *archetypes*, the basics of which include the hero, the mentor, and the quest. Archetypes also include more specific plot devices, such as the magic sword, and the lake or pool that hides a secret beneath its surface. These archetypes show up in everything from the King Arthur legends to Harry Potter to online role-playing games. The existence of universal archetypes might explain why people all over the world fall in love with the same kinds of stories, and why you can find similar myths in very different cultures.

The struggling filmmaker used the archetypes and rewrote his script to be more of a mythic hero's quest. That filmmaker was George Lucas, and his movie, *Star Wars,* went on to become one of the most popular films ever made.

But myths offer a lot more than box office boffo. Long before there were books or movies—or philosophers, literature professors, or psychologists—these universal stories were the way people passed along key life lessons. And one of the lessons conveyed in myth after myth is that trying to dodge the things we're most afraid of is a very bad idea. Time and time again in myths, the hero ultimately has no choice but to go into a dark and spooky place—a swamp, a cave, the Death Star—and confront head-on whatever is lurking there.

In modern life, we often find ourselves at the edges of our own dark places—all the more terrifying for being inside us. Sometimes these places are filled with demons; sometimes there are only a few little spooklets hiding in the corners. But whether the creatures represent major traumas or minor embarrassments, terrors or tics, they can keep us hooked.

Most of our own personal stories aren't particularly epic. Few of us would have much to offer Hollywood, not even a cheesy horror flick. Most people, fortunately, do not harbor repressed memories of, say, Grandma hacking Grandpa to pieces and serving him up on toast points. Our hidden demons are simply the residue of perfectly ordinary and almost universal insecurity, self-doubt, and fear of failure. Maybe you still resent your sister for flirting with your boyfriends in high school. Maybe you feel undervalued by your new boss. This is not even the stuff of a good, tear-soaked *Oprah* episode. But it can be enough to hook you into behaving in ways that don't serve you.

So, can't we just send in somebody with a lightsaber to wipe out these bad guys and blow up the Death Star?

Nope. That's not how it works in this galaxy.

Oddly enough, one example of what does work, at least metaphorically, comes from a genuine horror film called *The Babadook*. In it, a single mother is tormented by a shadow monster that emerges from one of her son's storybooks. It eventually becomes clear that the monster represents her feelings about motherhood and the resentment she felt toward her son since her husband, the boy's father, was killed while driving her to the hospital to give birth. Thus, the monster also represents her grief. In the end (spoiler alert!), she disempowers this big, scary bundle of unwelcome emotions not just by confronting it, but also by letting the Babadook live in the basement, where she feeds and cares for it. In other words, she learns to tame and accommodate it without letting it dictate her life. It seems an odd ending for a movie—shouldn't the protagonist vanquish the monster?—but if you understand emotions, it makes beautiful, perfect sense.

As with every hero's journey, our movement toward a better life begins with *showing up*. But that doesn't mean we have to smite or slay all the demons, Babadooks, or even the spooklets that trouble us. It does mean we must face up to, make peace with, and find an honest and open way to live with them. When we show up fully, with awareness and acceptance, even the worst demons usually back down. Simply by facing up to the scary things and giving them a name, we often strip them of their power. We end the tug-of-war by dropping the rope.

Decades of psychological research shows that our life satisfaction in the face of inevitable worries, regrets, and sad experiences depends not so much on how many of these things we experience, or even their intensity, but on the way we deal with them. Do we bottle or brood, allowing them to govern our behavior, or do we "show up" to them compassionately, with curiosity and with acceptance— no failures, regrets, or bad hairstyles turned away.

Showing up is not a heroic exercise of will but simply looking our personal tormentors in the eye and saying, "Okay. You're here, and I'm here. Let's talk. Because I am big enough to contain all my feelings and past experiences, I can accept all these parts of my existence without being crushed or terrified."

The Italian Jewish writer Primo Levi, like Frankl a survivor of the Nazi death camps, spoke of the unexpected anguish of his return home to Italy at the end of World War II. People gathered around him and his emaciated fellow survivors and asked, "What has happened to you?" As the survivors began to try to find words to convey their experience, people slowly turned and walked away—unable or unwilling to listen and accept what they were hearing.

Originally trained as a chemist, Levi took a job as an ordinary laborer in a paint factory, but he found his means of coping by jotting down remembered fragments of his experiences on train tickets and old scraps of paper. At night, at the factory dormitory, he would type them up. Over time, a manuscript emerged that became his first book, *If This Is a Man*. Levi had discovered the vital importance of having your feelings and experiences acknowledged, not just by other people but also by oneself.

In learning to see and accept your full self, warts and all, it helps to remember one thing that all our favorite heroes and heroines have in common: They're far from perfect. Perfection is one-dimensional, unrealistic, boring. That's why the most engaging protagonists have flaws or a dark side, and why the truly interesting villains have enough humanity that we at least partly identify with them.

A satisfying movie is one in which the complex positives and negatives of hero and villain get resolved. In real life, our successes come from how well we're able to live with and learn from our own flaws or dark side. And the path to that resolution, and that learning, begins with showing up.

In a survey of thousands of respondents, researchers in England found that of all the "happy habits" science has currently identified as being keys to a more fulfilling life, self-acceptance was the one most strongly associated with overall satisfaction. Yet the same study revealed that this particular habit was also the one people practiced least! Respondents reported they were good at helping and giving to others, but when asked how often they were kind to themselves, almost half gave a rating of 5 or less out of 10. Only a handful of respondents—5 percent—rated themselves as a 10 on self-acceptance.

SELF-COMPASSION

According to folklore—in a story I heard from many sources growing up in South Africa but have never been able to confirm—when a member of a certain tribe acts badly or does something wrong, he must take his place alone at the center of the village. Every member of the tribe gathers around him. Then, one at a time, each person— man, woman, and child—lets him have it. But they aren't describing what a jerk he is. Instead, the villagers carefully catalog all his *good* qualities. Whether true or not, the legend illustrates the power of a kind word (or two, or two thousand). It's a tribal version of that scene in *It's a Wonderful Life* in which all the citizens of Bedford Falls remind George Bailey of the huge impact his simple existence as a small-town banker has had on his friends and neighbors.

Imagine if we each treated ourselves with that same kind of compassion and support rather than the self-recrimination we so often fall into instead? That doesn't mean soft-pedaling the negatives, or

twisting ourselves into knots trying to work around them, or denying that they exist. Rather, it means forgiving ourselves for our mistakes or imperfections so we can move on to better, more productive
things.

Showing up takes guts. It's scary to consider what we might learn
about ourselves when we look inward. What if we unleash some
truth that could destabilize a relationship? Or call into question a
way of life that, while it may be far from perfect, is at least familiar?

But showing up doesn't mean wielding a wrecking ball. It means
bringing history and context into the equation to find the full sig-
nificance of what's there, and then putting that understanding to
work to make things better.

Showing up involves acknowledging our thoughts without ever
having to believe they are literally true. (Brooders especially should
take note of this, because the more often we hear some dubious state-
ment repeated, even just inside our own heads, the more likely we
are to accept it as truth.) Showing up starts the process of getting us
off that hook.

My homeland's racial segregation finally ended in 1994, with the
election of Nelson Mandela, the country's first black president. Part
of Mandela's genius was that as he worked to undo the damage done
by institutionalized hatred, he led his country beyond the blood lust
and score settling that has kept hostility alive for centuries in other
parts of the world. When it came to facing up to South Africa's
deeply painful past, Mandela's government established a Truth and
Reconciliation Commission, whereby people would show up, own
up to what they had done or what had been done to them, and then
move on. It was not about an eye for an eye or punishment or re-
crimination, but about healing and moving on with building a new,
just and democratic society.

Even with truth and reconciliation, though, we can't control the world, which means that it will never be a perfect place. The only way to get anywhere is through the practice of acceptance.

In fact, one of the great paradoxes of human experience is that we can't change ourselves or our circumstances until we accept what exists right now. Acceptance is a prerequisite for change. This means giving permission for the world to be as it is, because it's only when we stop trying to control the universe that we make peace with it. We still don't like the things we don't like; we just cease to be at war with them. And once the war is over, change can begin.

To continue the battle analogy, you can't rebuild a city when it's still under bombardment, but only when the attacks stop and peace prevails. The same goes with our internal world: When we stop fighting what *is*, we can move on to efforts that will be more constructive and more rewarding.

I often advise my clients that a good way to become more accepting and compassionate toward yourself is to look back at the child you once were. After all, you didn't get to choose your parents, your economic circumstances, your personality, or your body type. Recognizing you had to play the hand you were dealt is often the first step toward showing yourself more warmth, kindness, and forgiveness. You did the best you could under the circumstances. And you survived.

The next step is to think of yourself as the hurt child you once were, running up to you, the adult you are now. Would you first mock the child, demand an explanation, tell her it was her fault, and say, "I told you so"? Not likely. You would first take that young, upset child in your arms and comfort her.

Why should you treat the adult you any less compassionately?

Showing yourself kindness gets even more important during life's rough patches. People who are going through a breakup, have lost a job, or missed out on a promotion are often quick to scold, blame, and punish themselves. That internal chatterbox starts in with the "shoulda, woulda, coulda"s and the "I'm just not good enough"s. Seriously, it can sound like a nasty little troll, can't it?

In a study of people going through divorce, researchers found that those who expressed compassion for themselves at the beginning of this painful experience were doing better nine months later than those who'd beaten themselves up over "faults" such as not being attractive enough.

When it comes to facing up to all our emotions through tough times, it's also important to remember the distinction between guilt and shame. Guilt is the feeling of burden and regret that comes from knowing you've failed or done wrong. It's no fun, but like all our emotions, it has its purpose. In fact, society depends on guilty feelings to keep us from repeating our errors and misdeeds. A lack of guilt is actually one of the defining features of a sociopath.

While guilt is focused on the specific misdeed, shame is a very different animal. Linked to the feeling of disgust, shame focuses on a person's character. Shame casts one not as a human being who did a bad thing, but as a human being who is bad. This is why people who are shameful often feel diminished and worthless. It's also why shame rarely leads us to take action to make amends. In fact, studies show that people who feel shame are more likely to respond defensively, perhaps trying to escape blame, deny responsibility, or even pin it on others. In studies, prison inmates who exhibited shame at the time of their incarceration ended up reoffending more often than those who exhibited guilt.

The key difference between the two emotions? Self-compassion. Yes, you did something wrong. Yes, you feel bad about it, because, hey, you should. Maybe you even did something really wrong. Even so, this transgression does not make you an irredeemably awful human being. You can make amends, apologize, and get to work paying your debt to society, whether that means sending flowers or serving time. You can strive to learn from your mistakes and do better in the future. Self-compassion is the antidote to shame.

If you suspect that showing yourself some compassion is just an excuse to go soft on yourself, here are some things to keep in mind:

SELF-COMPASSION IS NOT ABOUT LYING TO YOURSELF

In fact, it's the opposite. It means looking at yourself from an outside perspective: a broad and inclusive view that doesn't deny reality but instead recognizes your challenges and failures as part of being human. In one study, people took part in mock job interviews in which researchers asked them to describe their greatest weakness. The more self-compassionate people didn't downplay their weaknesses any more than anyone else did. However, they were far less anxious and threatened by the whole experience.

Treating yourself with compassion is, in fact, at odds with deceiving yourself. You can't have real self-compassion without first facing the truth about who you are and what you feel. It's when we lack compassion that we're more likely to develop false bravado and grandiose overconfidence in an effort to deny the possibility of failure. When we lack compassion, we see the world as just as unforgiving as we are, so the very idea of failure is crippling.

Imagine an exceptionally bright, hardworking student who graduates at the top of her high school class and heads off to one of those best-of-the-best colleges everyone wants to get into. She arrives at college to find that everyone around her is just as smart and dedicated as she is. In fact, some of her new classmates are even more accomplished, come from sophisticated families, and went to fancier high schools. If our student identifies too narrowly with herself as the "geeky brainiac" or "the smartest kid in the class," as she always has, what's going to happen to her sense of self? As she struggles to keep up with all the elite students surrounding her, she'll need a healthy dose of emotional agility to define herself in a new, broader, and fluid way. To do that, she'll need to have compassion for her struggles as a small fish in a suddenly bigger and more competitive pond.

Compassion gives us the freedom to redefine ourselves as well as the all-important freedom to fail, which contains within it the freedom to take the risks that allow us to be truly creative.

SELF-COMPASSION DOES NOT MAKE YOU WEAK OR LAZY

Industrialized society, especially now that it's amped up with so much technology, encourages us to push ourselves to our limits. Certain professions—law, medicine, investment banking, business, technology—bake that intensity right into the job description. But even people in less competitive careers feel the pressure. We all now run faster, work harder, stay up later, and multitask more aggressively just to keep up. In this environment, in which we're expected to approach life like an endless Ironman competition, showing yourself compassion can be seen as a sign that you lack ambition or don't care about success as much as the person next to you does.

There's a misconception that you need to be tough on yourself to maintain your edge. But people who are more accepting of their own failures may actually be *more* motivated to improve. Self-compassionate people aim just as high as self-critical people do. The difference is that self-compassionate people don't fall apart when, as sometimes happens, they don't meet their goals.

It could be that self-compassion actually *sharpens* your edge. After all, it's associated with health behaviors such as eating right, exercising, sleeping well, and managing stress during tough times, which is when you need to care for yourself the most. It even strengthens your immune system, helping to ward off illness, while encouraging social connection and positive emotion. All of this helps you to keep on truckin' and be your best self.

Unfortunately, the postmodern consumption-driven environment in which we live is much more interested in selling us smart phones and Big Gulps than it is in advancing our physical or emotional health. One of advertising's basic jobs is to make us feel discontented so we crave stuff whether we need it or not, and whether or not it's good for us. Self-acceptance and self-compassion do not move the merchandise. So what we're confronted with instead are relentless invitations to compare ourselves with others—and, inevitably, to come out lacking.

Previous societies offered the encouragement and support of extended families, and the stable social structure of small villages. We citizens of the industrialized world, however, often live hundreds or thousands of miles away from our nearest relative, in anonymous and isolating cities, where we're bombarded by images not just of all the cool gadgets and other gleaming goodies we do not possess, but also of gorgeous men and women who set a standard of photoshopped perfection that is impossible to meet. Meanwhile everyone is posting online snapshots of their fancy dinners and selfies of themselves being fabulous on vacation, so each of us is constantly comparing ourselves not only with the rich, gorgeous, and airbrushed but also with every other person we know, including the kid you thought was a dope in eighth grade but who now drives around in a Lamborghini.

It will come as no surprise to anyone that, according to the research, being exposed to people who are hotter, richer, or more powerful than we are can send our own self-image into the toilet. It's called the *contrast effect,* and it means that while you may feel perfectly comfortable sunbathing in your Lands' End tankini at your family's place on Lake Okoboji in western Iowa, a stroll amid the thong-wearing models on the beaches of Rio de Janeiro or the Venice boardwalk in Los Angeles might be tough on the ego. Even more insidious, men rate themselves as being less in love with their wives or partners after looking at sexy magazine centerfolds. You might be content living in your tract house and proud of your husband who teaches special-needs children, but you might be less so after running into your old boyfriend who's now a thoracic surgeon who volunteers for Doctors Without Borders and just published his first novel.

Self-acceptance usually takes a big hit anytime we start making comparisons. In one study, the young men and women who had spent the least amount of time comparing themselves with others in terms of looks or intelligence or money also reported the least amount of self-blaming, guilt, and regret.

And social comparison doesn't just bring us down when we come out on the short end. In a follow-up to the study just mentioned, researchers asked police officers to compare themselves with security guards. Those who most wholeheartedly endorsed the idea that real cops were superior scored lowest on measures of mental health such as sense of self and life satisfaction. It seems that once you start comparing yourself with others, even if you believe yourself the winner, you get hooked on one-upmanship and external validation to buoy your own sense of value. That's a losing game. Heaven knows there will always be somebody who has a faster car, or flatter abs, or a bigger house than you do. In a world that contains Tom Brady, Jennifer Lawrence, Nobel Prize–winning scientists, bestselling novelists, and twenty-five-year-old billionaires, seeing your value in terms of comparison-worthy "product features" is a surefire way to make yourself miserable.

So, in the interest of your emotional agility, here's my advice: Keep your eyes on your own work. Remember that phrase from your school days? Teachers used it as a warning to students not to cheat during a test. But it had a second purpose too: to stop you from second-guessing yourself.

Teleport yourself back to high school for a moment. There you are, taking a test, with your two sharpened No. 2 pencils and a head full of facts. You're working through the questions, completely confident because you've studied all week. And then you inadvertently glance across the aisle and notice the supersmart kid to your left, the one who always raises his hand in class, has a completely different answer to one of the questions than you do. That gets you worrying: Is he right? Am I wrong? I was sure the answer was "Magna Carta," but that kid knows everything. Maybe the answer really *is* "Bhagavad Gita." And then guess what happens? You change your answer and get it wrong. It turns out that kid isn't any smarter or better informed than you are.

Keeping your eyes on your own work is even more important when you're tempted to compare yourself with a person completely out of your league. Looking to someone whose accomplishments are just a notch or two above your own might be inspiring, but judging yourself against a true superstar or a once-in-a-lifetime genius can be devastating. That's in part because we tend to focus on the end result rather than on what it takes to get there.

Let's say you play violin in a chamber group, just for fun. If you think about process, the fact that the first-chair violinist is a little better than you gives you a benchmark for improvement. Work harder and maybe you can rise to that level. But measuring yourself against a virtuoso like Joshua Bell will simply make you crazy. You have to remember that aside from being incredibly gifted, Bell began taking lessons at age four, after his mother found him using rubber bands stretched across the handles of his dresser drawers to pluck out music he'd heard her play on the piano. Once he started taking lessons, how many hours over the next twenty years do you suppose he spent in a room by himself practicing the violin? Would you have been willing to be so disciplined and committed? Think of all the things he didn't get to do because of all that time playing scales. And even if you think you might have been willing to work that hard, you weren't given the opportunity, so why torture yourself? Comparing yourself with the Joshua Bells or Mark Zuckerbergs or Michael Jordans or Meryl Streeps of this world is like learning to swim and comparing yourself with a dolphin. What's the point? You have to be you, as you are, rather than a desperately striving, lesser version of somebody else.

YOUR INNER CRITIC

We've all heard of the "inner critic," but some of us have an inner prosecuting attorney, or maybe an inner hanging judge. Where the compassionate view might be to see ourselves as a work in progress— "Okay, I didn't make the team, but I'm getting there"—we flagellate ourselves with self-loathing self-descriptions like "fake" or "imposter" or "loser."

How would you respond if your child was falling behind in class or hitting the cookie jar too hard? Most of us would try to find a tutor, switch out the cookies for apple slices, or suggest that the whole family get into hiking. But when we as adults hit a rough patch at work, or put on a few pounds, the first thing we do is start trashing ourselves, which is no way to find the motivation to change.

When we're anxious, we call someone we love. Why? Because warmth and kindness make us feel safe, valued, and that we can cope. So why can't we be that kind of loving friend to ourselves, turning that kind of compassion inward?

And why do we take someone else's occasional bad review of our behavior or performance more to heart than we take our friends' much more frequent compliments? People can be harsh, biased, unkind, narcissistic, self-serving, and just plain mean, which is why it's vitally important to remember that someone else's negative evaluation of you is rarely objective, and that there is absolutely no reason to interpret that bad review as the truth, much less to incorporate it into your own self-evaluation.

Stories that do carry some element of truth can actually be the most troublesome, because we put a lot of stock in "truth," no matter how selective and partial it may be. Perhaps, as your classmates years ago never failed to point out during dodgeball, you were bad at sports. Okay, but maybe you were bad at sports because you preferred painting, reading, or writing code to hurling a ball at other kids. Or maybe you thought sitting out the game to keep your friend with asthma company was more important than being the fourth-grade PE champ. Which truth do you hold on to? Your story is your story. You need to own it, rather than it owning you, and to honor it with compassion.

Your mother-in-law may call you impulsive, but maybe you're just spontaneous. Your husband may say that you're a control freak, but you have the choice of accepting that term or choosing to see yourself as organized. Your wife may be bugging you about your love handles, but hell—you're fifty! A little bit of belly fat is normal. The question is, in every case, how well does the evaluation serve you? If your cholesterol is high and you can't climb stairs anymore without getting winded, maybe you should head to the gym. If you get stress headaches and are regularly up until midnight folding laundry, maybe you could lighten up on being "organized." The point is, the person who has the final say over what's of value in your life should be you.

Developing meaningful compassion for yourself does not mean deluding yourself. You need to be deeply aware of who you are, for better and for worse, and fully attuned to the world around you. But even when we're dealing with the real world as it really is, you have enormous leeway in how you respond to it.

CHOOSING WILLINGNESS

We want life to be as dazzling and painless as possible. Life, on the other hand, has a way of humbling us, and heartbreak is built into its agreement with the world. We're young, until we're not. We're healthy, until we're not. We're with those we love, until we're not. Life's beauty is inseparable from its fragility.

One of the greatest human triumphs is to choose to make room in our hearts for both the joy and the pain, and to get comfortable with being uncomfortable. This means seeing feelings not as being "good" or "bad" but as just "being." Yes, there is this relentless assumption in our culture that we need to *do* something when we have inner turmoil. We must struggle with it, fix it, control it, exert brute-force willpower over it, remain positive. What we *really* need to do, though, is also what is most simple and obvious: nothing. That is, to just welcome these inner experiences, breathe into them, and learn their contours without racing for the exits.

If you were trying desperately to quit an addiction to smoking, you'd expect to crave cigarettes for a while. The craving would be normal and physiologically based—so why would you be judgmental about it? In fact, it's feeling the need to control a craving that can turn the craving into an irresistible compulsion. Which is why an open acceptance—ending the tug-of-war by dropping the rope—is the way to go.

You can't choose or control your desires. You *can* choose whether you light that cigarette, eat a second helping of dessert, or go home with somebody you just met at a bar. When you're emotionally agile, you don't waste energy wrestling with your impulses. You simply make choices that are connected to what you value.

In one study, researchers asked participants who were trying to quit smoking to allow the intense physical yearnings, thoughts, and emotions about tobacco to come and go without trying to control them. The program centered on the metaphor of a car journey with the participant as the driver, heading toward a destination of personal importance—namely, quitting. In the backseat are all the driver's thoughts and emotions, behaving like your bad-influence friends from high school yelling, "Do it! Go on—just one puff!" and "You'll never make it, wimp!" Participants in the program allow room for these unruly "passengers" while continuing to drive toward their destination, with their eyes on the prize.

The participants randomly assigned to this "willingness" group—the ones who learned to open their hearts and willingly accept and allow the presence of the cravings without having to give in to them—were compared with those in another group in the gold-standard smoking-cessation program recommended by the National Cancer Institute. Sure enough, the willing "drivers" group had a quit rate that was more than double the other group's.

Sometimes, in our struggle with difficult circumstances, we make things much worse for ourselves. We take raw pain and convert it into real suffering. After Theresa had a miscarriage in her mid-forties, doctors told her she would not be able to conceive naturally or via in vitro fertilization, which meant that this pregnancy had been her last chance. That was upsetting enough on its own. But then, rubbing salt in her own wounds, Theresa told herself that she should get over it, that women had miscarriages all the time, and that her troubles were her own fault for trying to get pregnant so late. She chastised herself for not focusing on the many other blessings that gave her life meaning. Not surprisingly, none of this did her any good.

What Theresa needed to do was to show up: show up to her sadness and disappointment and be fully present with it. This meant acknowledging the true extent of her grief, saying goodbye to the child she'd lost, honoring the memory of that life that would never be, and then allowing herself to fully experience whatever she was feeling. This would not necessarily mean she'd get over her loss or be happy about the fact that she'd never give birth to a child of her own. But by confronting her pain and acknowledging it, and then by embracing every stage of her sorrow, she would be able to move through the experience, learn from it, and come out the other side, rather than being stuck, paralyzed by sadness.

But to maintain this kind of equanimity, we do need some basic emotional equipment, including a nuanced emotional vocabulary.

An infant screams because she can't express her unhappiness any other way. Any form of unpleasantness—hunger, a wet diaper, fatigue—elicits an inarticulate and overwhelming bawl of distress (which her parents may be able to interpret, but the folks in the next apartment can't). Over time we teach our children to define and articulate their needs and frustrations. We say, "Use your words, honey."

Unfortunately, many adults still don't use their words to define and understand their experiences and the emotions surrounding them. Without the subtle differentiation in meaning provided by language, they're unable to make sense of their personal issues in a way that might allow them to "get a handle" on them. Merely finding a label for emotions can be transformative, reducing hugely painful, murky, and oceanic feelings of distress to a finite experience with boundaries and a name.

Many years ago, I worked with a client named Thomas who had once been a senior executive. One morning he'd come into his office with a busy day ahead only to suffer a seizure, completely out of the blue. Thomas had no history of seizures, and after his doctors put him through a series of tests, they concluded it was highly unlikely he would have another.

But Thomas started to obsess. Eventually, he became so crippled with the fear of having another seizure that he simply couldn't get on with his life. By the time he was referred to the community clinic where I worked, he was homeless. He had become so hooked on the certainty of having another seizure that he'd stopped going to work. That's how he had lost his job, and eventually his wife, and was reduced to living on the streets.

Each time I met Thomas, I greeted him with some variation on the usual "How are you feeling?" But no matter how I phrased the conversational prompt, he responded the same: "Just a little bit of bother." Which left me incredibly curious. Here was a man who lived on the streets in a state of near-constant panic, but all he could say about his situation was that it was "just a little bit of bother."

During one weekly session, we got to talking about Thomas's mother, the only person he was still connected with. She had looked out for him after everyone else had given up, and he'd visited her often at her nursing home. When I asked him how she was, he said, "It's been just a little bit of bother. She died."

After this rather graphic demonstration of his inability to differentiate among his emotions, I realized that Thomas had a condition called alexithymia, which literally means "no words for mood." People with this problem often struggle to convey how they're feeling and rely on vague, black-and-white labels like "I'm stressed." They are either "fine" or "not so great." It's a bit like the Black Knight from *Monty Python and the Holy Grail* saying, "Tis but a scratch!" or "Nothing but a flesh wound!" every time he loses another limb.

Words have enormous power. The wrong word has led to wars, not to mention the end of countless marriages. There's a world of difference between stress and anger, or stress and disappointment, or stress and anxiety. If we can't accurately label what we're feeling, it becomes difficult to communicate well enough to get the support we need.

If a client says, "I'm stressed," and I take that at face value, I might advise her to list out her priorities or to delegate more. But under the rubric of "I'm stressed," her real meaning might be "I thought my career would be more satisfying than it is, and I'm disappointed with my life," which is a whole different ball game. When the truth of that struggle is laid bare, tips on delegating or setting priorities just aren't going to cut it.

Alexithymia isn't a clinical diagnosis, but it's a difficulty that millions of people struggle with every day. And it carries very real costs. Trouble labeling emotions is associated with poor mental health, dissatisfaction in jobs and relationships, and plenty of other ills. People with this condition are also more likely to report physical symptoms like headaches and backaches. It's as if their feelings are being expressed physically rather than verbally. It's also true that sometimes, when people can't clearly express their feelings in words, the only emotion that comes through loud and clear is anger, and the unfortunate way they express it is by putting a fist through the wall—or worse.

Learning to label emotions with a more nuanced vocabulary can be absolutely transformative. People who can identify the full spectrum of emotion—who realize how, for example, sadness differs from boredom, or pity, or loneliness, or nervousness—do much, much better at managing the ups and downs of ordinary existence than those who see everything in black and white.

WHAT THE FUNC?

Along with the importance of precisely labeling our emotions comes the promise that once we do give them a name, our feelings can provide useful information. They signal rewards and dangers. They point us in the direction of our hurt. They can also tell us which situations to engage with and which to avoid. They can be beacons, not barriers, helping us identify what we most care about and motivating us to make positive changes.

My clients live all over the world, so I travel a lot. When I travel, I often find myself in some variation of the same setting: I'm in a nice hotel room with a beautiful view, a room-service dinner, and a sneaky feeling that I label as "guilt." I feel guilty that I'm not spending time with my kids, Noah and Sophie. I feel guilty that my husband, Anthony, is at home without me. It's not a comfortable feeling, but time and time again, there it is.

I used to get hooked on old stories: I'm a bad mom; I abandon the people I love. But over time, I have learned to show up, not only by identifying the feeling as guilt, but also by seeing how that feeling can be useful. I have realized that my guilt can help me set my priorities and sometimes realign my actions. After all, we don't feel guilty about the things we don't care about.

A good question to ask yourself when you're trying to learn from your emotions is, "What the func?"

No, that's not a typo for a more explicit question. "Func" is short for "function," so "What the func?" is shorthand for "What is the purpose of this emotion?" What is it telling you? What does it get you? What's buried underneath that sadness, frustration, or joy?

My on-the-road guilt signals to me that I miss my children and value my family. It reminds me that my life is heading in the right direction when I'm spending more time with them. My guilt is a flashing arrow pointing toward the people I love and the life I want to lead.

In the same way, anger can be a sign that something that matters to you is being threatened. Have you ever been mad at a colleague for trashing one of your ideas in front of your boss? On the face of it, that anger could seem like, well, just anger. But deeper down, it also could be a signal that teamwork is a value you hold dear, or that you feel less secure in your job than you'd realized. Anger is no fun to experience, but the awareness it provides can be channeled into active steps. It can be a flashing arrow pointing you toward positive changes like finding a new job or scheduling time for a performance review with your boss.

Once we stop struggling to eliminate distressing feelings or to smother them with positive affirmations or rationalizations, they can teach us valuable lessons. Self-doubt and self-criticism, even anger and regret, shine light into those dark, murky, sometimes demon-haunted places that you most want to ignore, which are places of vulnerability or weakness. Showing up to these feelings can help you anticipate the pitfalls and prepare more effective ways of coping during critical moments.

If you can confront both your internal feelings and your external options—while maintaining the distinction between the two—

you'll have a much better chance at having a good day, not to mention a meaningful life. You'll make important decisions in light of the broadest possible context. This requires the honesty and integrity to incorporate our experiences into a narrative that is uniquely our own, as well as one that will serve us, helping us understand where we've been so that we can better see where we want to go.

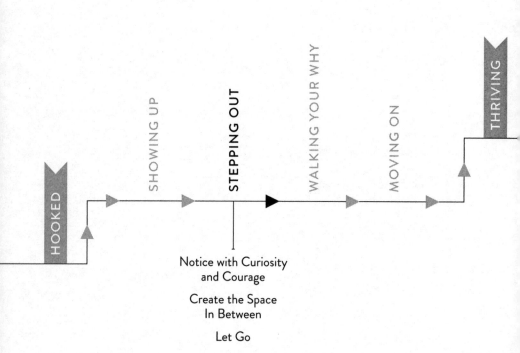

HOOKED

SHOWING UP

STEPPING OUT

WALKING YOUR WHY

MOVING ON

THRIVING

Notice with Curiosity
and Courage

Create the Space
In Between

Let Go

CHAPTER 5

STEPPING OUT

James Pennebaker, a distinguished professor at the University of Texas, got married right out of college in the early 1970s. Three years after his marriage, he and his wife started to question their relationship, and Pennebaker, confused and unsettled, sank into a depression. He ate less, drank more, and started smoking. Embarrassed by what he saw as emotional weakness, he became increasingly isolated.

One morning about a month into this decline, Pennebaker climbed out of bed and sat down at a typewriter. He stared at the machine for a moment and then started writing freely and frankly about his marriage, his parents, his sexuality, his career, and even death.

As he wrote, and continued to write in the days that followed, something fascinating happened. His depression lifted and he felt liberated. He began to reconnect with his deep love for his wife. But the writing had an even further-reaching impact. For the first time, he started to see the purpose and possibilities in his life.

Pennebaker's own experience getting through this rocky period sparked forty years of research into the links between writing and emotional processing. Over and over again Pennebaker did studies in which he would divide people into two groups and ask one group to write about emotionally significant experiences and the other to write about everyday things: their shoes, or maybe the cars passing on the street. Both groups wrote for the same time span—about twenty minutes a day, three days in a row.

In Pennebaker's experiments, some participants in the "emotionally significant writing" group wrote about sexual abuse by once-trusted family members; some about catastrophic failures; others about the devastating losses of their deepest relationships through breakups, illness, and death. One woman described unfathomable guilt stemming from an incident that had happened when she was ten. She'd left a toy on the floor and her grandmother had slipped on it and fallen, ultimately leading to the grandmother's death. Another man wrote about a warm, summery night when he was nine years old. His father had taken him outside and calmly announced that having children had been the biggest mistake of his life and that he was leaving.

In each study, Pennebaker found that the people who wrote about emotionally charged episodes experienced a marked increase in their physical and mental well-being. They were happier, less depressed, and less anxious. In the months after the writing sessions, they had lower blood pressure, better immune function, and fewer doctor visits. They also reported higher quality relationships, better memory, and more success at work.

When I first discovered Pennebaker's research, I was struck by the way it echoed my own teenage experience journaling about my father's cancer. While my father was dying, and then when he was gone, my life was painfully different, and the writing helped me voice my regret about all the time I hadn't spent with him and all the things I hadn't said. I also wrote about the moments I didn't regret, and how I'd done the best I could. Through that writing, I learned to sit with all my emotions, both the pleasant and unpleasant ones. This, in turn, gave me insight about myself, the most important revelation being "I am resilient." I realized that I can live with my full self, even the parts I'm not so thrilled about.

Still, I was skeptical of Pennebaker's results, which seemed too good to be true. How could writing for just twenty minutes a day for three days have had such a positive and lasting effect on people's lives? I kept Pennebaker's research tagged in my notebooks. Then, many years later, when I was doing my PhD on emotions, I had a chance dinner with him. This meeting led to much animated discussion, after which I took a deeper dive into his work.

I read about an intervention Pennebaker had conducted at a Dallas computer company that had laid off one hundred senior engineers. Most of these were men over fifty who had worked at the company since college. This was the only work life they knew, and getting pushed out had left them panicked and confused. They faced the real likelihood of never working in their field again. After four months, not one of them had found a new job.

Pennebaker and his team wondered if writing about their experiences could help the "downsized" engineers. Eager to try anything that might improve their employment prospects, the engineers agreed to participate. Pennebaker had one group of engineers write about being laid off. They delved into their feelings of humiliation, rejection, and outrage; the related strains on their health, marriages, and finances; and their deep worries about the future. The two control groups either wrote about time management or didn't write at all.

Before the writing began, there were no differences between the groups in terms of motivation or the effort they were making to land a new job. But afterward, the degree of change between them was astonishing. Just months after the emotionally charged writing sessions, the men who had delved into how they truly felt were *three times* more likely to have been reemployed than those in the control groups. The writing not only helped the men process their experiences; it helped them step out from their despondent inertia and into meaningful action.

After many more studies, with many thousands of participants—children and the elderly, students and professionals, the healthy and the sick—we can say with confidence that showing up and applying words to emotions is a tremendously helpful way to deal with stress, anxiety, and loss. (For people who don't like putting pen to paper or fingers to keyboard, there is nothing magical about the act of writing per se. Talking into a voice recorder, for example, can deliver the same results.)

But after showing up, there's another critical aspect of agility: stepping out. Deeper analysis over the years shows that unlike brooders, or bottlers, or those who let it all hang out in big venting rants, the writers in these experiments who thrived the most began to develop insight, using phrases such as "I have learned," "It struck me that," "the reason that," "I now realize," and "I understand." In the process of writing, they were able to create the distance between the thinker and the thought, the feeler and the feeling, that allowed them to gain a new perspective, unhook, and move forward.

Make no mistake: These people had not found a way to *enjoy* being betrayed, lost, jobless, or critically ill. But by dissolving the entanglement that had built up between their impulses and their actions so they could see their experience in context, and from a broader perspective, they flourished despite it all. More often than you might expect, they found ways of turning these obstacles into opportunities to connect more directly with their deepest values.

PENNEBAKER'S WRITING RULES

Set a timer for twenty minutes. Open up your notebook, or create a new document on your computer. When the timer starts, begin writing about your emotional experiences from the past week, month, or year. Don't worry about punctuation, sloppiness, or coherence. Simply go wherever your mind takes you, curiously and without judgment. Write just for yourself and not for some eventual reader. Do this for a few days. Then, throw the paper away (or stick it in a bottle and cast it out to sea), or close the document without saving it. Or if you're ready, start a blog or find a literary agent. It doesn't matter. The point is that those thoughts are now out of you and on the page. You have begun the process of "stepping out" from your experience to gain perspective on it.

THE SECRET LIFE OF WHAT YOU SEE

C. W. Metcalf was a comedian on television before he became a "humor consultant" to large organizations. (If you think that's pretty funny—as in a ridiculous job title—then you've probably never worked in a large organization.) He does wonderfully amusing routines onstage that also teach people how to deal with the stress of downsizing or growth—or whatever aspect of corporate life is killing them at the moment. One of my favorites is when he pulls out an empty chair, identifies it as "his job," and then goes into a hilarious rampage about just how utterly, utterly horrible his job is, every day, in every way. He takes a breath, points to the chair a few feet away, and says, "My job really sucks." Then he delivers the punch line: "Thank god I'm over here."

We've all experienced this ability to separate ourselves from our experience and see it from a different perspective. Years ago I found myself thoroughly hooked, raging over the phone at a customer-care agent about a phone bill that was wrong yet again. I worked myself into a froth about the hours I'd wasted trying to resolve the issue and the company's inability to correct its own error.

Then, for no reason that I can explain, I simply stepped out from all the rage. It was almost like one of those out-of-body experiences in which the soul is said to rise up to the ceiling and look back down at the scene from above. With this new perspective, I was able to notice my anger for what it was: blind rage, directed at the wrong person. I was able to experience compassion for the poor customer-service woman—what a terrible job she had, listening to lunatics like me all day!—and to understand that my alienating her would get me nowhere. I switched gears, apologized, and then from a perspective that included another's point of view, we moved on to a space of constructive and collaborative problem solving.

I had just stepped out—created the gap between stimulus and response. In the process I'd even recovered a bit of my humanity. This is the place from which you can choose behaviors based on your values rather than indulging in what your thoughts, emotions, and stories are insisting that you do. This newly created space allows you to be sensitive to the context, to shift your actions to what will work in the here and now, rather than being driven by mindless impulses—like *Justice! Revenge! You can't treat me like this!*

When you've stepped out, you can see things you haven't seen before. (Why do you think they call it "blind" rage?)

Take a look at this line drawing. What do you see?

A B C

Obviously it's the first three letters of the alphabet. But maybe there's another possibility.

When we're hooked, we typically have only one perspective, one answer, one way of doing things. We're entangled with our thoughts, emotions, and stories. They dominate us, direct our actions, and make us inflexible, often leaving us to wonder after the fact, "What was I thinking!?" Only when we step out can we see that there might be more than one way of looking at the situation.

The center squiggle above is obviously a "B." But now look at the exact same middle squiggle on the next page.

This is an illustration of what can happen when you see the same thing from a different view. We become sensitive to context, see more possibilities, and can respond in different ways. We become more agile.

You can purposefully cultivate the ability to create the kind of distance that I inadvertently did during my unfortunate phone rage. In fact, to live an intentional, meaningful life and to really thrive, one of the most critical skills to develop is this ability to take a *meta-view*, the view from above that broadens your perspective and makes you sensitive to context. This skill helps you gain new perspective on your own emotions and on how others might be feeling, and is a key factor in our ability to self-reflect.

A meta-view can be particularly useful when we make mistakes.

We can torture ourselves over the simplest screwups, alternately brooding and bottling, waking up in the middle of the night ten or twenty or forty years later to relive some stupid thing we did in junior high.

A B C

12 13 14

A mistake is often a matter of life not going as we'd planned. When we blow it, we blame ourselves for failing to make the right choice or do the right thing. A mistake, however, often supposes a predetermined course—that we have failed to navigate a static world that "is" a certain way. But as the famous nineteenth-century German field marshal Helmuth von Moltke the Elder was fond of saying (and I paraphrase), No battle plan ever survives first contact with the enemy. No matter how certain we are about the best course of action, the world is constantly changing, and circumstances are unpredictable. And since no one knows for certain what will happen, in battle or otherwise, everybody is bound to make a few decisions that turn out to be not so effective.

But you can view your mistakes from other perspectives. "Good" mistakes, for example, can teach us something of value, such as "Don't rush up to pet dogs you don't know." When we look at it that way, we find a lesson to be learned and a potential for growth. To find that knowledge, we need to be able to examine our gaffes from multiple angles.

For ages, monks and mystics have used practices such as meditation to dissolve the fusion between thought and thinker, impulse and action, freeing the mind from some of its tighter constraints and distorted interpretations.

When these sorts of practices first became popular with Westerners in the late sixties, the operative phrase was "Be here now." The idea was that the undisciplined mind is easily distracted, whipsawing back and forth in time, engaging with "push" memories of the past and "pull" projections of the future. It's only by being fully in the present, fully attuned to the "now," that we can deal with the moment in an emotionally agile way.

Since the days when the Beatles and the Beach Boys and Mia Farrow went to India to sit at the feet of the Maharishi, research in the behavioral and cognitive sciences has worked to demystify these gauzy imports from the East, and much of their focus has been on a technique for paying attention, on purpose and without judgment. That technique is called *mindfulness*.

Harvard researchers recently performed brain scans on sixteen people, before and after they took an eight-week mindfulness-training program to reduce stress. The results showed changes in the brain regions associated not just with stress but also with memory, sense of self, and empathy.

It appears that practicing mindfulness improves connectivity inside the brain's networks that keeps us from being distracted. By helping us focus, mindfulness also increases competence. It improves memory, creativity, and our moods, as well as relationships, health, and longevity in general. By paying attention to what's going on around us, rather than ignoring it or just going along with the program, we can become more flexible and insightful.

One of the leaders in mindfulness research, the Harvard psychology professor Ellen Langer, has found that musicians who play "mindfully" produce music that audiences like better. Magazine salesmen who sell mindfully sell more subscriptions. Women who make presentations mindfully are viewed as being more forceful and successful, because, it turns out, the speaker's mindfulness trumps any gender bias the audience might have. It's that quality of being fully present and available that audiences relate to most. Meanwhile, when we're in the audience, attending mindfully helps us break through our own distractions or premature judgments and see what others have to offer.

Unfortunately, the term has become such a buzzword, especially in business circles, that there's now a bit of a backlash. (You know a concept is overdone when you see *Mindful Leadership for Dummies* in bookstores.) And certainly, the idea that everything you do, every moment of the day, should be approached with purposeful in-the-moment attention is ridiculous. You really don't need to take out the recycling mindfully, or comb your hair mindfully—that is, unless you find it rewarding. (See the "Ways to Become More Mindful" sidebar on page 100.)

To many people, the practice also seems veiled in the flowery language left over from the ashram. That's why it may be easier to understand what mindfulness is really all about by first looking at its opposite: mindlessness.

Mindlessness so easily leads us down the path of getting hooked. It's the state of unawareness and autopilot. You're not really present. Instead you're relying too heavily on rigid rules or shopworn distinctions that haven't been thought through.

You know you're being mindless when . . .

You forget someone's name as soon as you hear it.

You put the card credit in the trash and your food wrappers in your handbag.

You can't remember whether you locked your door on your way out of the house.

You bump into or break things because you're not really "in" the space you're in.

You're so focused on what's coming up that you forget something you need to do right now.

You don't notice that the words "credit" and "card" are swapped in the example a few sentences above.

You eat or drink without being hungry or thirsty.

You feel an emotion just "came out of nowhere."

On the other side of the ledger, it's mindfulness that allows you to notice your uncomfortable feelings and thoughts rather than be entangled in them. When you're mindful of your anger, you can observe it with greater sensitivity, focus, and emotional clarity, perhaps discovering where the anger is actually coming from. You might even discover that your "anger" is really sadness or fear.

But the calm awareness—the *just being*—that's associated with hard-core mindfulness does not come easily to everyone.

Blaise Pascal, the seventeenth-century mathematician and philosopher, famously wrote, "All men's miseries derive from not being able to sit in a quiet room alone." A series of studies at Harvard and the University of Virginia put this idea to the test. Psychologist Timothy Wilson and colleagues asked participants to sit alone with their thoughts for a period of about ten minutes. Most of the subjects were miserable. Some went so far as to choose the option of giving themselves a mild electric shock rather than simply sitting there and being present.

This illustrates just how uncomfortable people can be with their inner world. It could be they're unaware that we all have a "self," an entity that exists apart from our appetites and attitudes, something more than our social-media presence, our résumé, or our status;

more than what we own, what we know, whom we love, or what we do.

Mindfulness can help us get more comfortable with this inner essence and help us follow the original commandment of self-improvement, straight from the Oracle of Delphi in ancient Greece: *Know thyself.*

We can't read the instructions when we're stuck inside the jar. Mindfulness guides us to become more emotionally agile by allowing us to observe the thinker having the thoughts. Simply paying attention brings the self out of the shadows. It creates the space between thought and action that we need to ensure we're acting with volition, rather than simply out of habit.

But mindfulness is about more than knowing "I'm hearing something," or being aware "I'm seeing something," or even noticing "I'm having a feeling." It's about doing all this with balance and equanimity, openness and curiosity, and without judgment. It also allows us to create new, fluid categories. As a result, the mental state of mindfulness lets us see the world through multiple perspectives and go forward with higher levels of self-acceptance, tolerance, and self-kindness.

WAYS TO BECOME MORE MINDFUL

BEGIN WITH THE BREATH

For a full minute, do nothing but focus on your breath. Start by breathing in and out slowly, counting to four as you inhale, and counting to four as you exhale. Naturally, your mind will try to wander. Notice that, and then just let it be. Don't berate yourself for "not being good at this." Each time a thought pops into your head, just try to bring your focus back to your breath. That's the whole game. It's not about winning. It's about engaging in the process.

MINDFULLY OBSERVE

Pick an object in your immediate environment—a flower, an insect, your big toe—and focus on it for one minute. Really look at it and try to see it as if you've just arrived from Mars and are seeing this thing for the very first time. Try to isolate and identify its various aspects and dimensions. Focus on the color, the texture, any movement it makes, and so on.

REWORK A ROUTINE

Pick something you do every day and take for granted, like making coffee or brushing your teeth. The next time you do it, focus on each step and action, each element of sight and sound and texture and smell. Be fully aware.

REALLY LISTEN

Select a piece of music such as quiet jazz or classical and really tune in—use headphones if you can—as if you'd grown up in a cave and this was the first music you'd ever heard. Don't judge it: Just try to identify different aspects of rhythm, melody, and structure.

Ultimately, your efforts at mindfulness should take you beyond intellectual or even emotional classifications of your thoughts and experiences. You can be like the poet Andrew Marvell, heading into a garden and aiming for "a green thought in a green shade." Or maybe no thought at all. Maybe just a deeper appreciation of green.

This is when the mind stops insisting on being rational, stops being a problem-solving or indexing machine, and becomes more of a sponge than a calculator. It just is.

That kind of calm receptivity makes a natural partnership with curiosity, and when the two align, great things can happen.

I often read my daughter, Sophie, to sleep with *Harold and the Purple Crayon,* a delightful book about a curious four-year-old who draws things into existence. He wants to visit the moon, so he draws a path skyward and he's there. He draws an apple tree, and then a dragon to protect the fruit. He's afraid of the dragon, so he draws water that covers his head. He gets lost and draws windows to find his way back home.

Harold doesn't know where he's going or what's ahead of him, but he keeps using his purple crayon to draw out potential experiences.

Curiosity like Harold's is a decision. When we decide to curiously explore the world inside us and outside, we can make other decisions more flexibly. We can intentionally breathe space into our reactions and make choices based on what matters to us and what we hope to be.

Whenever I read this story to my daughter, I notice that Harold doesn't try to stop his emotions. When he's scared, he doesn't run away. Rather, he looks at his fear and then moves forward with creative solutions, like drawing water over his head to hide from the dragon and creating a new window to slip through. Harold, the fictional four-year-old, can teach us all a thing or two.

CREATING THE SPACE IN BETWEEN

Sonya was a partner at a leading accounting firm who came to me for help because, despite her MBA and many other accomplishments, she felt like a fraud. Her fear of being exposed made her tongue-tied as she fumbled and tried to prove herself every day. Psychologists call Sonya's form of fear the *imposter syndrome*. She lived her life convinced that someday, someone was going to discover the awful "truth" that she didn't deserve to be where she was. Even though she had never received a negative performance appraisal, she felt stressed, unfulfilled, and anxious.

Sonya was hooked in the "thought-blaming" way that we discussed earlier. She treated her "I'm a fake" fears as facts. She didn't put her hand up for projects she would have loved to take on and approached her work with an overly narrow view of her talents and abilities, as if she were looking at herself through a telescope turned the wrong way. When she learned to bring a mindful curiosity to her experiences, she was able to step out, to turn the telescope around to take in a wider perspective.

"Okay, I'm having a thought that I'm a loser," a person with thoughts like Sonya's might say. "What else is new? That's my 'wounded child' speaking up. I have lots of thoughts. I can notice and acknowledge all of them, good or bad, but I reserve the right to act on only those thoughts that will help me live the life I want to live."

When I work with executives in groups, I often do an exercise that seems like a silly game for little kids but that has a surprisingly profound effect. I ask everyone to write on a sticky note the deepest fear they have about themselves, or any unsurfaced "subtext" they carry with them into their work, relationships, and lives: "I'm boring," or "I'm unlovable," or "I'm a fraud," or "I'm a bad person." Then I invite each executive to slap that sticky note onto his or her chest, and we put on some music and pretend we're at a party. Everyone shakes everyone else's hand, looks that person in the eye, and introduces himself or herself with "Hi, I'm boring. Nice to meet you," or whatever they've written down. (By the way, "I'm boring" is my label. I was always "the boring one," or so it seemed to me.)

This is an enormously powerful experience. Afterward, the executives invariably tell me that the ugly "truth" they have stuck on themselves, the harsh evaluation that has had so much power over them, has been tamed. I get emails years later in which people tell me what a relief it is to be able to see a thought as just a thought. They've given their fear a name, and then are able to have had some fun at its expense. By doing so, they create more space to be themselves. They've stepped out.

You can get a hint of this phenomenon simply by staring at the letters that spell your name. You've seen them so many times that you skip over multiple levels of representation and interpretation and immediately get to something along the lines of "that's me." But when you really look at the Roman symbols that represent certain sounds in a written language, you begin to see their shapes, some of which are pretty funny-looking. (I'm looking at you, lowercase *d*.)

Or say a simple word like "milk" aloud. Now repeat it for thirty seconds. As you do this, you'll notice a change. At the start of the experiment, you identify the word's literal meaning: the white stuff you pour on your cereal or in your coffee or dunked Oreos into as a child. Yet, as you repeat the word, something different starts to happen. The typical ways you relate to "milk" fade away and you begin to notice the way it sounds, the way your mouth moves when you say it—the word as just a word.

Now try the experiment with the aspect of yourself that you most dislike or even with a challenging everyday experience. "I'm fat," "Nobody loves me," or "I'm gonna screw up the presentation." Pick your phrase, then say it ten times. Now say it backward or mix up the order of the words. What you'll see is that these sounds turn from something meaningful and evocative, which may hold great sway over you, into something remote, devoid of power, and slightly ridiculous. No longer are you entangled and looking out at the world from the perspective of the negative thought. Rather, you're looking *at* it. You've created space between the thinker and the thought. You've turned your telescope.

This wiggle room and breathing space you create gives you the great gift of choice. You begin to experience thoughts as just thoughts—which is all they really are—rather than as directives that must be followed, or even agonized over. You can have the thought that you're a fake, notice it, and then purposefully choose to set it aside, because what's more important is making a meaningful contribution to this meeting you are in right now. You can experience and even rationalize the thought that your spouse should make the first move to patch up the argument you had this morning, and then pick up the phone to call him or her. You can accept your craving for crème caramel, notice your "I want that!" thoughts, and then choose not to reach out your hand. This is not bottling, because you are not ignoring or denying or trying to suppress the thought, emotion, or desire. Rather, you are curiously noticing it and the information it brings but not letting it call the shots.

If you rise high enough in an organization, eventually you'll get a staff, and the staff will send reports. But you, the executive, need to decide which report to act on and which to set aside, remembering that, like self-serving courtiers, thoughts and emotions don't always speak the truth and that they come and go. Which is why we need to treat these reports as mere position papers, subject to our evaluation, rather than as representations of solid reality leading to action points. Thoughts and emotions contain information, not directions.

Some of the information we act on, some we mark as situations to be watched, and some we treat as nonsense to be pitched into the circular file.

Emotional agility means having any number of troubling thoughts or emotions *and* still managing to act in a way that serves how you most want to live. That's what it means to step out and off the hook.

A different kind of linguistic stepping out popped up during the summer of 2010, when basketball superstar LeBron James faced a tough decision that would ultimately bring howls of complaint down on his head, but also two back-to-back world championships: Should he stay in Cleveland, Ohio, with his hometown Cavaliers, the team that had nurtured his career from the start? Or should he move to Florida to join the Miami Heat, a move that would help take him to a new level in his career? He decided to go to Florida, and shortly thereafter described his thought process: "One thing I didn't want to do was make an emotional decision. I wanted to do what's best for LeBron James and to do what makes LeBron James happy."

Notice how he initially referred to himself using the first-person pronoun "I," but then, when discussing how he didn't want to make an emotional decision, he switched to the third-person "LeBron James." At the time, many of his detractors attributed his choice of words to nothing more than his king-size ego (certainly understandable given the reputation of famous athletes). But subsequent events—after his highly successful stint in Miami, he came back to play in Cleveland—suggest that he may indeed have been highly conflicted about his decision. If so, he used a sophisticated verbal strategy to manage his emotions.

Research shows that using the third person this way is an effective technique for distancing yourself from stress (or anxiety or frustration or sadness) that can help you regulate your reactions. It also leads people to view future stressful situations more as challenges and less as threats.

TECHNIQUES FOR STEPPING OUT

1. **Think process.** See yourself as being in it for the long haul and on a path of continuous growth. Absolutist statements drawn from old stories ("I'm bad at public speaking" or "I suck at sports") are just those—stories. They are not your destiny.

2. **Get contradictory.** In Zen Buddhism it's common practice to contemplate paradoxes such as "What is the sound of one hand clapping?" There are probably paradoxes from your own life that you could chew on in a Zenlike fashion: You may love and loathe your hometown, your family, or your body. You can feel that you're both the victim and the person responsible for a relationship breakdown. Embracing and accepting these seeming contradictions improves your tolerance for uncertainty.

3. **Have a laugh.** Humor can be a stepping-out practice because it forces you to see new possibilities. As long as you aren't using humor to mask genuine pain (bottling), finding something funny about yourself or your circumstances can help you accept and then create distance from it.

4. **Change your point of view.** Try to consider your problem from the perspective of someone else—your dentist, perhaps, your child, or even your dog.

5. **Call it out.** Anytime you get hooked, identify that thought for what it is (a thought) and that emotion for what it is (an emotion). You can do this by introducing the language "I'm hav-

ing the thought that . . ." or "I am having the emotion that . . ." Remember you have no obligation to accept your thoughts' or emotions' opinions, much less act on their advice. (This, by the way, is my go-to stepping-out hack. It's easy to do on the fly or when you're in the midst of a difficult interaction.)

6. **Talk to yourself in the third person.** As in the LeBron James example, this strategy allows you to transcend your egocentric viewpoint and regulate your reaction.

LETTING GO

With a receptive, open, broader view, we can hold our thoughts and emotions lightly, not be hooked on old stories, and not prejudge new experiences as they come along. We can let go.

Monica is married to a guy named David. They love each other deeply, but Monica has one gripe: Every day, her husband comes home from work and drops his coat on the floor. Now, this complaint might sound petty, but anyone whose relationship has lasted beyond a particular length knows that these small annoyances—the toothpaste tube left uncapped, the slurping of the morning coffee—can hook us into an obsessive cycle of projections and negative interpretations.

Trouble is, when we're hooked, that one dimension takes over. We stop seeing the people involved in our hooks as fully rounded human beings who exist outside our perception of them, or beyond what we need from them.

"Every day I say, 'David, can you please not drop your coat on the floor?'" Monica told me. "And every day he does! He says it's because he's so tired and so excited to see me that he just doesn't think about hanging up his coat."

Monica tried to understand his explanation, but she still became irritated—and he still dropped the coat on the floor. She tried to ignore the coat lying there. She obstinately walked on the coat when it was in her path. She tried hanging up the coat herself—often with a big show of it so David was acutely aware of her effort. By this time, the coat on the floor had become way more than just a coat on the floor. It had become a symbol of the "fact" that David wasn't taking Monica seriously on an issue that was important to her. The coat was proof David was ignoring and belittling her. Even though the coat was trivial in the all and all, whenever they argued, the coat came up.

Then one day, right around David's birthday, Monica found the perspective that let her change the game. She did it by distancing herself from her thoughts—the interpretation that "he's doing it to belittle me." She created space between this simple annoyance and the profound emotions that came up in response. She made a conscious decision, going forward, to let go of the subjective threads she'd woven into that coat and to assume only the most generous intentions on David's part. Instead of being hooked on what David was or was not doing by leaving it on the floor, she would give him a birthday gift: She would accept this was simply a part of David, a person whom she loved, and that without a sense of injured pride or resentment, she would lovingly pick up his coat. She would end the tug-of-war by dropping the rope.

"I didn't do it begrudgingly," she said to me. "Or in defeat. I did it in a willing, kind, accepting, and compassionate way because I love him, and I value our relationship. I know if anything ever happened to David, there would be a million things I would trade to have him and that coat back in my life again."

A friend, Richard, told me about a fifteen-year exercise in frustration with his wife, Gail. Richard worked at home, and Gail had a horrible commute, so he took on the role of househusband in charge of daily operations, including shopping and meal preparation. Over time, Gail had less and less to do with the kitchen, and Richard became a pretty good cook. Still, on weekends, and especially when company was coming, he always hoped she'd pitch in—mostly because it would be more fun to prepare food together. She never did. Richard became increasingly angry and frustrated. Was Gail taking advantage of him? Why did she treat him like the houseboy? Who did she think he was, Cinderella?

Then one day, as he was whipping up a lamb tagine for their guests, he had a revelation. He knew Gail loved him and that she was not a selfish person. He also knew that she did not enjoy cooking, but that she did enjoy pulling out the nice china and setting the table and arranging flowers, activities that also contributed to their dinner parties. Any other interpretation he might apply toward her resistance to helping in the kitchen was a choice on his part, and not one that helped his relationship with his wife.

He chose to let go of any sense of unfairness, and along with it, any expectation that his wife would ever lend a hand chopping vegetables or stirring the gravy. That recognition, and his acceptance of it, gave him enormous relief and a deep sense of inner freedom. It also gave him new energy and vigor to pour back into his relationship with Gail.

What you let go of will be different from what another person chooses to let go of. Sometimes it is letting go of a past experience. Sometimes it means releasing an expectation or a relationship. Sometimes letting go means forgiving others. Sometimes it means forgiving yourself.

Just saying the words "let go" is enough to bring a sense of hope and relief. But those same words can bring up the anxiety that we will be left with nothing—that we have resigned ourselves to a hopeless situation. In truth, though, when we let go of that one thing, we are left with everything else. Clinging to that one small piece of emotional driftwood prevents us from feeling part of the dynamic system that is the universe itself.

I've talked about the value of turning the telescope around to get a broader view. Astronauts take this broader view to its most literal extreme. They speak of the "overview effect," the transformation they experience after traveling deep into space, and then glancing back to see our entire planet, with all the rest of us and our problems, large and small, looking like a tiny blue beach ball floating in the blackness. That's "stepping out" to get a fresh perspective big-time.

One of the astronauts most associated with the overview effect is Edgar Mitchell, who was the lunar module pilot of Apollo 14, and, in 1971, the sixth person to walk on the moon. Mitchell described his moment of epiphany this way: "On the return trip home, gazing through 240,000 miles of space toward the stars and the planet from which I had come, I suddenly experienced the universe as intelligent, loving, harmonious."

Not everyone will be able to embrace quite such a mystical vision, but for everyone, "let it go" can at least become "hold it lightly," and when that happens, the heart expands. This does not mean a passive resignation to fate, but rather a vital engagement with the way things actually are, unfiltered and undistorted by rigid mental lenses.

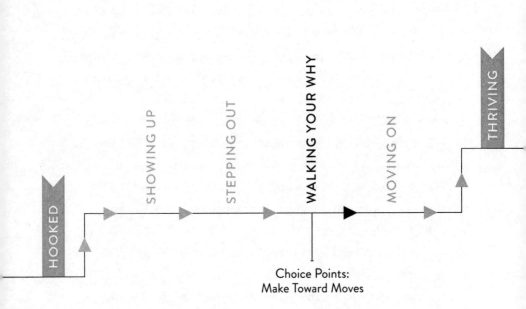

HOOKED

SHOWING UP

STEPPING OUT

WALKING YOUR WHY

MOVING ON

THRIVING

Choice Points:
Make Toward Moves

CHAPTER 6

WALKING YOUR WHY

Tom Shadyac gave Jim Carrey his first big role in *Ace Ventura: Pet Detective,* and then went on to direct him in huge hits like *Liar Liar* and *Bruce Almighty.* He's also worked with Eddie Murphy, Robin Williams, Morgan Freeman, and Steve Carell.

By the early 2000s, Shadyac's movies had grossed more than two billion dollars, and Shadyac himself was worth more than fifty million dollars. He owned a seventeen-thousand-square-foot mansion in Los Angeles and a fleet of luxury cars, and he traveled in private jets. By most people's standards, he'd achieved success in the super-competitive movie business, but by his own standards, not so much.

"The lifestyle was fine," he wrote, "but it certainly didn't deliver on the promise of elevating happiness. I simply found it all neutral, and in some ways, negative. And when I considered the needs of others—how others couldn't meet their basic needs for food, medicine, etc.—it didn't feel right. No one runs up to you and hands you all of that money. You have to ask for it. And by asking for it, what's implied underneath is that I am more valuable than others; more valuable than the cook, the maintenance man, the janitor. And I simply don't believe that. I know our economic textbook will tell us otherwise, but my heart is telling me otherwise."

Shadyac realized that the cultural validation of his "value" notwithstanding, he needed something different. So he sold his mansion and moved to smaller digs that, while by no means ascetic, felt more suitable for him. He began flying economy class on commercial airlines and riding his bike for local transportation. He became a lot choosier about his film projects and started donating money to organizations he believed in. Shadyac didn't renounce his material possessions altogether; he just winnowed them down until they had an appropriate place in his life, so he had more time and energy to devote to his true priorities.

He also made sure that the choices he made were for himself alone. "I can judge no one," he said in an interview, "and my path is different than someone else's. I haven't given up everything. I simply met myself at my needs."

Because Shadyac used closely held principles to realign his life, chances are they'll continue to serve as powerful guides regardless of what's going on around him. "[We have] a very extrinsic model of success," he explained. "You have to have a certain job status, a certain amount of wealth. I think true success is intrinsic . . . It's love. It's kindness. It's community."

Some of his Hollywood buddies thought he was nuts and didn't hesitate to tell him so. Others praised Shadyac for his decisions. But neither reaction mattered much to him. Asked in another interview whether he was happier since his lifestyle change, he answered, "Unquestionably." He knew he was doing the right thing for himself, and it gave him the courage to follow his own path regardless of criticism or admiration.

In short, he was walking his why.

"Walking your why" is the art of living by your own personal set of values—the beliefs and behaviors that you hold dear and that give you meaning and satisfaction. Identifying and acting on the values that are truly your own—not those imposed on you by others; not what you think you should care about, but what you genuinely do care about—is the crucial next step of fostering emotional agility.

WE MAKE DECISIONS THAT ARE NOT OUR OWN

Identifying what you value and acting on it is not always easy. We're constantly bombarded with messages—from culture, advertisers, our upbringing, our religious training, and our families, friends, and peers—about what is important and what makes us worthy. Most of us aren't in the market for private jets and sprawling ultra-prime real estate, but nevertheless, we all experience the same kind of cultural pressures Shadyac did. It may be that your neighbor drives a fancier Toyota than you do, or buys five-dollar coffees at Starbucks instead of making Folgers at home. She may take nicer vacations or have more household help, or seem more fulfilled in her career, happier in her marriage, or a more adept parent than you are.

No matter the context, the act of making comparisons is the same. In the same way Shadyac continued on what he thought was his chosen path in Hollywood until realizing that it wasn't *his* choice, we all have a tendency to simply plow ahead with blinders on, just getting through the day. If we need guidance, we look around to check out what other people are doing, mindlessly choosing all sorts of things that we've been told are universal keys to satisfaction, such as a college education, home ownership, or having children. In fact, these are not for everyone. It's just a lot faster and easier to follow what we see than to work it out for ourselves.

Other people's actions and choices affect us more than we realize, on every level, through a fascinating phenomenon called *social contagion*. If the term brings to mind a virus, spreading through a population via seemingly random casual contact, that's exactly the idea. Studies show that certain behaviors really are like colds and flus— you can catch them from other people. Your risk of becoming obese increases with each obese person you come into contact with. Your chances of getting divorced, a decision you'd think would be deeply personal and individual, are higher if other couples in your peer group are also splitting up.

And then things get really weird. Unlike infectious diseases, which tend to be transmitted from person to person, you can "catch" some behaviors from people you've never even come into contact with. One study found that couples are more likely to divorce not just when their friends do but also when friends of their friends do. That's right: Your personal life can be affected by people you don't even know.

That's even true of smaller decisions. A Stanford University marketing professor tracked more than a quarter of a million airline passengers and proved that you're a whopping 30 percent more likely to make an in-flight purchase if your seatmate does. When you're trapped in a plane with nowhere to go, that 30 percent can add up to a lot of bad films and snacks you could just as easily have done without.

These kinds of choices are based on mindless decision making, an approach in which there is no space between impulse and action, thinker and thought, and where the herd instinct comes into play. Sometimes, this behavior is okay (one more airplane movie isn't going to kill you); sometimes it's even beneficial: If all your friends exercise regularly, you might be more likely to get off the couch.

But make too many mindless, autopilot decisions over the long haul, and eventually you'll find yourself living what feels like somebody else's life—a life aligned with values you don't necessarily ascribe to. (Not to mention that you might be carrying several extra pounds' worth of in-flight snacks you didn't really want, and might have spent hours *not* reading books you'd been planning to read but somehow didn't have time for.) As the Talking Heads song goes, "And you may ask yourself / Well . . . how did I get here?"

Just "going with the flow" drains the purpose from your work and life, makes personal and professional relationships seem tenuous and uncertain, and almost guarantees that you'll fail to live with intention. All this means you may not accomplish things you'd really like to accomplish.

To make decisions that match up with the way you hope to live going forward, you have to be in touch with the things that matter to you so you can use them as signposts. If you've never taken the time to sort out your values, you're always winging it, which is how we wind up frittering away our time—surfing the Internet, forwarding pointless email chain letters, cycling through hours of reality TV— and feeling unfulfilled. You see this lack of clear intention played out in people's choices (or lack thereof) in everything from romantic partners to vacations. (Then again, if everyone liked the same things that I do, my favorite little hotel would be way too crowded.)

Not knowing your values doesn't always lead to autopilot decisions. Another danger is you may make choices that seem thought-out and deliberate but that don't serve you, such as deciding to buy a family home two hours away from your job, without acknowledging that the long commute will cut into the family time you truly believe is precious.

We expend a lot of energy on these kinds of counterproductive decisions, energy that would be better put toward achieving our goals.

Making choices and negotiating relationships without a clear set of governing values at the front of your mind is taxing labor. It not only involves the confusing work of facing the world each day with everything up for grabs, but also sometimes means retrofitting your emotions so they appear to line up with what you think is expected of you—such as acting thrilled at yet another vacation trip to Walley World, even if you'd rather be anywhere else.

WHAT DO I WANT MY LIFE TO LOOK LIKE?

Psychologists asked a group of people in their early twenties to write a letter about their current selves to their future selves. Some were asked to cast their minds just three months ahead, to their "near selves," and the others to jump forward two decades, to their "distant selves." They were then instructed, "Think about who you will be [then] . . . and write about the person you are now, which topics are important and dear to you, and how you see your life." In other words, they were asked to think about and articulate what mattered to them.

After writing these letters, the two groups were presented with a questionnaire made up of three illegal scenarios—buying a computer they knew to be stolen, committing insurance fraud, or downloading media illegally—and asked how likely they would be to participate in them. The people who wrote letters to their distant selves were significantly less likely than those who wrote letters to their near selves to say that they would participate in any of the three unsavory actions.

At first glance it may not be clear how something like writing a letter—to yourself, no less—could possibly change your attitude about behavior. But these writers were creating what's called *continuity of self*. By connecting with their distant selves and with their values, they were able to understand themselves as people with core beliefs and a moral keel that would remain stable, even as other elements and situations in their lives changed.

By contrast, the people who were asked to look only three months ahead continued to think of their distant selves—as research has shown we often do—as abstract strangers. They went on to make their choices accordingly, as if they were making them for someone else. After all, if you believe the person you'll be twenty years from now has little relation to the person you are now, why would it matter if you bought stolen goods, cheated your insurance company, or—to give some more common real-world examples—took up smoking, squandered your retirement money, or loaded yourself up with credit card debt?

Creating continuity of self can both help to prevent bad choices and encourage good ones. In another experiment, college-age participants were told to pretend they'd just received one thousand dollars out of the blue. Then they were asked to allocate it into four different categories: "use it to buy something nice for someone special," "invest it in a retirement fund," "plan a fun and extravagant occasion," and "put it into a checking account." But before the subjects divvied up their imaginary windfall, researchers put each participant into a virtual-reality environment. Half the group saw digital avatars of their current selves, while the other half saw digital avatars of themselves as they might look at the age of seventy. As you might expect, the group who saw older avatars allocated more than twice as much of their theoretical windfall to their imaginary retirement funds. Taking time for the long view leads to actions that benefit the long term.

Jeff Kinney is the author of the bestselling kids' series *Diary of a Wimpy Kid* (150 million copies sold in forty-five languages). And while he's thrilled by the success of his work and plans to keep doing it, he also knows that this one single creation isn't going to be enough to sustain him forever. "If my whole life were 'Wimpy Kid,'" he told the *New York Times,* "it wouldn't be very fulfilling. I don't want to be designing 'Wimpy Kid' pillowcases for the rest of my life."

By connecting with his future self, Kinney found the motivation to alter his path to more fully align with his values. He opened a bookstore in his hometown, where he occasionally teaches cartooning classes and works the odd shift at the cash register and in the café. For him, it's about giving something back to the world that has given him so much, and it feels right. "If one kid's life is changed because of this bookstore," he said, "then the whole thing was worth it."

Kinney and Shadyac's stories also illustrate a much bigger truth: If you know your own personal values and generally live by them, you are also likely to be comfortable with who you are. You don't need to compare yourself with other people because you're a success—by your own definition. Shadyac interprets success as living a life filled with love and community; Kinney interprets it as giving back. By their own standards, both men have made it big.

IDENTIFYING YOUR VALUES

The word "values" can have a scolding, Sunday-school connotation that's pretty unappealing. It feels restrictive, or punishing, or, worse, judgmental. We hear a lot about having the "right" values (or the wrong ones), but what does that really mean? And who decides what values are worth having?

First off, I don't think that inflexible notions of right and wrong help us much. And they certainly don't belong in a book about emotional agility! Instead, I see values not as rules that are supposed to govern us, but as qualities of purposeful action that we can bring to many aspects of life. Values aren't universal; what's "right" for one person may well not be for someone else. But identifying what matters to you, whether that's career success, creativity, close relationships, honesty, altruism—there is an almost infinite list to choose from—gives you a priceless source of continuity. Values serve as a kind of psychological keel to keep you steady.

And you don't have to settle on just one. A colleague of mine describes values as "facets on a diamond." Sometimes, he says, "when you turn one to face you squarely, another may have to move away—but it is still there, part of the whole, and visible through the prism."

Here are some other characteristics of values:

They are freely chosen and have not been imposed on you.
They are not goals; that is, they are ongoing rather than fixed.
They guide you rather than constrain you.
They are active, not static.
They allow you to get closer to the way you want to live your life.
They bring you freedom from social comparisons.
They foster self-acceptance, which is crucial to mental health.

Above all, a value is something you can *use*. It helps you place your feet in the right direction as you journey through life, no matter where life leads you.

When the author Elizabeth Gilbert was writing her memoir *Eat, Pray, Love,* she had many moments of doubt about herself, the book, and the whole project of writing. "I had a strong mantra of THIS SUCKS ringing through my head," she remembered. She agonized and cursed the universe for making her a writer. And then, from the endless loop of negative self-evaluation in her mind, she emerged with a value she hadn't known she had.

"The point I realized was this—I never promised the universe that I would write brilliantly; I only promised the universe that I would write. So I put my head down and sweated through it, as per my vows."

By identifying and then staying true to the tenet of being a creator through writing, which was paramount to her, she finished her book. The rest, as we know, is publishing history.

Here are a few questions to ask yourself in order to start identifying your values:

Deep down, what matters to me?

What relationships do I want to build?

What do I want my life to be about?

How do I feel most of the time? What kinds of situations make me feel most vital?

If a miracle occurred and all the anxiety and stress in my life were suddenly gone, what would my life look like, and what new things would I pursue?

The answers to these questions can help you start to figure out the guiding principles of your life, many of which are probably inherent, even if you're not explicitly aware of them. Are there particular areas in which people consistently seek your advice and expertise? Are you most alive doing certain activities and work projects? Is there a time when you feel most yourself?

The thing to ask is not whether something is "right" or "wrong," but rather how it relates to the way you want to live your life. When you know what you *do* care about, you can be free from the things you *don't* care about.

If, for example, being a good parent is something you value, understanding what that looks like for you, specifically, is far more important than trying to conform to some general notion of what a "good parent" is supposed to be. There are all kinds of parents in the world, and there is no single right way to be one, even within your city or neighborhood or group of friends.

Some potential questions to ask yourself about parenting: "What do I want people to observe when they see me with my child? What would I observe if I watched myself? Is my behavior reasonably consistent from one setting to the next? Does my behavior align with my core beliefs about what a good parent is?"

Parenting is just one example, of course. You can apply the same kinds of questions to almost any aspect of daily life. One way to start doing this is to answer a single question, in writing, each night before bed: "As I look back on today, what did I do that was actually worth my time?" This isn't about what you liked or didn't like doing on a particular day; it's about what you found to be valuable.

If you discover after a few weeks that you have very little to write down in answer to this question, press the issue another way by asking yourself when you wake up each morning, "If this were my last day on earth, how would I act to make it a great final day?" For example, if you value your relationship with your wife but have gotten into the habit of not saying a real hello when she gets home after work, you might decide to stop whatever you're doing when she comes through the door and greet her with a warm hug. Once you've done something new, you can decide whether it was worth your time, and before long you'll have a list of actions and experiences that align with what you believe to be important.

THE WHISTLE-BLOWER

At the age of twenty-four, Sergeant Joseph Darby was a U.S. Army reservist. Called up during the early days of the Iraq War, he was posted to the now infamous Abu Ghraib prison, where, unbeknownst to the rest of the world, U.S. soldiers were subjecting detainees to physical and sexual abuse. Within the prison walls, this behavior had come to seem normal, and as one soldier after another began to participate in these abuses, Darby looked the other way. Even when his fellow guards gave him a CD that included some of the abuse photos on it, he initially played along.

"It was amusing at first," he told an interviewer. But the more he witnessed, the more he realized that the abuse "violated everything I personally believed in and all I'd been taught about the rules of war." After a few days of stressful deliberation, he handed over the CD to a superior officer, an action that ultimately led to the prosecution of many of the soldiers in the photos.

Conformity and loyalty are key concepts in military culture. And under stressful conditions, members of tightly knit military units can fall prey to dangerous groupthink, exhibiting violent and dehumanizing behavior that in other contexts they would condemn as wrong. The atrocities committed at Abu Ghraib are a textbook example of the powerful phenomenon of group coercion. Resisting the pull of group behavior takes a great deal of strength, and Darby was able to make the dramatic switch by acting from a place of truth within himself. By staying aligned with his values, he was able not only to break free from the group's behavior but also to muster the courage to make the abuse public, even though he was so afraid he'd be found out as the whistle-blower that at one point he slept with a gun under his pillow.

Though its results were shattering, Darby's choice was actually quite simple. He had a powerful personal sense of acceptable behavior, so the decision to become an informant was ultimately straightforward.

When you connect with your real self, and what you believe to be important, the gulf between how you feel and how you behave closes up. You begin to live your life without as many regrets, and without as much second-guessing.

Most of us will never find ourselves in circumstances as dire as Sergeant Darby's, but we all face many other choices: whether to sell credit-default swaps for a living, where to settle down, how to educate our kids. Even the trivial choices—cook dinner or order pizza? walk or drive?—add up. As Aristotle told his Greek friends long before they joined the European Union, "You are what you habitually do."

This is why having a clear understanding of your own values is critical to finding change and fulfillment. It's not just that values are nice things to have. Rather, research shows that values actually *help* us access greater levels of willpower and grit and safeguard us from negative social contagion. They also protect us against subconscious stereotypes and beliefs that limit us without our even knowing they're there—and yet can have a real, negative impact on our ability to face challenges.

Say you're a female first-year college student dreaming of becoming a doctor, but you've grown up in a culture that constantly tells you "girls are bad at science." Then you have a setback, such as a bad grade on your first test in freshman biology. You may be more likely to drop the class and give up your dreams.

Unless, that is, you're clear about what matters to you. One important study found that just identifying their personal values helped protect a group of minority students from absorbing the dangerous cultural message that they couldn't perform as well academically as their more privileged peers. In the study, African American and Latino middle schoolers were asked to complete a ten-minute exercise in which they wrote down what mattered most to them. Their answers included everything from dancing to family to politics, and the effect of this simple exercise was astonishing. After focusing on their connections to the world and people outside themselves, the students were able to improve their GPAs enough to close the achievement gap between them and their white classmates. In many cases, the effect lasted into high school. And all because these kids took a few minutes to think about their core values.

A similar scenario played out for a group of female college students enrolled in an introductory physics course—a classic setting in which doubts about gender and scientific ability can flourish. The students who were randomly assigned to do a values affirmation exercise performed better on their physics exams and in the course overall than those who hadn't done the exercise. By thinking about what was important to them, they unleashed their true potential, regardless of cultural skepticism about their abilities.

We are on this planet for only a limited time, and it makes sense to try to use that time wisely, in a way that will add up to something personally meaningful. And study after study shows that having a strong sense of what matters leads to greater happiness, as well as to better health, a stronger marriage, and greater academic and professional success. The subjects of one such study, who affirmed just one core value, responded better to warnings about potential health problems (and more strongly voiced their intention to address them going forward) and were more accepting of others' cultural worldviews.

When we make choices based on what we know to be true for ourselves, rather than being led by others telling us what is right or wrong, important or cool, we have the power to face almost any circumstance in a constructive way. Rather than being caught up in pretending or social comparison, we can stride forward with confidence.

WALKING YOUR VALUES

Of course, determining what you truly care about is only half the process of walking your why. Once you've identified your values, you then have to take them out for a spin. This requires a certain amount of courage, but you can't aim to be fearless. Instead, you should aim to walk directly into your fears, with your values as your guide, toward what matters to you. Courage is not an absence of fear; courage is fear walking.

When Irena Sendler was a seven-year-old living in Poland, her father, a doctor, told her, "If you see someone drowning, you must jump in to save them." When the Nazis invaded her town during World War II, this value of helping that she held so dearly led her to shelter and feed her Jewish neighbor.

As the war progressed, Sendler moved on to creating, with her like-minded friends, thousands of false papers to aid Jewish families in escaping from the notorious Warsaw Ghetto. From there, disguised as a social worker checking for typhus, she started smuggling children out of the ghetto herself.

It was terrifying, but she never wavered, not even when the Gestapo arrested her and sentenced her to death. She later described a sense of relief at the news; at last she would be free from the fear that had come with the brave path she had chosen.

Then a guard helped her escape and go into hiding. Yet, instead of protecting herself for the remainder of the war, Sendler remained true to her values and continued, at enormous risk, to work to save Jewish children—at least 2,500 in all. She stayed the course when it would have been far easier, and safer, to duck and run. But Sendler knew that without action, a value is just an aspiration, rather than the way we really are.

Whether your values-based actions are a matter of life and death, as Sendler's were, or of the blessedly mundane "should I go to sleep on time or indulge in another hour of Netflix?" variety, you will eventually arrive at what I call a *choice point,* a metaphorical fork in the road where you are presented with just that, a choice. But unlike many choices—black shoes or brown? latte or cappuccino?—each choice point presents you with the opportunity to walk your why. Will you move *toward* your values and act like the person you wish to be, or will you move *away* from your values and act against them? The more you choose moves that are *toward* your values, the more vital, effective, and meaningful your life is likely to become. Unfortunately, when we're hooked by difficult thoughts, feelings, and situations, we often start making moves away from our values.

If you value relationships and hope to get married, you can put that value in motion by Internet dating, taking a cooking or rock-climbing class, or joining a book club where you might meet someone who shares your interests. Insisting that you're too shy or nervous to take such actions is allowing yourself to make a move away and is directly opposite from what you say you value.

If you hope to be healthier, you can start by changing what you eat, or by going to the gym, or even just by taking the stairs instead of the elevator. But it can't be just an intellectual commitment. You have to actually walk the talk—or should we say "walk your why"? After all, when you ride a bicycle, you can stay balanced and upright only when you're in motion. It's the same with values.

GOAL CONFLICTS

How many times have your found yourself torn between two options, both of which you feel strongly about? Work versus family? Caring for yourself versus caring for others? Spiritual leanings versus worldly ones? Or to put it differently, what if moving toward each of your values leads you in opposite directions?

The key is to think about these choices not as better or worse but as equal and different. Then it's up to you to find the reason for making the choice, not because one thing is better than the other, but simply because a decision *has* to be made. To come to a decent decision, we'd better know ourselves pretty well.

"Choices," the philosopher Ruth Chang said, "are chances for us to celebrate what is special about the human condition . . . that we have the power to create reasons for ourselves to become the distinctive people we are."

Often, what we view as a values conflict is really an issue of goal conflict (and, importantly, values are not goals), or of time management, or of the difficulty in committing to a plan or a course of action. Or it may be that as mere mortals, we simply cannot be in two places at once. One of the biggest issues many people face on this front is creating a work-life balance. For many of us—myself included—there's a constant tug between working and spending time with our kids and partners.

But what if the choice is not really between work and home? What if the choice is about being fully committed to both rather than conflicted and torn?

If you say, "I value being a loving parent; I will bring that love to my interactions with my kids," and "I value being a productive worker; I will bring that productivity to my desk every day," that is very different from saying, "I value being a loving parent, so I will leave the office at five every day regardless." With the former approach, you're no longer experiencing a conflict but an expansion of what is possible in your life.

Since values relate to quality—rather than quantity—of action, the amount of time you spend enacting your values doesn't necessarily reflect how much they matter to you, or limit the degree of engagement you bring to the precious moments you have with your loved ones or to the limited time you have at work. If you need to put in a twelve-hour day at the office to complete a project, something as simple as sending a quick email or text to your spouse can keep you connected to your value of being a loving partner. (In psychology departments it's called "social snacking.") You may have to travel on business, but you can usually call your kids every night at bedtime while you're away and really focus on them while you talk. Holding these values may mean working a bit harder and more efficiently at the office, so you can get out the door at something like a reasonable hour. And you may have to give up running the March Madness betting pool or pitching on the company softball team, but when you frame these activities in terms of how much you value your family life, such trade-offs become easier.

Sometimes, of course, the decisions get more complicated. If your job absolutely requires you to travel on your son's birthday, chances are you're not going to stay home no matter how much you value your relationship with your child. (You also value being able to pay the bills and *provide for* your child.) But since you value being a loving parent, you can find another way to show your love, like organizing a celebration before you leave town, having something special delivered to him on the big day, or video calling into the party.

We all spend time in different value domains depending on our circumstances, and being in one doesn't mean you value the others any less.

Making hard choices can actually be liberating because it helps you define who you truly are and demonstrates the power we all have to shape our lives. If you can willingly accept the pain associated with giving up the road not taken, you can embrace the decision you did make and move forward with clarity.

Values, in fact, are not limiting or restrictive. Instead, they give us latitude we might not otherwise allow ourselves by providing a continuous web of support. Knowing our values also makes us flexible and open to new experiences. We can use our values to make more deliberate, satisfying "toward moves" and fewer reflexive, unproductive "away moves."

Living your values—walking your why—however, will not bring you a life free of difficulty. We all face dilemmas, no matter how solid our beliefs and regardless of our specific decisions. Moving toward your values isn't always fun or easy, at least in the moment. If you're socially anxious, for example, and a friend invites you to a party, the easiest response might seem to be to send your regrets. But if you truly value friendship and let these values guide you, you'll make a toward move instead and say yes. When you arrive at the party, you will experience another bout of discomfort—more than if you had stayed at home. But this initial discomfort is the price of admission to a meaningful life.

As Elizabeth Gilbert discovered, even after she had begun to focus just on her writing, the process still remained a tough slog. Sergeant Darby and Irena Sendler learned that being true to their beliefs meant following paths that would make their lives more challenging, not less. I recall a profound interaction I had with Jane Goodall, the famous primatologist. She told me that at a certain point in her illustrious career, which she has devoted to conservation and animal welfare, she went through a period in which she cried frequently. She later discussed this with a friend, who asked her why she thought she'd been so sad. "And I said something which really startled me. It had never come into my mind before," Goodall told me. "I said, 'I think I was crying because I knew I was giving up the right to feel selfish.' That's what I said. Isn't that strange?"

A colleague of mine described the dilemma this way: "Your mind says, 'Hey, I thought if I did this values thing, I wouldn't feel so bad or so conflicted after making the choice.' But the simple fact is you still have to choose."

There is loss inherent in choice. You give up the path not taken, and with any loss comes a certain amount of pain, sorrow, and even regret. You can know why you're doing something—remember the question "What did I do that was actually worth my time?"—and still feel anxious or sad about it. The difference is that you will have a real investment in it that will help you navigate with agility through those difficult emotions. Even if your choice turns out to be wrong, you can at least take comfort in knowing you made the decision for the right reasons. You can show up to yourself with courage, curiosity, and self-compassion.

I once heard a story about a woman who was told that she was dying. She asked her doctor, "Is there hope?"

The doctor replied, "Hope for what?"

What he was suggesting is that even when we are dying—and we are all, right now, in the process of dying—we can make choices, based on our values, about how to live out the rest of our days.

I was reminded of this story when a friend and colleague, Linda, was diagnosed with the fatal neurodegenerative disease amyotrophic lateral sclerosis, or ALS. Linda loved her children. She loved her friends. And she loved to dance. She suffered tremendously as her symptoms progressed, but she continued, despite her pain, to send social media updates that were filled with love and life. When Linda reached her choice point, she made a toward move and opted to remain connected. Just before she went into hospice and not long before she died, she wrote, "I plan on taking this quiet time in that sacred place to think about my life and death. I feel lucky. Many people are snatched from this life without a chance to measure their mission . . . In the meantime, dance if you can."

By knowing who you are and what you stand for, you come to life's choices with the most powerful tool of all: your full self. Dance if you can.

HOOKED

SHOWING UP

STEPPING OUT

WALKING YOUR WHY

MOVING ON

THRIVING

THE TINY TWEAKS PRINCIPLE

Tweak Mindsets

Tweak Motivations

Tweak Habits

CHAPTER 7

MOVING ON

THE TINY TWEAKS PRINCIPLE

Cynthia and David were fighting about money. She had been scrimping and saving for months, with no small amount of sacrifice, to create an emergency nest egg for . . . well, you just never know. Now her husband wanted to use that money to take the family on a rafting trip through the Grand Canyon. It wasn't a bad idea—they could certainly use a vacation—but Cynthia wanted them to be *practical* for once. David, on the other hand, took a different approach. "The kids are going to be grown before we know it," he told Cynthia. "We're going to be creaky and old. We've been talking about this trip for years. If not now, when?"

The discussion went back and forth, the tension rising with each round, as more old business—"You're just like your father!" "Well, you're just like your mother!"—got thrown into the vortex.

Then Cynthia glanced down. "What happened to your socks?" she asked.

David looked down, a little off guard, and examined his blackened feet as if for the first time. "I had to chase a raccoon out of the garden last night," he said after a moment. "I didn't have time to put on my shoes."

They looked at each other, and then they both cracked up, the tension between them clearing like the air after a heavy rain.

Families bicker about money all the time in households around the world. The only thing unusual about the argument between Cynthia and David was that psychologists were filming it. Researchers had wanted to observe couples "in their natural habitat." Since moving into these couples' homes would have been a little awkward, the researchers did the next best thing and created a studio apartment at their lab. The makeshift dwelling was located in a park-like setting at the University of Washington in Seattle and consisted of a single room with a kitchenette, some furniture, a TV, and a music system. Couples agreed to spend twenty-four hours on view—one couple at a time—usually beginning on Sunday morning. Each was asked to bring groceries and whatever else they'd need for their usual indoor weekend activities—movies, books, even work. The only other instruction was to spend the day as they would at home. During twelve of their twenty-four hours, usually nine a.m. to nine p.m., they were filmed.

One of the things the research team was most struck by was the way individuals made and responded to "bids for emotional connection" or efforts to reach out, like Cynthia's question about David's grimy socks. The researchers organized these bids into a hierarchy based on how much emotional involvement each demanded. Moving from lowest to highest, this is what the bids looked like:

A simple bid for a partner's attention: "There's a pretty boat."
A bid for a partner's interest: "Didn't your dad sail a boat
    like that?"

A bid for enthusiastic engagement: "Hey, with a boat like
   that, we could sail around the world."
A bid for extended conversation: "Have you called your
   brother lately? Did he ever get his boat fixed?"
A bid for play: Rolling up a newspaper and bopping a
   partner lightly on the head, saying, "There. I've been
   meaning to do that all day."
A bid for humor: "A rabbi, a priest, and a psychiatrist go
   out sailing . . ."
A bid for affection: "I need a hug," or something similar,
   but often nonverbal.
A bid for emotional support: "I still can't understand why
   I didn't get that promotion."
A bid for self-disclosure: "What was it like when you sailed
   with your grandfather growing up?"

The researchers noticed that after each of these gambits, the
partner receiving the bid would respond in one of three ways: by
"turning toward" his or her partner with enthusiasm that varied
from a grunt of acknowledgment to wholehearted participation; by
"turning away," usually by simply ignoring the comment or question; or by "turning against" ("Please, I'm trying to read!").

How the couples reacted to these emotional offerings revealed
volumes about each couple's future. Although they may have seemed
inconsequential on the surface, these tiny behaviors were the best
predictors of how well each couple would fare in the long term. In
one follow-up six years later, the couples in which either partner had
responded with intimacy to only three out of ten bids were already
divorced, while those who had responded with intimacy to nine out
of ten bids were still married.

In marriage, these micro-moments of intimacy or neglect create a culture in which the relationship either thrives or withers. The tiny behaviors feed back on themselves and compound with time, as every interaction builds on the previous interaction, no matter how seemingly trivial. Each person's moments of pettiness and anger, or generosity and lovingness, create a feedback loop that makes the overall relationship either more toxic or happier going forward.

In the early fifties, a singer named Kitty Kallen had a huge hit with a torch song called "Little Things Mean a Lot." And she was right. Tweaking the little things can have a powerful impact when doing so allows us to align our behavior more closely with what really matters to us.

Nature favors evolution, not revolution. Studies from many different fields have demonstrated that small shifts over time can dramatically enhance our ability to thrive. The most effective way to transform your life, therefore, is not by quitting your job and moving to an ashram, but, to paraphrase Teddy Roosevelt, by doing what you can, with what you have, where you are. Each little tweak may not look like much on its own, but think of them as frames in a movie. If you alter each frame, one at a time, and put them all together, you'll end up with a totally different film, and one that tells a totally different story.

Or (to continue the boat metaphor used earlier) if you've ever sailed, you know that a shift of a degree or two can dramatically change where you wind up across the bay. Imagine how much greater the effect would be if you were sailing across the ocean.

When our approach to problems is too grand ("I need a new career!"), we invite frustration. But when we aim for tiny tweaks ("I'm going to have one discussion a week with someone outside my field."), the cost of failure is pretty small. When we know we have little to lose, our stress levels drop, and our confidence increases. We get the feeling "I can handle this," which helps us become even more committed and creative. Equally importantly, we tap into the fundamental human need to make progress toward meaningful goals.

In looking for the right places to make these tiny changes, there are three broad areas of opportunity. You can tweak your beliefs—or what psychologists call your mindset; you can tweak your motivations; and you can tweak your habits. When we learn how to make small changes in each of these areas, we set ourselves up to make profound, lasting change over the course of our lives.

A NEW OUTLOOK: TWEAKING OUR MINDSETS

Alia Crum, a professor of psychology, conducted a study in which she made a tiny tweak to the mindsets of eighty-four female hotel cleaners. The hardworking women Crum recruited spent long hours at their jobs, and at the end of their shifts, they went home to look after their families. They didn't have time to exercise at the gym, and they likely ate a standard American diet overloaded with caffeine and sugar. Most were overweight or markedly obese.

Crum's idea was elegantly simple. What if she simply asked the cleaners to think differently about their work? What if instead of feeling guilty about not getting enough regular exercise, the cleaners recognized that the activities they spent a large part of their day doing were, in fact, exercise?

Unless you've lived a truly charmed life, you probably know how tiring it is to clean a house from top to bottom (which is why few of us actually do it). Imagine, then, how exhausting it must be to spend your day bending, pushing, lifting, dusting, and vacuuming about fifteen hotel rooms and bathrooms several days a week. The hotel cleaners didn't see their work as formal exercise because they weren't sweating it out at the gym or swimming laps. But in reality, their daily exertion far exceeded the U.S. surgeon general's exercise recommendations for a healthy life.

Crum divided the cleaners into two groups. While both groups received descriptions of the benefits of exercise, only those in one group were informed that they met the surgeon general's daily exercise requirements.

In terms of intervention—that was it.

Four weeks later, with no other changes in the women's lives, those in the "aware" group had lowered their blood pressure compared to those in the "unaware" group. They'd also shaved off pounds and improved their body-fat and waist-to-hip ratios. The tiny tweak in mindset had made a huge difference.

When I first started to train as a clinical psychologist, I worked as a student therapist, seeing patients at the university clinic in Melbourne, Australia. About once a week I'd discuss my toughest cases with Mike, a senior colleague and supervisor.

In the beginning, my patients' problems seemed so complex, and the resources I had to solve them so woefully inadequate, that I felt completely overwhelmed. Some of the people had been coming to the clinic week in and week out for years, with no apparent improvement. To be honest, after a few weeks I thought that everything I was being asked to do was pointless and that I stood no chance of helping anyone. Then I met Carlos—after which I was *convinced* I stood no chance!

At thirty-seven, Carlos had been out of work for nine years and divorced for eight. At our first interview I could smell alcohol on his breath.

"I've been depressed for as long as I can remember," Carlos told me. He believed something inside himself was broken, and he self-medicated with alcohol, which made all his problems worse.

"I don't think I can help this guy," I told Mike that evening. "He's had depression all his life. He doesn't have any support. He's unlikely to consistently come to therapy, and even if he does come, he still won't stop drinking! I just can't see that he'll change."

Mike smiled and told me I was approaching Carlos's problems with a "fixed mindset."

Many people have heard of the concept of "fixed" versus "growth" mindsets, thanks to the work of Stanford psychologist Carol Dweck and her book, the aptly titled *Mindset*. People with a fixed mindset follow an "entity" theory of self and believe important qualities such as intelligence and personality are fixed traits that cannot be changed. People with a growth mindset believe that these basic qualities are "malleable" and can be improved through learning and effort. Whether you have a fixed or a growth mindset can differ depending on the quality in question. You might be "fixed" with regard to your math skills ("I'm just no good with numbers") but "growth" when it comes to your social skills ("I just need to get to know my new coworkers better").

Studies show that these beliefs about change can have a profound effect on behavior. Children who believe their intelligence is fixed underperform in courses that they find difficult relative to those who believe they can improve their effective intelligence by working hard. After all, those who are open to change and believe they can do better—and that their efforts matter—have a sense of agency over their performance and rise to the challenge. So setbacks or failures don't keep them down, and they persevere, even when they're frustrated.

We also know that one's mindset can be developed and shifted.

The parent who praises a child's accomplishment by saying, "You studied hard!" promotes a growth mindset. The parent who says, "Look at your A, son! You're a genius!" promotes a fixed mindset. If a child comes to believe that success depends on innate intelligence, and that intelligence is a fixed commodity, then he's more likely to think there's nothing he can do when the going inevitably gets tougher and he finds himself struggling in Spanish or pre-calculus.

Dweck, however, notes that it is important not to confuse having a growth mindset with simply working harder. If a child spends hours and hours studying, but her grades stay the same or her understanding of the subject doesn't improve, it's time to consider other strategies. Nor should parents stop at simply praising a child's effort. If your daughter fails her history test, "Good try!" might make her feel better but won't help her improve. Though, Dweck says, "Let's talk about what you tried, and what you can try next" just might.

In a recent study, researchers wondered whether they could improve the success rates of two hundred community-college students who hadn't yet mastered basic high-school math. Not surprisingly, community-college students whose math skills aren't up to par face a lot of obstacles trying to catch up, especially if they hope to transfer to a four-year college. But being placed in a remedial math class can make them feel as if they're hopeless at the subject.

In the study, researchers sent half the students an article explaining that people's brains—even adults' brains—can grow and improve with practice, and then asked the subjects to summarize what they'd read. Compared with a control group that was sent a different article, the students who had received the message that their brains were malleable dropped out of their math classes half as often and got better grades, all because of this tiny change in their mindsets.

When it came to my client Carlos, my mindset was fixed. I didn't believe that I had it in me to help him and that he would make it through therapy. Mike, my supervisor, saw it differently. He helped me tweak my mindset toward viewing the situation as an opportunity rather than a fool's errand. Most important, he helped me focus on small steps in the process (like what skills I needed for different phases of treatment, and how to develop a true relationship with Carlos) rather than on the outcome (my being a "success" at helping to "cure" Carlos). This freed up my thinking and allowed me to direct my knowledge and energy in positive ways. Change is often seen as a onetime event that happens after, say, setting a New Year's resolution. But change is a process, not an event. A focus on this process gives individuals the sense that they can make mistakes, learn from them, and still improve their performance over the long run.

While theories of mindset are most often associated with intelligence and academic success, they have a reach far beyond these areas. They are at the heart of how we position ourselves in the world at large. They can even mean the difference between life and death.

How would you respond to the following?

True or false?

1. Old people are helpless.
2. As I get older, things in my life will get worse.
3. I have less pep this year than I did last year.

Becca Levy from the Yale School of Public Health is interested in researching participants' answers to questions just like these. She then follows them for decades, tracking their health. People who answer "true" on the questions above—those who see aging in terms of inevitable decline or disability—are more likely to suffer from conditions ranging from respiratory illness to hearing loss to premature death as they get older.

In one of Levy's studies, for example—and nearly forty years after being asked for their beliefs about aging—those with negative views on aging were twice as likely to have experienced a heart attack or stroke than those with positive views. And here's the kicker: This dramatic difference held up even *after* Levy had controlled for known risk factors such as age, weight, blood pressure, chronic health conditions, cholesterol, family history, and smoking history. So it wasn't these physical markers at the study's start, but rather the respondents' mindsets at that time—mindsets about a fixed negative future—that truly mattered to their long-term health. In a different analysis, Levy showed that people with fixed negative views on aging die about 7.5 years earlier than those who are more open to a positive future.

This isn't to say some negatives about aging aren't real. There's nothing particularly fun about having a stiff back and creaky knees and discovering strange brown spots on the back of your hands. But certainly when it comes to our minds and coping abilities, many of our perceptions of decline are tied up with our assumptions. When you were twenty-four and you couldn't find your car keys, you might have thought, "Whoa. Out too late last night." Or even just, "Too much on my mind." When you're fifty and you can't find your car keys, you may jump to "Uh-oh. Senior moment." The fact is, fifty-year-olds can simply have too much going on as well. So can eighty-year-olds. Studies show that, on average, seniors have greater life satisfaction and make fewer errors at work relative to their younger counterparts, and that various aspects of thinking and memory actually *improve* with age. Yet when we have fixed negative assumptions, we tend not to take any of these facts into account.

Our brains care deeply about what we believe. A few milliseconds before we make a single voluntary move, our brains fire electrical waves in preparation. Only after that do they send activation signals to the necessary muscles. This preparation for action—called *readiness potential*—is outside our conscious awareness but it is activated by our intention. When we have a reduced sense of our own agency and effectiveness, it weakens the "readiness potential" in our brains.

A malleable sense of self is a cornerstone of emotional agility. People who have a growth mindset and who see themselves as agents in their own lives are more open to new experiences, more willing to take risks, more persistent, and more resilient in rebounding from failure. They are less likely to mindlessly conform to others' wishes and values and more likely to be creative and entrepreneurial. All this adds up to better performance, whether that's in the C-Suite, R&D, Ranger training, or relationships.

Tweaks that activate one's sense of self can also have a profound effect, even when the tweak is purely grammatical. In one study, eligible voters were asked before a major election to respond to survey questions in which voting was conveyed either as a verb—"How important is it for you *to vote* in tomorrow's election?" or a noun: "How important is it to you *to be a voter* in tomorrow's election?" In the first version, voting was presented as just one more errand to be checked off a to-do list on a busy day. The second version, though, positioned voting as an opportunity to be someone of value—"a voter." Just that one change in phrasing from "to vote" to "to be a voter" boosted the officially recorded voter turnout by more than 10 percent.

We all have personal qualities and parts of our identity we wish we could change. But when we try to make changes and run into difficulty, we sometimes focus too much on what we assume is our destiny. We'll say, "I am fat. I have always been fat, and I will always be fat." Or, "I'm just not creative," or even "I was always going to grow up to be a doctor or an accountant."

Tweaking your mindset starts with questioning notions about yourself and the world that may seem set in stone—and that might be working against what matters to you—and then making the active choice to turn yourself toward learning, experimentation, growth, and change, one step at a time.

WAGGING FINGER OR WILLING HEART: TWEAKING OUR MOTIVATIONS

My mom is a tough cookie, and when I was growing up, she eschewed the typical womanly wisdom so often dispensed from one generation to the next. She never told me to "play hard to get" or to "never wear white after September 1." Instead, she used to tell me, "Susan, you should always, always have 'screw you' money!"

After my father passed away, my mother was left to raise three children and spent years simply trying to get by. She did this by selling stationery to businesses—self-employed in a job she detested. She'd wake up at five a.m. so she could pack parcels of pens, pencils, and other sundries; deliver them all over Johannesburg; come back to take customer orders and do bookkeeping; and then collapse, exhausted, into bed at midnight. She managed to do this while simultaneously grieving the loss of my father, who was her lifelong sweetheart; helping my brother, sister, and me through our own loss; and ensuring we were fed, clothed, and educated.

My mother understood firsthand how horrible it feels when you're trapped by your circumstances, basing each decision on what you *have* to do instead of what you *want* to do, and she wanted to protect me from such a fate. "You always need to have just enough money to say, 'Screw you!'" she advised. That way, I would never have to stay in a job I hated or in a relationship that wasn't working for me because I didn't have the financial resources to make a move.

By urging me to set up my own personal screw-you fund, my mother wasn't simply doling out sound personal finance tips. She was also emphasizing the fundamental importance of autonomy, the motivating power of being able to do things out of your own free will and volition, as opposed to being coerced by some outside force. Engaging our autonomy—the power of *want to* rather than *have to*—is the second prerequisite for tweaking your way to significant change.

Ted was a London-based client of mine who eventually became a good friend. He was forty pounds overweight and, because he traveled a lot for work, he found it difficult to get into a healthy routine. After a long flight, he'd show up at a hotel tired, hungry, and missing his family and seek out comfort in a cheeseburger and a couple of beers. Then, while watching TV, boredom would send him over to graze from the snacks in the minibar. His wife and doctor were after him to lose weight and exercise, but somehow, knowing what he "had to" do never actually got him to do it.

Ted had married late in life, and he and his wife couldn't have children, so they'd adopted a boy from Romania named Alex. Alex had been orphaned at a young age and had spent his early years in truly heartbreaking circumstances. He'd been kept almost exclusively in a crib, which prevented him from walking or exploring. He'd barely been held, touched, or spoken to, and was so malnourished he developed long-term learning disabilities.

Despite these difficulties, Alex was a very talented artist who expressed his inner life in incredibly evocative drawings and paintings. One day, when Alex was ten years old, he drew a picture of himself alone, desolate, and abandoned. He titled his picture "The Orphan." Now, Ted was not surprised at the theme of the work—Alex often depicted his early memories. This time, however, Ted noted that the figure in the picture was not a toddler but a young adult. When Ted asked about it, his son began to cry. Through sobs, Alex explained that he "just knew" his dad would die in the next couple of years because of his poor health habits, leaving Alex fatherless yet again.

In that moment, he later explained to me, Ted immediately went from feeling that he "had to" change his health habits to feeling that he "wanted to." Suddenly, he was intrinsically motivated to get healthy purely out of love for his child and the desire to see Alex grow up. Ted began to make small changes—ordering salad instead of fries, placing the minibar candy out of sight when he traveled, and exploring cities on foot rather than by cab whenever he could—and those changes added up over time. He lost weight and kept it off, and even now, whether he's on or off the road, he stays with his routine because he wants to.

In trying to bring our actions more in line with what really matters to us, we can double down on discipline and willpower, but—as most of us have learned the hard way—this rarely leads to the best results. You may drag yourself to the gym, but how often does that lead to a great workout or sticking with an exercise routine? Or you may call up your relatives out of a sense of obligation, but how often do you have a meaningful conversation? When we enter into something this way—compelled by a wagging finger instead of a willing heart—we end up in an internal tug-of-war between good intentions and less-than-stellar execution, even when the end goals—improved health, better relationships with family—are supposedly in line with our values.

Twenty-five hundred years ago, Plato captured this inner conflict with his metaphor of a chariot being pulled by two very different horses. One horse was passion—our internal urges and yearnings—and the other, intellect: our rational, moral mind. In other words, Plato understood that we are constantly being pulled in two opposing directions by what we want to do and what we know we should do. He saw that it was our job, as the charioteer, to tame and guide both horses in order to end up where we want to be.

It turns out Plato wasn't too far off the mark. Modern neuroimaging tells us that whenever the impulsive, reward-seeking system in our brain (passion) conflicts with our rational, long-standing goals (intellect), our brain tries to—pardon the pun—rein things in. Let's say you're trying to eat more healthily. You're at a restaurant, and you spot a delicious-looking chocolate mousse on the dessert tray. That triggers activity in your nucleus accumbens, an area of the brain associated with pleasure. Boy, do you want that chocolate mousse. But, no, you remind yourself. Can't have it. As you muster up the strength to pass on dessert, your inferior frontal gyrus, a part of the brain associated with self-control, kicks in. With both these areas activated, our brain is literally fighting with itself while we try to make a decision about whether to dig in or abstain.

To make matters even more complicated, our baser instincts have a head start. Again, according to brain imaging, when we're faced with a typical choice, basic attributes like taste are processed on average about 195 milliseconds *earlier* than health attributes. In other words, our brain is encouraging us to make certain choices well before willpower even enters the picture. This might explain why, in one study, 74 percent of people *said* they would choose fruit over chocolate "at some future date," but when fruit and chocolate were put right in front of them, 70 percent grabbed the chocolate. Because this is the way our brains actually work—primitive drive trumping well-considered judgment—it's highly unlikely that your inner schoolmarm wagging her finger at you is going to get you where you want to be in the long term.

Fortunately there is a tiny tweak we can make to help us sidestep this ancient competition between the two horses pulling our chariot. Just like Ted, we can position our goals in terms of what we *want* to do, as opposed to what we *have* to or *should* do. When we tweak our motivation in this way, we don't have to worry about which part of us prevails—our passion or our intellect—because our whole self is working in harmony.

Want-to goals reflect a person's genuine interest and values (their "why"). We pursue these kinds of goals because of personal enjoyment (*intrinsic interest*), because of the inherent importance of the goal (*identified interest*), or because the goal has been assimilated into our core identity (*integrated interest*). But most important, these goals are freely chosen by us.

Have-to goals, on the other hand, are imposed, often by a nagging friend or relative ("You've gotta lose that gut!") or by our own sense of obligation to some internal narrative or external goal, typically related to avoiding shame ("Good grief! I look like the Goodyear blimp! I can't go to the wedding looking like this!").

You can choose to eat a more healthful diet because of feelings of fear, or shame, or anxiety about your looks. Or you can choose to eat well because you view good health as an intrinsically important quality that helps you feel good and enjoy life. A key difference between these two kinds of reasons is that although have-to motivations will allow you to make positive changes for a while, eventually that determination is going to break down. Invariably, there will be moments when impulse gets ahead of intention—and 195 milliseconds is all it takes.

Studies show, for instance, that two people with the same goal of losing five pounds will see that same serving of chocolate mousse very differently depending on their motivation. The person with a want-to motivation will physically experience it as less tempting ("The dessert looks nice, but I'm just not that interested") and will perceive fewer obstacles in the process of sticking to the goal ("There are lots of other, healthier options on the menu"). Once she's tweaked her motivation, she no longer feels like she's struggling against irresistible forces.

Want-to motivation is associated with lower automatic attraction toward the stimuli that are going to trip you up—the old flame, the glimmer of a martini passing by on a waiter's tray—and instead draws you toward behaviors that can actually help you achieve your goals. Have-to motivation, on the other hand, actually *ramps up* temptation because it makes you feel constricted or deprived. In this way, pursuing a goal for have-to reasons can actually undermine your self-control and make you more vulnerable to doing what you supposedly don't want to do.

Anyone who's ever been around a six-year-old knows how balky they can be anytime you insist that they have to do something, whether it's going to bed, or brushing their teeth, or saying hello to Aunt Lola. One evening my son, Noah, was complaining that he had to do his math homework, even though he actually loves math. This gave me the perfect opportunity for what in parenting parlance they call a teaching moment. "Have to or want to?" I asked. He grinned. "Want to!" he said, and bounded away to do his homework.

If life is a series of small moments, each of which can be adjusted ever so slightly, and all of which, in combination, can add up to significant change, imagine how much ground you could gain by employing this simple tweak and finding the "want to" hidden in the "have to." Once again, that's where knowing what we truly value becomes critical. Understanding what we want in the big picture helps us find the desire in circumstances where we otherwise might only see obligation.

For instance, it might be easy for me to say that I "have to" work on yet another beautiful Sunday to finish this book. And if I head to the library to write, I might start to resent the time spent away from my kids or away from the sunshine, and while I might get some work done, I won't have put my full self into it. However, if I position the work as a "want to" by reminding myself that no one forced me to write a book and that, by doing so, I'm helping spread the important message of emotional agility, my feelings of joy and energy are activated. I'll become open to new ideas and interpret my editor's notes as collaboration rather than criticism or commands. And at the end of the day, I'll likely still be energized enough to enjoy some time with my husband and kids before turning in for the night.

We all fall into these subtle traps of language and thinking: "I have to be on dad duty today," or "I have to attend another boring meeting." When we do this, we forget that our current circumstances are often the result of earlier choices we made in service of our values: "I want to be a father," or "I love the work that I do and want to excel at my job."

To be clear, I'm not suggesting we should all simply "think positive" and ignore real underlying concerns. If you can't find a "want to" in some particular facet of your life, then that could be a sign that change is in order. If you entered your field because you wanted to make a difference in the world but your company is focused more on the bottom line, it may be time to switch jobs. Or if you've come to realize that your significant other is not the person you thought he was, you might need to seek a new relationship. Finding a "want to" is not about forcing any particular choice; it's about making it easier to choose things that lead to the life you want.

BUILT TO LAST: TWEAKING OUR HABITS

Even if we've adopted a growth mindset, and even if we're in tune with our most heartfelt, intrinsic, "want to" motivations, there's still a chance that our efforts will wind up in the attic of good intentions, right next to that fancy exercise bike or the expensive juicer we used maybe twice. The only way we can really be sure the changes we make are lasting is by taking the intentional behavior we've consciously chosen and turning it into that old bugaboo: a habit.

We began this book with all sorts of warnings about the pitfalls of automatic, System I responses, the autopilot behaviors we follow when we're not living life intentionally. But we've also acknowledged just how powerful habits can be, as evidenced by how difficult it often is to break them. It follows, then, that if we want to direct our behavior toward our values—if we want to reach the master-class level of emotional agility—we should transform our *intentional* behaviors into habits, making them so deeply ingrained that we no longer have to be "intentional" about them at all.

The beauty of deliberately cultivating habits in line with our values and associated want-to motivations is that they can persist over time with almost no further effort, on good days and on bad, when we're really paying attention and when we're not. No matter how frazzled we are in the morning, we always remember to brush our teeth and to fasten our seat belts as soon as we get in the car. The ability to form values-connected habits not only makes our good intentions durable; it frees up our mental resources for other tasks as well.

Luckily, scientists have uncovered a few secrets to help make the process of creating habits easier. In their bestselling book *Nudge*, the economist Richard Thaler and the law professor Cass Sunstein show how to influence other people's behavior through carefully designed choices, or what they called "choice architecture." You can't force everyone to become an organ donor, for instance, but you don't need to. All you have to do is set up the choice so that it's easier for an individual to become a donor than not. In Germany you must explicitly consent to becoming an organ donor by checking a box to opt into the organ-donation program. As a result, the donation rate in Germany is 12 percent. In neighboring Austria, by contrast, you are presumed to be an organ donor unless you deliberately opt *out* of the program. There, the rate for organ donation is almost 100 percent.

We may not be able to switch our behavior simply by checking a box, but we can still apply the concept of choice architecture to our own lives. In doing so, we prime ourselves to form the good habits that will bring us closer to our goals.

Habit is defined as an externally triggered automatic response to a frequently encountered context. We encounter dozens, if not hundreds, of these familiar contexts every day, and generally respond to them automatically and unconsciously. But when we approach these situations intentionally, seeking opportunities to act in line with our values, we can use them to trigger better habits. Let's look at some potential values-based intentions, the contexts in which you have the option to follow or not follow those values, and the tiny tweaks you can put to work.

Intention: You want to make better use of your time when you're on the road for work.

Context: Hotel room.

Choice point: Turn on the TV as soon as you enter, or leave it off?

Intention: You want to keep the romance alive in your marriage.

Context: Evening at home.

Choice point: Mumble a greeting when your spouse comes in the door and go back to what you were doing, or get up and emotionally engage?

Intention: You want to savor your limited time with your children.

Context: Morning at home.

Choice point: Check email first thing, or spend pajama time clowning around with your little one?

If you generally turn on the TV, mumble a greeting, or check email as soon as you wake up, changing these behaviors will likely require some effort at first. But soon the new choices will become ingrained, allowing your unconscious brain to direct you to where you need to go.

Researchers in a series of studies of more than nine thousand commuters put up two different signs at a train station. One sign was written in want-to language that appealed to the commuters' desire for autonomy: "Will You Take the Stairs?" The other sign was written in have-to language that commanded people, "Take the Stairs."

When the signs were placed some distance from the stairs-versus-escalator decision point, giving commuters enough time to deliberate on their behavior, the "Will You Take the Stairs?" sign had the greatest impact. Commuters who received this sign even chose to take the stairs at a subsequent decision point where there was no sign posted at all. So, the message that promoted autonomy—the one that allowed them to want to rather than have to—resulted in more lasting behavior.

However, in an interesting twist, when the signs were placed right at the stair-versus-escalator decision point, people were more likely to obey the "Take the Stairs" command. Connecting with want-to motivations is key when it comes to creating effective change. But when you're starved for time (or tired or ratty or hungry), knowing exactly what you need to do—in other words, taking the active choice out of the choice—is enormously helpful. Here, again, we see the power of automatic response—of habits—at work.

Functional magnetic resonance imaging (fMRI) shows that exposure to cues we associate with rewards—tasty food, money, sex, cigarettes for smokers, drug paraphernalia for addicts—activates the brain's reward areas, the structures and systems that drive people to seek out the pleasure that's readily available. Limit the exposure, limit the temptation, and you make life easier for the "executive brain," the part that integrates the cognitive and the emotional to arrive at an appropriate course of action.

In the manner of Thaler and Sunstein, here are some more tweaks you can make to alter the architecture of your choices.

1. The no-brainer: Switch up your environment so that when you're hungry, tired, stressed, or rushed, the choice most aligned with your values is also the easiest.

Let's say that you want to drop a few pounds. Studies show that people tend to eat 90 to 97 percent of what is on their plate, regardless of the size of the plate. So use smaller plates. Based on that math, a plate that's 10 percent smaller should reduce food intake by 10 percent.

Remember the study I cited earlier about how most people *say* they would choose fruit over chocolate at a later date but then don't actually make this healthy decision when the fruit and chocolate are right in front of them? Do your future self a favor the next time you go to the grocery store by stocking up on healthful items and skipping the stuff that isn't. That way, when you're tempted to binge on cookies later on at home, you will have set up your environment to promote the healthier choice—there will be no cookies to seduce you. After a while, you may discover that munching on nuts or an apple provides all the satisfaction you need, and you'll no longer crave the fat-filled sugar bombs you once did.

Research also shows that people tend to snack when they're bored and that most people, most of the time, are bored when they watch TV. So remove the gateway drug and cancel your cable subscription. Instead, get into a book that really excites you. Play charades. Dig out that ukulele you bought on a whim and learn a few chords. Organize all those shoe boxes of family photos into the elegant series of leather-bound albums you've always dreamed of lining up along your shelves.

Plants and animals are pretty much stuck with the environment they have, but our big brains allow us to act on our environments, instead of merely having them act on us. This provides the opportunity to create the space between the impulse and the action to live the kind of life you truly want to live. If there is some other behavior or habit that you'd like to change, consider what might be getting in your way. There is likely a small tweak you can make to address it.

2. The piggyback: Add a new behavior onto an existing habit.

Studies show that when participants choose a new specific action to piggyback onto an existing habit—add some fruit each time I eat my daily granola—they have significant success transferring that new action into a habitual behavior.

Let's say you value having more quality time with your kids, but you always end up thumbing your smart phone while you're with them instead of being present. You can tell yourself, "I won't check my phone," but as long as it's right there, the urge to check it "just for a second" will be warring with your intention.

Perhaps you're already in the habit of putting your keys in a drawer or bowl as soon as you walk in the door. Create the new habit of stashing your cell phone in the same place you put your keys. And turn it off.

Want to create opportunities for more face-to-face time with your team at work? Make your daily mid-afternoon coffee run a group effort and use it as quality connecting time.

You ease the creation of a new behavior by piggybacking it on an existing habit, meaning you don't have to make a major adjustment to your routine.

3. The precommitment: Anticipate obstacles and prepare for them with "if-then" strategies.

Let's say you've had a fight with your boyfriend and want to smooth things over. You know you both have a tendency to lose your temper when things get tense, but that yelling at each other makes you both miserable, and you sometimes say things you regret. You want to resolve the situation, not continue as you have in the past.

Often, when we can anticipate unpleasant situations or reactions like this, we allow ourselves to get hooked by them. And even though we may want to change, when confronted by these emotional triggers, we can't. But emotional agility allows you to take a step back and see these moments as opportunities to make a values-based commitment to yourself. Before you even talk to your boyfriend, you can commit to the idea that *if* he raises Explosive Topic X, *then* you'll hear him out with an open mind.

Similarly, you may know that when the alarm goes off at five a.m., you'll be tempted to roll over and hit the snooze button instead of getting up for a morning run. So the night before, tell yourself that if you're tempted to sleep in, then you'll immediately haul yourself out of bed no matter how tired you feel, because, as grumpy as you might be for a few minutes, you'll feel a thousand times better an hour later when you've started your day with a bit of exercise. Even a sleep-addled brain will remember this *if-then* commitment, and the more you get up to exercise, the easier it will become, until it's finally a habit.

4. The obstacle course: Offset a positive vision with thoughts of potential challenges.

Earlier, we discussed how positive thinking can hinder emotional agility. Changing your habits is a case in point.

Researchers asked some women in a weight-reduction program to imagine they had completed the program with new, slim figures. They asked a second group to imagine situations in which they might be tempted to cheat on their diets. One year later, the women who had imagined their transformative weight loss had lost *fewer* pounds than those who had been forced to think realistically about the process.

Similar studies in various countries have looked at people with a wide range of goals—college students wanting a date, hip-replacement patients hoping to get back on their feet, grad students looking for a job, schoolchildren wishing to get good grades, and so on. In each case, the results were the same. Fantasizing about smoothly attaining your dreams doesn't help. In fact, it hinders you by tricking your brain into believing that you've already achieved the goal. In essence, these positive fantasies let the fizz out of the bottle, dissipating the energy we need to stay motivated and really follow through.

Those who achieved the best results did so through a combination of optimism and realism. It's important to believe that you can achieve your goal, but you also need to pay attention to the obstacles most likely to get in the way. This is called *mental contrasting.*

In a recent study on healthful eating and exercise, people who practiced this mental contrasting were working out twice as long each week and eating considerably more vegetables four months down the road than those in the control group. Mental contrasting has been shown to help people recover more quickly from chronic back pain, find more satisfaction in relationships, get better grades, and better manage workplace stress.

By imagining the future while clearly assessing the present reality, you link the two to each other. This creates a mental pathway that includes both the obstacles and your plans for getting past them. That path can lead from where you are now to where you want to be. And that's a proper thoroughfare for change.

A mind that is open to growth and change is a hub from which values and goals can be brought to life and realized. There is tremendous empowerment in appointing yourself the agent of your life—in taking ownership of your own development, career, creative spirit, work, and connections.

Tweaking your mindset, motivation, and habits is about turning your heart toward the fluidity of the world, rather than planting your feet on its stability. It's bringing a playful sense of curiosity, experimentation, and what-ifs to bear in the service of living. It's setting aside ideas about "what you will become" (results, goals, and outcomes) and engaging freely with the process and journey, taking life moment by moment, habit by habit, and one step at a time.

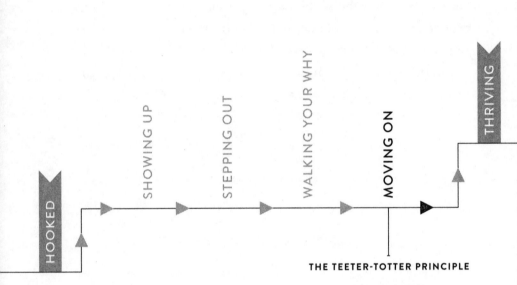

HOOKED

SHOWING UP

STEPPING OUT

WALKING YOUR WHY

MOVING ON

THRIVING

THE TEETER-TOTTER PRINCIPLE

Live at the Edge
of Your Ability

Choose Courage
over Comfort

Opt for
What Is Workable

CHAPTER 8

MOVING ON

THE TEETER-TOTTER PRINCIPLE

A friend of mine—I'll call him George—grew curious one day when he realized that his four-year-old son had been in the bathroom long enough for things to become, in the parlance of an old cowboy movie, "quiet . . . too quiet."

George knocked on the bathroom door, then opened it to find George Jr. standing on a stool in front of the sink. George later recounted how time slowed to a crawl as he took in the scene. First he noticed white stuff everywhere—on the lavatory, the mirror, the floor, and all over his son's face. Then he saw the red stuff—less of it, but also widely distributed—on the sink, the mirror, and the boy's chin, where it was streaming from a slash just below his mouth.

Wanting to emulate his father, George Jr. had been trying to shave, and even though he'd been using a relatively innocuous plastic-handled safety razor, he'd made an unfortunate lateral movement with the blade. Happily, the cut was not serious (facial wounds tend to bleed above their weight class), and the only lasting effect was that the boy learned a valuable, albeit painful and scary lesson.

This story is a (messy) reminder that humans are innately curious creatures with an inherent desire to learn and grow. Like George Jr., we all yearn to be competent, and we increase our competencies by trying new things, even though, yes, we sometimes get ahead of ourselves. Ideally, the challenges we take on, and the competencies we work to develop, will help move us closer to the life we deeply want.

As preschoolers, we're eager to take on the challenge and master the skill of tying our shoes, and this milestone can be pretty thrilling for children and parents alike. But after a while—in fact, very quickly—competence leads to complacency. Once you've got the hang of tying your shoes, there's not much to celebrate each morning as you lace 'em up.

As we saw in the last chapter, that kind of routine competence is not necessarily a bad thing. When we make habits out of once-novel tasks, we free up mental energy, allowing us to get out the door and into the world so we can climb much higher mountains. As we've also seen, making habits out of behaviors we've consciously chosen, and that are connected with our values, is a key aspect of emotional agility.

In certain areas of life, though, there is such a thing as being "too competent." When we get too good at something, we can quickly find ourselves lulled back into autopilot mode, reinforcing not just rigid behavior but also disengagement, lack of growth, and boredom—in short, we fail to thrive.

In one way or another, we've all experienced this kind of *overcompetence*. You're overcompetent in your job when you could do it with your eyes closed, when you already know what the day will bring, or when you're no longer experiencing an expansion in your skills or sense of possibility. You're overcompetent in your marriage when you know precisely what your wife's opinion about the movie will be, or when you may as well order your husband's dinner for him because you know what he's going to want from the menu. It happens in families when you can predict exactly how the conversation will go around the Thanksgiving table ("Please don't get Uncle Lou started on politics!"). It happens to you as a parent when you ask your teenager, "How was school today?" without looking up from your phone, and he responds, "Fine" without looking up from his. There is no challenge or joy or discovery when everything is reduced to routine, when every aspect of life has been staked out and subdivided, as bland and predictable, perhaps even as comfortable, as a Sunbelt suburb.

By the same token, the opposite of overcompetence, *overchallenge*, isn't great either. When we're juggling so many complexities that Superman and Wonder Woman together couldn't get it all done working double shifts, or when we're walking on eggshells in an unpredictable relationship, we can become stressed in ways that inhibit our ability to be creative, to be appropriately responsive, and to thrive. Staying emotionally agile requires us to find the equilibrium between overcompetence on the one hand and overchallenge on the other. This is the teeter-totter principle.

On the playground, a teeter-totter, or seesaw, is all about balance. When you're at one end, you need some resistance at the other so you don't crash down unceremoniously (and painfully) on your backside. At the same time, if there's too much weight on the opposite side, you'll be left hanging high and dry.

In life, the teeter-totter principle means finding that give-and-take, that place where competence and the comfort of the familiar exist in a kind of creative tension with the excitement and even the stress of the unknown. We get to that zone of optimal development in a very specific way: when we *live at the edge of our ability,* a place in which we're not overcompetent or complacent, but also not in so far over our heads that we're overwhelmed.

We move to the edge of our ability when we incrementally advance ourselves beyond the level of our competence and comfort. Ideally, the advances are the kind of small, incremental tweaks we discussed in Chapter 7.

In our relationships, creative lives, personal development, and work, we can promote this advancement in two ways—expanding our *breadth* (*what* we do: the skills we acquire, the topics we talk about, the avenues we explore) and our *depth* (*how* well we do what we do: the quality of our listening, our level of engagement with the world). A helmsman wants to keep the sails trim, never luffing; for tennis players, it's always more fun and more rewarding to play with someone who's just a little better than they are.

But we also need to be mindful of how we expand and why— choosing breadth and depth in line with what truly matters to us instead of adding to them arbitrarily, simply because we can or be- cause we feel pressure to be the best, smartest, or most fabulous. Remember, this is about building the life you want, not about being busy for busy's sake, or creating more "should"s for yourself.

THE CURSE OF COMFORT

The idea of reaching our own personal zone of optimization sounds pretty appealing. It's like a Tony Robbins speech just before the fire walk, or "Climb Every Mountain" sung at your high school gradua- tion. Certainly it taps into our inner four-year-old's drive to learn and grow. So why are we so often left immobilized, with one side of our teeter-totter high and dry and the other side stuck in the mud?

The biggest reason is fear. Just as we're wired to explore, we're also wired to keep ourselves safe, and our brains confuse safety with comfort, a comfort that can get us hooked. If something feels comfortable—as in *familiar, accessible,* and *coherent*—our brains signal that we're just fine where we are, thank you very much. And if something feels new, difficult, or even slightly incoherent, fear kicks in. And while fear comes in all shapes and sizes, and sometimes it appears in disguise (as procrastination, perfection, shutting down, unassertiveness, or excuses), it speaks only one word: no, as in "No, I'll just screw it up." "Nah, I won't know anyone there." "Nope, that will look awful on me." "Nuh-uh, thanks; I'll sit this one out."

That "no" has its roots in evolution. At its most basic level—and other than being frozen to the spot in fear—animal behavior consists of two options: approach or avoid. Millions of years ago, if one of our proto-human ancestors saw something that looked like food or a mating opportunity, he'd approach it. If it looked like trouble, he'd avoid it. Run and hide!

Eventually, evolution began to favor certain pre–*Homo sapiens* whose big brains led them, in the course of normal, healthy development, to approach all sorts of new experiences just for the heck of it. Like George Jr. with the safety razor, the young of these species could be fearless—except under stress, when evolution saw to it that the other half of the ancient dichotomy would kick in, and the otherwise curious creatures would avoid anything the least bit unfamiliar, even Grandma, until she'd hung around for a while and maybe served up some applesauce.

Even today, children withdraw to their tattered and stinky old stuffed animals if they're feeling discomfort or fear. And our adult behavior is not all that different. Pretty much everyone has a beloved old sweatshirt they wear or a favorite place to which they retreat (maybe one "where everybody knows your name") when they're sad, tired, or under pressure.

Studies show that when we make judgments about risk, we show a bias toward the familiar. For example, people assume that technologies, investments, and leisure activities are less risky or difficult the more familiar they seem, even when the facts suggest otherwise. That helps to explain why people can be terrified of flying when, according to the statistics, they're at far greater risk of dying in a car accident. For most people, driving is a familiar, everyday activity, while air travel is, relatively speaking, unusual and unfamiliar.

Accessibility—the degree to which something is easy to understand—is another proxy in our brains for safety and comfort. In one study, participants were given two sets of the same instructions for the same routine. One set was printed in an easy-to-read font, while the other was in a font that took a little effort. Participants were asked to estimate how much time would be required to complete the described routine. When they read the instructions in the more accessible font, they guessed the routine would take about eight minutes, but when they read the exact same instructions in lettering that was less user-friendly, they estimated the routine would take them almost twice as long.

Our bias in favor of the familiar and the accessible can even influence what we accept as the truth: We give more credence to opinions that appear to be widely held. Trouble is, we're not very good at tracking how often we've heard something or from whom we've heard it. This means if a simplistic (easily accessible) idea is repeated often enough, and we aren't listening to it with a critical ear, we may accept it as truth, even if the source is merely one zealot (or one critical parent) parroting the same ideas over and over.

The *curse of comfort*—defaulting to the familiar and accessible— wouldn't matter so much if the only place it led you was down the supermarket aisle, past the unfamiliar and difficult-to-pronounce exotic foods, and straight to your favorite brand of peanut butter. Its impact, though, is much more insidious and far-reaching. It can lead to mistakes that waste our time and keep us from getting where we want to go—sometimes literally.

Imagine you're running late for an important appointment, and the traffic on your usual route is snarled up. You know there's a quicker back way that requires bushwhacking through some side streets, but you've driven it only once or twice. When you're under pressure and you really have to be on time, research shows you're more likely to stick with the devil you know—the familiar main road, even though it's jammed—than to try the unfamiliar shortcut, thus pretty much guaranteeing you'll be late. In the same way, the stress of having your doctor tell you that you need to lose weight, lower your cholesterol, and exercise more, can actually increase the comforting appeal of those familiar Krispy Kremes.

Neuroimaging bears out the ways we react to the discomfort of uncertainty. When we face known risks—a bet, let's say, with odds that can be calculated—there is increased activity in the reward areas of the brain, especially the striatum. But when we have to place a bet with nothing quantifiable or familiar to go on, our brains show increased activation in the amygdala, an area associated with fear.

In one study, a small amount of uncertainty made participants significantly less willing to take a modest gamble. Oddly enough, the risk was not whether they would win or lose, but *how much* they would win. Even though it was all upside, that lack of clarity was enough to make almost 40 percent of the participants opt not to take the bet. Anytime there are gaps in our knowledge, fear fills in those gaps—a fear that overshadows the possibility of a payoff.

THE COHERENCE OF BAD DECISIONS

The fear factor actually increases in subtlety and complexity the more that insecurity and loneliness enter the picture. That's because humans evolved as a social species that always needed to be part of the family or the pack for survival. This means that, even today, feeling cut off from our tribe is still life-or-death scary.

The bigger and more sophisticated brain that makes us explore as part of our nature evolved primarily because it enabled an otherwise unimpressive ape to manage a larger and more complex social structure. More brain power made us better at judging reliability and trustworthiness beyond kinship, thereby becoming better at creating and maintaining mutually beneficial coalitions that allowed the scrawnier but brainier species (the one that led to us) to outcompete the brawnier but dumber and less cooperative ones (that led to the chimps and gorillas).

Eventually, this organ for "making sense" of the social environment became so sophisticated it began trying to make sense of everything. The big-brained apes developed an awareness of the passage of time, and of the trajectory of their own lives, and began trying to account not just for their place in the social fabric but also for their place in the universe. They became self-aware, possessed of something called consciousness, and with consciousness came free will, empathy, and a moral sense, even religious awe.

But all this awareness required that the big brain perform one more very important task, which was to provide a coherent picture of the otherwise confusing rush of information made available through the portals of our senses and the newly developed subtlety of our perceptions.

Managing social connection is vital to our survival because we still depend on family and tribe, friends and loved ones, for our well-being. But oddly enough, when push comes to shove, coherence seems to be our top mental and emotional priority.

I need the coherence provided by my cognitive brain to remind me that I am the same person today as I was yesterday, that someday I will die, and that, between now and then (if I last long enough), I will grow old, so it would be wise to plan for that and to make the most of the time I have. Mental coherence is what helps me to understand that the sound of the baby crying from the next room is important and deserves my attention, but that the annoying hum of the refrigerator can be tuned out. Without coherence, we'd be like schizophrenics, unable to filter the stimuli around us and responding to perceptions that don't matter or that may not even jibe with external reality.

Coherence—like familiarity and accessibility—is a crude proxy in our brain for "safe," *even* when the desire for coherence leads us to go against our own best interests. For example, numerous studies have shown that people who think poorly of themselves prefer interacting with individuals who also view them negatively. And it may astonish you to hear that people with low self-esteem tend to quit their jobs more often when their earnings *increase* over time. In their minds, it just doesn't seem coherent to be appreciated and rewarded. More logically, workers with healthier self-esteem tend to leave their jobs sooner when they don't get appropriate raises. For these people, it doesn't make sense *not* to get the reinforcement they feel they deserve.

It's the comfort we take in the familiar and the coherent that leads us to continue seeing ourselves based on how we saw ourselves as children. How we were treated as children is then used by us as adults to predict how we'll be seen and received today, as well as how we *deserve* to be treated, even when it's derogatory and self-limiting. By the same token, information that challenges these familiar and therefore "coherent" views can feel dangerous and disorienting, even when the disconfirmation shines a new, positive light.

Fear of success, or fear of even being "okay," can lead to self-sabotage, including underperformance in school, being a slacker, or ruining an otherwise healthy relationship because you haven't "earned" it. We can undermine ourselves in service to coherence when we stay in a dead-end job, allow ourselves to get dragged back into a family drama, or, in extreme circumstances, when we take back an abusive spouse.

As if seeking the comfort of coherence wasn't damaging enough, sometimes it conspires with the even more basic hook of immediate gratification, also known as "comfort *now*."

Imagine a freshly minted college graduate named Scott who has always been "the funny one," delivering sharp one-liners—and getting attention for it—ever since he could string two words together. Scott just started a new job in a new city where he doesn't know anyone, and it's been a tough transition. So he reverts to his tried-and-true class-clown approach to breaking the ice, cracking wise about his colleagues whenever the opportunity comes along. Some people find him amusing, but many others are put off by his sarcasm. Even as he's struggling to fit in, Scott is ostracizing himself from his officemates. He understands what is happening here, and he knows he should take a different approach, but in his lonely and alienated circumstances, it's hard to give up the little hits of affirmation—or at least attention—he gets when he makes some of his colleagues chuckle. Much of the laughter may be awkward, but it's still laughter, which has always been his drug of choice.

By definition, immediate gratification makes us feel good a lot faster than do the tiny tweaks and disciplined, steady work that can actually get us to higher ground. You may have heard about studies in which lab mice are given access to two levers, one that delivers a food pellet and another that delivers a hit of cocaine. No matter how hungry they get, the mice keep pushing that cocaine lever again and again until they die of starvation. Lesson for mice and men (and women): Cheap thrills (and even cozy comforts) can carry high costs.

A hot-fudge sundae may make you feel good *right now.* Of course, it may also make you feel regretful in about twenty minutes. Aligning your actions with your values and getting healthier by losing five pounds isn't as intensely pleasing as the sugar rush of ice cream covered in chocolate, but it can lead to satisfaction that lasts a lot longer.

These self-sabotaging responses are not what we choose to do; they're what we've been conditioned to do, and will continue to do until we unhook from the flight to the familiar and find the agility to shut down the autopilot, show up, step out, and take agency of our own lives. That's how we're able to continuously embrace the challenges that allow us to thrive.

For many people, the familiar and comforting identity that hooks them, especially in times of stress, is a holdover from way, way back. The high school baseball star and the beauty queen of Bruce Springsteen's "Glory Days" come to mind as perfect examples. But the more emotionally agile path involves letting go of the "moldy oldie" aspirations that were a very narrow and perhaps naive definition of self, and working to strengthen the meaning derived from actions that embody the more mature values appropriate to the here and now. When you've got three kids to put through college, it's time to file the glory days in the attic and explore something new.

CHOOSING CHALLENGE

In his bestselling book *Good to Great,* Jim Collins says, "Good is the enemy of great." I beg to differ. I think avoidance is the enemy of great. Avoidance—particularly avoidance of discomfort—is even the enemy of good. It's the enemy of the growth and change that lead to flourishing.

When we say, "I don't want to fail," "I don't want to embarrass myself," "I don't want to get hurt," we're expressing what I call *dead people's goals.* That's because the only people who never feel discomfort for having made fools of themselves are—you guessed it—dead. The same goes for people who don't change or mature. As far as I know, the only people who never feel hurt, vulnerable, mad, anxious, depressed, stressed, or any of the other uncomfortable emotions that come with taking on challenges are those who are no longer with us. Sure, the dead do not annoy their families or coworkers, cause problems, or speak out of turn. But do you really want the dead to be your role models?

There's an old adage that if you do what you've always done, you'll get what you've always got. But that actually may be too optimistic. Think of the executive who puts in eighty hours a week for twenty years in the same mid-level position at the same company, only to find herself competing for a new job against people half her age after she's been downsized. Or consider the devoted spouse who spends years faithfully plodding through a monotonous marriage only to come home one day to a half-empty closet in the bedroom and a note on the pillow.

To stay truly alive, we need to choose courage over comfort so that we keep growing, climbing, and challenging ourselves, and that means not getting stuck thinking we've found heaven when we're simply sitting on the nearest plateau. But, according to the teeter-totter principle, we also don't want to be overwhelmed by taking on unrealistic goals, or by thinking we can get to our personal mountaintop in one sudden burst of effort.

Perhaps the best term to describe living at the edge of our ability, thriving and flourishing, being challenged but not overwhelmed, is simply "whelmed." And a key part of being whelmed lies in being selective in our commitments, which means taking on the challenges that really speak to you and that emerge from an awareness of your deepest values.

In the early 1600s Pierre de Fermat was a distinguished judge in the southern French town of Toulouse. But while the law was his career, mathematics was his passion.

On a wintry day in 1637, when Fermat was reading an ancient Greek text called *Arithmetica*, he scrawled a note in the margin: "It is impossible to separate any power higher than the second into two like powers. I have discovered a truly marvelous demonstration of this proposition which this margin is too narrow to contain."*

Well, thanks a lot, Pierre. Talk about a tease.

Word of the intriguing proof for this odd mathematical theorem got around, and around, and by the nineteenth century, various academies and wealthy individuals were offering prizes to anyone who could find the solution. Proto–pocket-protector geeks from far and wide tried to find a proof, but without success. Fermat's last theorem remained elusive.

Then, in 1963, a ten-year-old British schoolboy named Andrew Wiles stumbled on the problem in a book at his local library. Immediately, he vowed to solve it. Thirty years later, in 1993, Wiles announced he'd found the proof. Unfortunately, someone uncovered a subtle flaw in his calculations, so he dived back in for another year, rebuilding his proof until it was perfect. Finally, nearly four centuries after Fermat first scrawled his provocation in the margin of *Arithmetica*, the greatest puzzle in mathematics was solved.

When asked why so many people, including himself, had put so

---

* A more accurate description is "I have discovered that $x^n + y^n$ does not equal z^n where n is bigger than 2. I'd explain how I figured that out, but there isn't enough room in the margin of this book for me to do so."

much effort into solving what amounted to an abstract mind game, Wiles answered, "Pure mathematicians just love to try unsolved problems—they love a challenge." In other words, what spurred Wiles on was not the hope of success or glory, but simply a deep intellectual curiosity in the beauty of math.

This is the same kind of curiosity that led our ancient ancestors to leave the rain forest, to explore the grasslands, to discover agriculture and found cities, and eventually to migrate across the globe. It's why our species is landing rovers on Mars while our genetic cousins, the chimps, are still looking for lunch by digging termites out of mounds with sticks.

Of course, the curiosity that will lead to the right kind of challenge, persistence, and success will be different for different people. A task that would have me pulling my hair out might be a breeze for you. Something that fascinates someone like Wiles might bore you or me. And while your colleague may be satisfied being a midlevel manager, you may not consider yourself a success until you own blocks of Manhattan real estate with your name plastered all over them in gold. Some people might need an Ironman race to get their juices flowing, but for others, walking around the block without getting winded might be just the right level of challenge for now.

Whatever we choose to take on, the trick is to remain whelmed, to get the balance right between challenge and competence.

STAYING WHELMED

In the 1880s, during the heyday of Morse code, two researchers from Indiana University, William Lowe Bryan and Noble Harter, wanted to find out what made an average telegrapher into a great one.

For a year, they monitored the telegraph operators' speeds, and from this data, they plotted a graph. What they found was that the more a telegrapher practiced, the faster he became.

No surprises there.

In fact, when I lead workshops, I sometimes ask participants to draw out a similar concept—the effect they think practice has on their own skills. They generally sketch something similar to Bryan and Harter's graph, which looks like this:

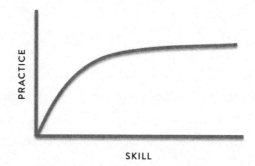

Most people believe that, after a while, practice matters less and their mastery of a particular skill begins to plateau. But while this is true for most people, Bryan and Harter discovered that the best operators' graphs looked more like this:

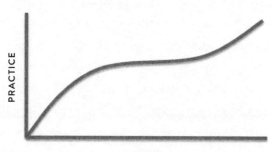

The majority—75 percent—of the operators gave up serious practice after they'd reached what they assumed was their peak skill level. From there, they settled on the plateau. But 25 percent were able to break through the plateau and start improving again. What was the difference between the telegraphers who kept improving and those who didn't?

Those who broke through the plateau embraced challenge. They took on new goals and tried to beat new targets with no incentive other than the same joy in personal growth that drives us to learn to tie our shoes, or write a proof for Fermat's last theorem.

In his book *Outliers,* Malcolm Gladwell popularized the idea that it takes ten thousand hours to burst through a plateau and truly master a skill. The consensus among psychologists and learning specialists, though, is that mastery is not so much a question of the time invested but the *quality* of the investment. Quality investment requires "effortful learning," a form of mindful practice that entails continually tackling challenges that lie just beyond our grasp.

And the proof is in the gray matter. In the past few decades, researchers have popularized the idea of *neuroplasticity,* which holds that the brain isn't "fixed" at some point in early childhood, but instead it continues to produce new cells. The more subtle discovery, however, is that most of those replenished cells die off. What prevents new cell death—and in fact connects the neo-neurons into synapses and integrates them into the brain's architecture and potential—are effortful learning experiences. Our brains don't grow if we simply spend ten thousand hours playing "Stairway to Heaven" on the guitar (god forbid), or simply repeat the well-practiced steps of gall bladder surgery (assuming one has the credentials and a willing patient). Effortful learning means mindful engagement that continues to expand the boundaries and increase the sophistication of one's knowledge and experience.

Most everyone engages in effortful learning when they first take up something new. But once we reach an acceptable level of performance—being able to keep up with our golf buddies or running partners, or mastering "Hot Cross Buns" on the glockenspiel for the school band—most of us relax into a kind of automaticity that typifies the comforts of the plateau.

Remember when you learned to drive? Before you first got behind the wheel, you were *unconsciously unskilled* in that you didn't know what you didn't know. Then, when you registered for driver's ed, you became *consciously unskilled* as you realized just how much you had to learn. ("Wait! You're telling me I have to parallel park?!")

It's in that receptiveness to new experience that effortful learning kicks in. Once that happens, you can then become *consciously skilled* as you go through the punch list in the driver's handbook, buckling the seat belt, carefully adjusting your seat, checking the mirrors, and putting the car into gear before you get the rocket rolling. And while you may panic the first time you have to merge onto the interstate, you start to get the hang of it after a few tries.

But not long after you get your license, *unconscious skill* takes over. You simply get into the car and drive, often arriving home without knowing quite how you got there. It's when you're in this autopilot phase that you are, in essence, parked on a plateau.

When you're consciously unskilled or consciously skilled, you're still within the zone of optimal development because you're open to receiving more knowledge. You may be a beginner, and therefore a little shaky, but at least you have the beginner's mind, which includes the desire to grow and the willingness to learn.

You might also be a little stressed—which is not a bad thing. For decades now we've been taught that stress is Psychological Enemy

Number One, a killer of well-being to be avoided at all costs. Certainly, stress does have its downside. Biochemically speaking, chronic stress can wreak havoc on our systems, fueling inflammation that contributes to heart disease, cancer, and compromised immunity to infections.

But the right amount of stress—whelmed but not overwhelmed—can be a great motivator. As uncomfortable as it feels at times, it's the stress that keeps us moving forward. It's seeing losing numbers on the scoreboard—down but not too far down—that spurs an exhausted team to pull off a come-from-behind victory in the last two minutes. It's the stress of a deadline—tight, but not too tight—that fuels the creativity and motivation needed to finish the project.

Stress is also pretty much a given if you want to do more in life than flip channels on the remote control. It is a natural and expected complement to challenge, and the learning and flourishing that comes with it. You can't climb Mount Everest without putting in a lot of effort and taking on a lot of risk. The same goes for raising a well-adjusted child, or staying happily married for fifty years, or running a business, or running a marathon. No one ever got anywhere that mattered without stress and discomfort.

LEAVING THE PLATEAU

So, how can we apply what we've just learned to our own efforts to leave the plateau?

CHOOSE COURAGE OVER COMFORT

Confusing safety with the familiar, the accessible, and the coherent limits our options. (The door you know because you came in through it is not necessarily the safest exit in an emergency.) To keep growing, you need to be open to the unfamiliar, even the uncomfortable. And leaning in to your uncomfortable emotions allows you to learn from them.

CHOOSE WHAT IS WORKABLE

Leaving the plateau means developing your full capacity for life over the full span. The ultimate litmus test for any action should be this: Is it going to get me closer to being the person I want to be? But you also have to exercise common sense and get through the next day, the next week.

The *workable* choice is the one that's appropriate for whatever short-term constraints you face, but that *also* brings you closer to the life you want to live over time. Walking out on a marriage doesn't always make sense. But neither does biting your lip and avoiding difficult conversations, allowing misery and misunderstanding to persist. The courageous solution is also the most workable: Have the uncomfortable conversation and get down to what is real.

KEEP GOING, KEEP GROWING

Flourishing means expanding both the range of what you do and the depth or skill with which you do it. As for range, ask yourself, "What have I done lately that scares me? When was the last time I tried something and failed?" If you draw a blank, you're probably playing it too safe.

As for depth, when was the last time you felt vulnerable because you were investing your full passion and really laying it on the line, perhaps in creativity on the job, perhaps in a relationship? Do you truly know the people around you, or do you rely on small talk to limit anything deep and real? If you were going to die this evening, what would you most regret not having said?

GRIT VERSUS QUIT

Even if we choose courage over comfort and engage with life at the edge of our ability, emotional agility is not always a matter of charging full steam ahead, damning all the torpedoes, and tackling your objectives no matter what the cost. If you're making choices genuinely aligned with your values, there may come a time when the only smart thing to say is "enough is enough."

The English are famous for their "stiff upper lips," and for putting phrases like "Keep Calm and Carry On" on tourist T-shirts. It's a refined way of saying, "When the going gets tough, the tough get going."

In America we tend to express the same sentiments through the frontier virtue of grit. Even our favorite T-shirt–worthy phrase, "the American dream," implies that we can accomplish anything we set our minds to as long we keep our heads down, one eye on the prize, the other eye on the bottom line, our nose to the grindstone, our shoulder to the plow, and so on.

Grit embodies—but is not the same as—resilience, ambition, and self-control. The University of Pennsylvania psychologist and researcher Angela Duckworth defines it as *passion* and sustained *persistence* in trying to achieve a goal over the very long haul, with no particular concern for rewards or recognition along the way. Resilience is about overcoming adversity; ambition, at some level, suggests a desire for wealth, fame, and/or power; self-control can help you resist temptations, but that doesn't necessarily mean you're persistently pursuing a long-term goal.

Grit is a special case that, according to Duckworth's research, is an important predictor of long-term success. Teachers who are gritty stay in the profession for longer and are more effective than those who aren't. Students who are gritty are more likely to graduate. Men who are gritty stay in marriages longer (a finding that, interestingly, doesn't apply to women).

Emotional agility can help one develop grit, since it allows us to unhook from difficult emotions and thoughts, manage setbacks, and identify our values so we move toward a long-term goal worth pursuing. But it also allows us to let go of those goals once they no longer serve us.

Earlier we established that a sign of being hooked is when your emotions drive you in ways that don't align with your values. While the passion part of grit is important, it's healthy only when you are managing the passion, rather than letting it manage you. Passion that becomes an obsession to the point of obscuring other important life activities is not going to help you thrive.

You can persevere—working like a dog at a project or task, and possibly even deriving a sense of accomplishment from it—but if all that effort and determination is not in service of your life's goals, then it's just not serving you.

While Duckworth's work accounts for the importance of values alignment, popular usage equates grit with a never-say-die attitude, and those who fail to press on no matter what get labeled as weak, lazy, or even cowardly. But emotional agility leaves room for the considered decision to quit something that is no longer helping you. And that can be a very good thing. How many lives have been wasted by sons doggedly following in their fathers' footsteps, pursuing a father's dreams, even though those steps and dreams led in directions that held no intrinsic appeal to the dutiful sons? And don't get me started on all the daughters who suppressed their own desires so they could keep the home fires burning and the old folks comfortable, because that was simply the gritty way to do things. How many political decisions have resulted from misdirected grit? During the Vietnam War, President Johnson's cowboy grit, expressed as his refusal to "be the first American president to lose a war," made him press on, even though he admitted privately, as early as 1965, that the war was unwinnable. Dylann Roof, the shooter responsible for the 2015 massacre of nine people at the Emanuel African Methodist Episcopal Church in South Carolina, was quoted as saying he almost didn't carry out his plan for the mass murder because the people of the congregation were so nice. But in the end he did because he had "to go through with his mission." That's an egregious and profoundly sad case of "grit" gone awry.

For the rest of us, hanging on to unrealistic or harmful goals, often driven by unexamined emotions, is the worst kind of rigidity, leading to all sorts of misery and missed opportunities. Many people invest years pursuing unsatisfying or unrealistic choices because they're afraid to admit their error or that their values have evolved, and by the time reality forces them to change course, other ships have sailed. It may be, alas, that the novel you've been laboring on just doesn't work and needs to be set aside for other pursuits. It may be that even though you got the lead in all your high school musicals, you're still not Broadway material. Or perhaps you've realized you're in the wrong romantic relationship, but you're reluctant to break it off because you've already invested years of your life in it.

Maybe your ambition wasn't unrealistic—maybe you've just chosen a very tough row to hoe. Perhaps you actually made it into the ballet company, or got the glamorous job in investment banking you always wanted. But after a while, the thrill has faded, and the life you're living remains really, really brutal. Meanwhile, waiting too long to face up to the cold hard facts can cost you plenty as the doors to other opportunities continue to close. Sometimes the truly courageous thing is to say, "I just can't do this to myself anymore."

We should be gritty, yes, but not stupid. The most agile and adaptive response to an unattainable goal is goal adjustment, which entails both disengaging from the unattainable goal and then reengaging in an alternative.

These are tough, often scary decisions to make, and it's easy to feel like a quitter if you're hooked on the idea that grit is a quality to be valued above all others. But there's no shame—in fact there's actually a lot of virtue—in making a logical, heartfelt choice. Instead of looking at these transitions as giving up, look at them as moving on. You're letting yourself evolve and grow along with your circumstances, choosing a new path that is full of possibility. That decision is filled with grace and dignity.

So, how do you know when to grit or when to quit? How do you act with that grace and dignity?

In some careers—sports, modeling—the answer is clear because those fields put such premium on youth. But what if you're a musician who gets gigs but can't quite make a living? Or an academic who has to make do with adjunct teaching positions? Or maybe you have the job of your dreams, for now, but everywhere you look you see cutbacks because your entire industry is in decline? What if you're an entrepreneur who's just shut down her third start-up? Or what if we're not talking about a job? What if your grit-or-quit decision is about a friendship that's really just getting you down?

There are plenty of stories about people who stuck with it, whatever "it" is, and finally broke through, but there are plenty more about people who persevered all the way to a very dead end. So, how do you know whether to adjust your goals and walk away or to give your endeavor one more shot?

In trying to balance the "grit versus quit" equation, the economist

Stephen J. Dubner compares two things: the sunk cost and the opportunity cost. The sunk cost refers to whatever investment—money, time, energy—you've already made in your venture that makes you reluctant to just drop it. The opportunity cost is what you're giving up by sticking with the choice you've made. After all, every extra cent or minute you continue to channel into this project, job, or relationship is one that you won't be able to put toward some other, possibly more satisfying project, job, or relationship. If you can take a step back and stop fretting about sunk costs, you can better assess whether it's worth investing even more time and money in the same effort.

The real answer to whether you should stick with it or throw in the towel can come only through the self-knowledge that underpins emotional agility. You simply have to show up and step out and move on, discovering and then pursuing your deepest values and goals.

If you're faced with a grit-or-quit decision, here are some things to ask yourself:

Overall, do I find joy or satisfaction in what I'm doing?
Does this reflect what is important to me—my values?
Does this draw on my strengths?
If I'm completely honest with myself, do I believe that I
    (or this situation) can really be a success?
What opportunities will I give up if I persevere with this?
Am I being gritty, or am I being stupid?

In invoking the teeter-totter principle, I'm using a piece of playground equipment to illustrate the idea of balance, the sweet spot in which challenge and mastery are in a state of creative tension. I'm certainly not using it to suggest that our goal in life should be to simply rock back and forth in the same spot.

Emotional agility is about getting on with life. It involves moving toward clear, challenging, yet achievable goals that you pursue not because you think you have to, or because you've been told to, but because you want to, because they're important to you.

When you continue to pursue new knowledge and richer experiences, when you follow your heart and your honest answers to the questions that matter to you, you'll find that you aren't stuck on a seesaw. Instead you'll be soaring, opening up not just your mind but also your world.

HOOKED

SHOWING UP

STEPPING OUT

WALKING YOUR WHY

MOVING ON

THRIVING

CHAPTER 9

EMOTIONAL AGILITY AT WORK

first met Erin at a training program I ran for executive women. She was decked out in a sweater set and pearl earrings, with her hair perfectly coiffed. I looked at her and thought, "Now there's a woman who's got it together."

As the day unfolded, the program participants began to talk about the sense of pressure they felt at work and the juggle-struggle of managing their personal and professional lives. To my surprise, Erin, who had earlier appeared so composed, burst into tears. "I'm just in this thing and I can't cope!" she blurted out.

Erin explained that she had three kids all under the age of five and worked a four-day week to spend more time with them. She'd arranged this plan with her employer, but it didn't always work as seamlessly as she'd hoped. Just a week earlier, her boss had scheduled an important phone call during her day off, and Erin felt she had no choice but to take it. But because she didn't want her boss to hear her kids in the background, she'd carried out this super-serious, ninety-minute business discussion . . . while crouched on the floor of her closet.

As she told this story, the other women in the group nodded and murmured in support. They acknowledged that her behavior was both very sad and hysterically funny. These women had all felt the same way—trapped in dark closets of their own, trying to please everyone and, in the end, making themselves miserable.

Erin was trapped, but not just inside her closet. She'd also been hooked on the idea of herself as the perfect employee, available around the clock no matter what else was going on. Concerned she'd never be taken seriously if she let on too much about her family life, she'd masked this hugely important part of her identity and her values: her role as a deeply involved mother.

As it happened, I knew her boss quite well—a lovely but somewhat disorganized man who struggled to keep track of where his more than thirty team members were at any given time. I suspected he would have been absolutely mortified at the idea of this young mother feeling that she had to take a business call in her closet—especially on a day when she wasn't supposed to be working to begin with!

After sharing her feelings with us, Erin decided to move toward her discomfort, in the service of her values, and to talk turkey with her boss. She walked him through what had happened and the pressure she'd felt when he called (though I don't think she disclosed the exact location of her impromptu home office).

Showing up to her feelings—desperation and resentment at the struggle to balance her life demands and her felt need to be the "perfect employee"—enabled her to gain enough distance from these hooks to step out and see them for what they were (feelings, not fate). This also allowed her to walk her why in a very open and honest conversation about her boss's expectations and her own aspirations, during which she made it clear that she treasured the intellectual growth she got from work, but that she also treasured the time she spent with her children. And on that fifth day of the week, she said, while she would of course be available for true emergencies, she was otherwise, and unashamedly, going to be home being a mom.

By articulating her full, emotional truth to her boss, Erin was able to remove a huge source of conflict and anxiety. Her work benefited from the newly clarified relationship she now had with her workplace, her children benefited from having their mother's full attention when she was with them, and Erin got a great night's sleep for the first time in months.

We now know that fulfillment and flourishing in your personal life do not come from doing what other people say is right for you, but from aligning more of what you do, minute to minute, with your deepest values. The same is true at work. While it's customary to accept certain constraints in exchange for a paycheck, employment is not bondage, and employees are not chattel. With practice, you can use the techniques of emotional agility to shape your professional life, rather than having it shape you.

HOOKED AT WORK

The prevailing wisdom of today's business culture is that uncomfortable thoughts and feelings have no place at the office, and that employees, particularly leaders, should be either stoic or eternally optimistic. They must project confidence and damp down any powerful emotions bubbling up inside them, especially the negative ones. But as we've seen, that goes against basic biology. No matter how good they are at what they do, all healthy human beings have an inner stream of thoughts and feelings that include criticism, doubt, and fear. That's just the human brain doing its job, trying to make sense of the world, anticipate and solve problems, and avoid potential pitfalls.

That's also why, at work, potential hooks jut out every which way you turn. Work draws on and integrates our hidden beliefs, our self-concepts, our sense of competition and cooperation, and all the life experiences that preceded that first day on the job. Were we good at fitting in as a kid, or did we feel left out? Did our parents have unrealistic expectations of us? Do we still expect too much of ourselves, or too little? Do we feel confident in our own self-worth and proud of our talents and ideas, or do we try to undermine them?

Even when the outward focus is on metrics and analytics, spreadsheets and coldly rational decisions, the office is actually a stage on which all these emotional issues play out—whether we're conscious of them or not. At work, especially when things get intense, we too often fall back on our old stories about who we believe ourselves to be. These dusty old narratives can really hook us at critical moments, such as when we get (or need to give) negative feedback, or when we feel pressured to take on more work or to work faster, or when we must deal with supervisors or coworkers with stronger personalities, or when we feel unappreciated, or when our work-life balance is out of whack or—you get the idea. The list goes on.

To advance in our careers, we need to update these narratives the same way we update our résumés. And just as we no longer list our summer jobs once we're out of college, some stuff from way back simply needs to be left behind.

In Chapter 1, I mentioned that the increasing pace and complexity of life has made emotional agility an ever more urgent necessity. The business world exists at the bleeding edge of these changes: Globalization, technological innovations, geopolitical instability, regulatory revisions, and demographic shifts make work unpredictable. Role descriptions can change every few months; goals from just last quarter become irrelevant; there are layoffs and consolidations and organizational transformations. It can be a tough-enough battle even without our emotions and thoughts running amok.

In this environment, now more than ever, effectiveness in our jobs demands that we be able to attentively examine our plans, which includes anticipating how our decisions will affect other aspects of the company or project, and to adjust as necessary. We need the resilience to deal with the only constants of each day—ambiguity and change. We also need the interpersonal skills to be able to draw on the power of the group to come up with fresh ideas and perspectives, and to get things done.

Unfortunately, the same forces of speed and change that demand flexibility conspire to keep us rigid. We have so much information coming at us, and so many decisions to make, that we can quickly default to the first, best guess, which usually involves black-and-white thinking. And with little time to interact, we often reduce our relationships to transactions. With three hundred emails in your inbox demanding a response, we can all too easily default to a quick "reply" to our colleague, never thinking to ask about his child who has cancer.

The result of all of this *meshugaas* is distraction, premature decision making, and simplistic solutions—also known as smart people acting dumb—not to mention stress, emotional strain, panic, guilt, and the false hope that, somehow, technology and multitasking will provide the solution. (They won't.)

INDIVIDUAL HOOKS

A few years ago, I met a woman named Livia who worked for one of my corporate clients. She was an intelligent go-getter, highly competent and well liked by her colleagues and superiors. In fact, in my meetings with the company's executive team, I learned that she'd been selected for a life-changing promotion. But her future job role was part of a larger corporate restructure that was still under wraps, so she had no idea great things were in store for her. (A confidentiality agreement kept me from sharing the good news.)

What she did know was that something was going on, and instinctively, she didn't like it. Senior management seemed to be treating her differently. Once or twice she'd sensed that they had stopped talking when she walked into the room. Over the next few months, as rumors of a massive reorganization swept through the office, Livia let these very subtle signs of "something's up" convince her that she was about to get fired. Her thorough misreading of the situation—if "something's up," it has to be bad—sent her into an emotional tailspin. She began to make negative comments about every proposed change, and she stopped contributing her ideas. I went on maternity leave, and when I came back, Livia's office was vacant. She had been fired.

Where Livia slipped up was in letting the hook of insecurity deter her from following through on the deepest value she brought to her work: the desire to contribute. Even if her slightly paranoid reading of the situation had been correct, the more emotionally agile approach would have been to say, "Okay, I may be on the way out. But damn it, I'll go out with my head held high, doing work I can be proud of." Better yet, at the first sign of unease, she could have set up a meeting with her boss in which she opened up and said, "I'm getting a strange vibe. Can you help me understand what's going on?"

Another client, Al, was writhing at the end of several hooks. A bold and intelligent graduate of a top business school, he was also the proud father of two children. Al came to me when he lost a promotion that, based on his talent and hard work, should have been his.

Al told me how he had promised himself not to be the kind of absentee father—always at the office—that his own dad had been. His commitment to that vow had only grown stronger after his second child had been born with special needs. The complexity of his family situation led Al to what he saw as an almost Solomonic decision, one that, to his credit, was based on his deepest values: He decided that he would conserve all his caring, emotional energy for his home life. At work, he would be all-business, getting on with it and getting things done, so he could go home to the people he loved and who needed him most. As a result, he had no time at the office for small talk or, for that matter, developing relationships of any kind. He saw himself as focused and efficient. But his coworkers saw him as robotic, abrasive, and lacking in empathy. That's why he hadn't gotten the promotion.

Ironically, Al had let an old hook—the pain of his father's unavailability—keep him from the goal he valued most. That goal was to truly be there for his kids. Because taking care of his family required not just his presence at home. It also required that he commit to and be successful in his career so he could take care of them financially.

Both Livia and Al had everything it takes to succeed—except for the emotional agility we all need to roll with the shock waves. That agility begins with unhooking ourselves from unhelpful thoughts, feelings, and patterns and aligning our everyday actions with our long-term values and aspirations.

There are about as many ways of being hooked at work as there are people in the workforce. Often when I'm coaching, I see executives who get hooked on "the task." They go into meetings with a checklist of items to be accomplished, mainly interacting with team members in relation to a specific to-do item ("Raphael, I need the marketing report by noon"), not as human beings with a common goal ("Does anyone have thoughts on how to make this project more efficient?") or a shared why ("How can we deliver something excellent to the customer—something we are really proud of?"). If a colleague doesn't seem to be doing his or her assigned task, the executive gets defensive or aggressive. Or she'll fixate on the minutiae of the task ("We need to lock down this brief by two forty-five sharp today, no excuses") and won't connect with the larger needs, thoughts, or desires of the team—failing to congratulate them on a job well done, for instance. Or she'll take a purely task-oriented approach to giving feedback: "Your numbers are down this quarter" instead of "I see your numbers are down. What issues are you facing and how can we work together to improve them?"

In contrast, emotionally agile managers can step out from their micro-focus. They know that details are important, but they also know how to elevate their thinking and planning from *task* to *objective*. Before a meeting, the emotionally agile leader might ask himself, "What is the (shared) goal of this meeting?" "How would I like my team members to be feeling when we adjourn?" "How will my feedback help them achieve their own objectives?"

Another surprisingly prevalent workplace hook is, oddly enough, caring too much. Decades ago, as often as not, a job was primarily seen as a means for putting food on the table, and certainly as just one aspect of a life that included social clubs, hobbies, and perhaps church or temple. Nowadays, for many of us, the workday is longer, the workplace has become our primary social outlet, and our careers have become inextricably bound to our sense of self. Meanwhile, we're also bombarded with the message that people can and should find "purpose" in their work. While it is true that work has the potential to enrich our psychological well-being, it's easier than ever to lose all perspective and sense of proportion.

Caring too much can manifest as defensively proclaiming our "expertise," always having to have the answer, or not being able to admit to a mistake. Interpersonally, it can manifest in stepping on coworkers' toes, overinvolving yourself in matters that aren't your business, or letting other people's irritations and quirks take up way too much space in your head (or conversations).

To someone who is hooked, "caring less" may sound like slacking off. It's not. It is actually a form of stepping out and letting go that opens us up to many more dimensions of life, while allowing us to work more effectively in service of the things we truly value.

GROUP HOOKS

Most of us work in teams, which means that our hooks aren't limited to those derived from our personal narratives or preoccupations; they can very easily include narratives about our colleagues. Without even realizing it, we make judgments about their weaknesses and strengths, and about how dedicated or talented they are—or are not.

The simple truth is that it's very easy to get people entirely wrong. Often this is the result of biases we'd never admit to in a million years. Making matters worse, humans are biased about their own objectivity, so we often have no idea that we're biased in the first place.

In one study, participants (both male and female) were asked to consider a male candidate (Michael) and a female candidate (Michelle) for the position of police chief. After they heard about the backgrounds of the two potential hires, the study subjects were asked whether they thought it was more important that the successful candidate be streetwise or formally educated. Over and over, the participants chose as more important whichever quality had been ascribed to the male candidate. If the man up for the job was said to be streetwise, the participants said it was more important that the police chief be streetwise. If the male candidate was said to be well educated, the participants went with that. Not only did they consistently show this gender bias, but also they were completely unaware that they had this bias.

Another experiment asked subjects to place bets in a game against the same opponent, who was either well-dressed and confident or poorly dressed and awkward. (The researchers playfully named these the "dapper" and the "schnook" conditions. Who says scientists don't have any fun?) When the results were tallied, the participants had bet far more aggressively against the unimpressive schnook, even though the game—choosing random cards from a deck—was based entirely on chance. The subjects looked at the awkward, ill-dressed loser guy across the table, and their biases kicked in right away, telling them they were better than the schnook and that, against all logic, their superiority would somehow enable them to come out ahead, even in a game of luck.

In an article for *Harvard Business Review,* I wrote about "Jack," a senior manager who worked at one of the companies I consult with. Jack's coworkers had always seen him as a good guy. Then one day he announced he was pulling the plug on a big project, and the disappointed people under him suddenly changed their tune. In their minds, Jack was no longer the nice guy everyone chatted with at parties. He was a phony, self-serving, risk-averse snake, just like all the other higher-ups.

It's all too easy to be hooked on the notion—known as correspondence bias—that someone else's behavior can be attributed to fixed personality *traits* like phoniness or risk aversion. In contrast, we generally explain away our own bad behavior as a reaction to *circumstances* ("What could I do? I was under pressure!"). The Harvard psychologist Daniel Gilbert assigns four root causes to correspondence bias:

1. WE LACK FULL AWARENESS OF THE SITUATION.

In the example of Jack the Project Killer, Jack's staff simply didn't know the entire story about their boss's decision, including how hard he may have resisted it, or how much of a beating he took from his bosses to go through with it.

2. WE HAVE UNREALISTIC EXPECTATIONS.

Even if Jack's colleagues understood that he was stuck between a rock and a hard place, they might have said to themselves, "What a turkey—I would never have caved like that."

3. WE MAKE EXAGGERATED ASSESSMENTS OF BEHAVIOR.

His team members are more likely to interpret that slight smile of Jack's as a sadistic smirk of pleasure at destroying his colleagues' dreams and ambitions than as a smile.

4. WE FAIL TO CORRECT OUR INITIAL ASSUMPTIONS.

Even if his disappointed team members eventually learn more about the circumstances behind his decision, they might never get around to revising their opinion of him.

———

In actuality, neither the positive assumptions Jack's colleagues made when they liked him nor the negative conclusions they leapt to after he did something they didn't care for were complete, or even particularly well-informed. The truth was they didn't know jack about Jack. It's only when we practice emotional agility that we're able to shift perspectives and move into continued investigation, discovery, and an evolving understanding of the people and situations we encounter.

HOOKED GROUPS

Sometimes in the collaborative world of work it isn't just one person who is hooked; it's the whole team.

In March 2005, Elaine Bromiley went to the hospital for a minor operation. She suffered from sinus trouble, and the doctors were going to straighten the inside of her nose to alleviate the problem. Her husband, Martin, waved goodbye to his wife and went off with their two children to do the weekly shopping.

Several hours later, Martin received a phone call: There had been difficulties keeping Elaine's airway open under anesthesia and she wasn't waking up properly. Her oxygen levels had plummeted and she was being moved to intensive care. When Martin arrived at the hospital, he found his wife in a coma. A few days later, he allowed doctors to turn off the life-support machines.

An investigation showed that Elaine's airway had collapsed almost immediately after the procedure had begun. Following standard medical practice, the anesthesiologist tried to give her oxygen using a ventilator. He called for help, which led to another anesthesiologist and a surgeon arriving on the scene. They then tried to place a tube in Elaine's airway—to "intubate" her—with no success.

A patient can survive without oxygen for only about ten minutes before suffering irreversible brain damage. So in a "can't ventilate, can't intubate" life-or-death situation, the cardinal rule is to stop trying to insert a breathing tube and instead find a direct way of getting oxygen into the patient's airway. This is most often done by making an emergency incision through the neck directly into the windpipe, or trachea. The three doctors in the operating room had sixty years of experience among them. They knew the guidelines, yet they failed to shift gears and kept trying to insert the tube, again and again. By the time the doctors finally got the tube in, more than twenty-five minutes had passed, and it was too late.

While the doctors were making their intubation attempts, one of the nurses who saw clearly what was happening offered a tracheotomy kit, but she was brushed off. Another nurse went to reserve a bed in intensive care, but when the doctors' expressions seemed to imply she was overreacting, she canceled it.

How could a routine operation like this get bungled so badly? An otherwise healthy thirty-seven-year-old goes to a modern hospital with experienced staff for a minor procedure and winds up dead? The answer in a word: rigidity. The doctors experienced tunnel vision: a loss of awareness of the situation and a narrowing of context meant that they didn't take a step back, process what was going on, and shift from Plan A to Plan B.

The nurses in the operating room later said they were surprised that not one of the doctors performed a tracheotomy, but they didn't feel they could speak up. They assumed the doctors would be biased against a nurse taking the lead in such a critical moment. But in this, they showed their own bias against the doctors.

While the results aren't always as tragic, this kind of group hook happens all the time in the workplace. It's the same kind of rigidity that had Erin, our well-coiffed executive at the beginning of the chapter, taking a call in her closet. And it's the same rigidity that can lead to the whole design team plowing forward with some fabulous product—despite the market data clearly predicting that it will fail. The difference in the case of Elaine Bromiley is that the misguided decision making resulted in a devastating loss of life.

No doubt you've sat in a meeting in which you've suppressed your doubt or disagreement because you either weren't willing to offer a different perspective or approach, or because you didn't feel you could. It's risky and scary to be the only one voicing a dissenting or unpopular opinion. But if you're not willing to show up to the difficult feeling of being in the minority, you'll never be heard. People can be silent in a constructive way—as when you decide to disengage from an argument that just isn't that important, or when you refrain from telling a colleague that you think his off-the-cuff idea is absurd. But while the idea that everyone on a team needs to be on the same side is comforting, it all too often leads to group-think fiascos instead of organizational agility.

SIGNS YOU'RE HOOKED AT WORK

You can't let go of an idea or of "being right" even when there is an obviously better course of action.

You stay silent when you know something is going wrong.

You busy yourself with small tasks without considering the bigger picture.

You become apathetic.

You volunteer for only the least difficult assignments or tasks.

You make backhanded comments about coworkers or projects.

You rely on assumptions or stereotypes about your colleagues.

You aren't taking agency over your own career development.

SHOW UP FOR WORK

To truly show up at the office means making room for and labeling your thoughts and emotions and seeing them for what they are: information rather than facts or directives. This is what allows us to step out to create distance from and gain perspective on our mental processes, which then defangs their power over us.

Only a relatively small percentage of Americans have jobs in which they routinely experience fear—by which I mean fear-for-your-life fear, the kind where the ship is going down, or the mine is caving in, or six drug dealers with itchy trigger fingers are cornering you. But nearly every working American is acquainted with fear's chemical cousin, stress—the stomach-clenching effect of that ancient fight-or-flight instinct, only now applied to a third-quarter budget report, a nasty customer, a dreaded conversation, or the threat of impending layoffs. In Chapter 1 we spoke about the kind of fear that manifests as a steady, protracted drip of anxiety-causing hormones (as opposed to the sudden rush of "*Aaaah!* A snake!" adrenaline). Psychologists call this *allostatic stress* or *allostatic load,* and the more of it we experience over time, the more physically and emotionally exhausted we become.

When you're in a group environment at work (which is to say, most of the time), in which everyone else is stressed (which is to say, most of the time), everyone adds to everyone else's allostatic load through another process we described earlier, known as *contagion*. Around the average workplace, stress seems to hang in oppressive clouds in the air above everyone's cubicle. And much like second-hand smoke, secondhand stress can have a profound effect on everyone in its vicinity.

In one study, a group of nurses were asked to keep a daily log of their mood, work hassles, and the overall emotional "climate" of their team. The logs, which covered a three-week period, showed that any one nurse's mood on any given day, whether bad or good, was significantly predicted by the moods of the other nurses on the team. What was astonishing was that this emotional contagion occurred even when the moods doing the influencing had nothing to do with work, and even though the nurses were spending only a few hours of the workday with one another. Over time, these infectious moods can spread through a given organization, contributing to the overall culture of the workplace.

Another study suggests that even just *seeing* a stressed-out person can increase the observer's own stress. Participants watched through a one-way mirror while a stranger was put through difficult arithmetic tasks and a high-pressure interview. The researchers measured a major uptick in cortisol—a hormone released during times of stress—in almost a third of the onlookers. About a quarter of the onlookers had the same reaction while viewing the stressful event on video.

And yes, while stress can be a killer, it turns out that stressing about stress (those Type 2 thoughts from Chapter 3) is the *real* killer. In a study of nearly thirty thousand respondents, people who had experienced a lot of stress but who didn't worry that their stress was harming them were no more likely to have died during the next eight years than the other respondents. But those people who had a lot of stress *and* who believed the stress was hurting them were over 40 percent more likely to have died.

The more basic truth to remember is that stress ain't all bad. Having deadlines and expectations keeps our feet to the fire and us—if you'll pardon the shift in metaphors—on our toes. At a more existential level, a certain amount of pressure is simply part of living, which makes "getting rid of my stress" one of those dead people's goals we talked about earlier.

The bottom-line, take-home message brought to you by emotional agility is this: Denying stress, bottling it, or brooding about it is counterproductive. Avoiding stress is impossible, but what we *can* do is adjust our relationship to stress. It doesn't have to own us. We can own it.

The first step is, rather than obsessing about stress as a torment that's destroying our lives, to simply accept that it exists: to show up to it by acknowledging that it's not going away anytime soon.

The second, vitally important step is to understand that "stressed" is not *who* you are. When you say, "I'm stressed," you conflate your whole self (I am = all of me) with the emotion. It may sound nit-picky, but the very phrasing fuses your entire identity to that feeling of stress. That's part of what makes the experience so suffocating. In Chapter 5, I suggested that calling a feeling out for what it is (a feeling) and a thought for what it is (a thought) can be a quick and enormously powerful stepping-out hack: "I am noticing . . . that I'm feeling stress." It immediately creates space between you and the feeling.

But this requires proper labeling to be effective. You may realize that what you're calling "stress" is actually exhaustion because you've taken on too much, or frustration with a team that isn't pulling together.

When you consider the func (as in, "What the func?") of that feeling, evaluate what it is trying to teach you. It may be signaling that you need to have a talk with the members of your team or appeal to a supervisor for a more equitable division of labor. Or maybe the feeling is just the price of the ticket—a not-so-pleasant aspect of a job you otherwise enjoy for the growth and challenge it provides. On the other hand, the lesson may be that you've had enough of this madness and are ready to move to, say, Portland, Oregon, to start making artisanal cheese. (Just don't kid yourself that the cheese business is entirely stress-free, nor is competing with a bunch of hipsters for that perfect sunlit loft. Still, those kinds of stressors might, for you, be worth the payoff.)

THE WHY OF WORK

Just a short train ride south of Vienna, Austria, lies Marienthal, an attractive town with orderly streets bordered by lovely green hills. In 1830, a cotton-spinning mill was built there, and it remained the region's primary employer for the next century. In the Great Depression of the 1930s the business went under and about three-quarters of the town's workers lost their jobs.

Shortly before the mill closed, however, Austria had made unemployment insurance obligatory for all citizens. This insurance would replace a significant part of the Marienthalers' lost wages, but there was a catch. To qualify for support, the laid-off workers were forbidden from taking paid jobs of any kind. Even informal work was prohibited. Reports from the period describe how one townsman lost his unemployment benefits by playing a harmonica on the sidewalk for tips.

From 1930 to 1933, researchers from the University of Graz observed a striking change in the local inhabitants. Over time, the whole town became lethargic. Walkers stopped walking. Hikers stopped hiking. Napping became the primary activity. Men quit wearing watches because time no longer mattered, and wives complained that their husbands were always late for dinner even though they had nowhere else to go.

The townspeople didn't even fill their new leisure time with reading, painting, or other artistic or intellectual diversions. In fact, over the three years of the study, the local library saw a 50 percent drop in the average number of books checked out. Their inability to work seemed to leave the residents of Marienthal demotivated to the point that they weren't interested in *anything*.

As we've already established, work provides far more than a meal ticket. It can give us a sense of identity and purpose, as well as a framework around which we organize our other activities and interests. Work can also bring substantial mental health benefits. Unless they replace their job with other engaging new activities, retired workers are at risk of accelerated cognitive decline.

Pay, of course, is part of what people expect from work, but my own research has shown that pay is far from the only aspect of a job that provides satisfaction and incentive. In a recent study for Ernst & Young, a global professional-services corporation, I examined what I referred to as "hot spots"—business units where employees were exceptionally engaged, meaning that they felt able to bring the best of themselves to the workplace. These hot spots were also performing outstandingly on metrics such as revenues and reputation—but it wasn't that these metrics were driving engagement. Instead, it was people's engagement that *predicted* these outstanding results. We were curious. What was accounting for these hot spots' engagement scores and leading to such remarkable success for them and for the business? What I discovered in my research was that only 4 percent of respondents mentioned their pay as a motivator. Instead, they highlighted their sense of connection with their teams, challenge in their work, being truly seen as individuals, and feeling empowered in their roles.

EMOTIONAL LABOR

I started working when I was fourteen, but my first postcollege "real" job was as a technical writer at a training organization in New Zealand. Until that point I hadn't really given much thought to what I wanted to do with my life, but soon I realized that technical writing was not it. I absolutely hated that job. Every day at lunch, I would go out with another young woman who worked there, and we would vent about our coworkers, our assignments, the boss lady, and pretty much everything else. Then we'd go back to the office and behave as though everything was just fine.

Spending my lunch hour co-brooding with my colleague, and then returning to the office to play nice, didn't make me feel better, nor did it do much for my job performance. Truth is, I needed to show up to my frustration and disaffection and examine what was fueling it: chronic under-challenge. Then I needed to step out from those feelings to develop a broader perspective that would help me to take steps toward what was most constructive. I needed to do my best work, develop all the skills and contacts I could, and use this boring job to help me learn more about what I really wanted to do. Ultimately, instead of using my energy to moan, I needed to put it to better use finding a new job!

Every job, of course, whether it's growing palm trees or selling napalm, involves physical or intellectual work, or both. But every job also involves emotional work—what psychologists call *emotional labor*—the energy that goes into maintaining the public face required in any job, and in fact in most any human interaction. If you're in the working world, you've no doubt laughed politely at a joke you didn't find funny because your boss was the one who made it. You've probably put on a happy face at some function when all you really wanted was to be home in bed with a book. To some degree, emotional labor is about what we call being polite, or getting by. We all do it, it's generally harmless, and it's more socially savvy, say, to smile at your hostess and compliment her on her (wretched) coq au vin than it is to spit it back onto your plate.

At work, though, the more you fake your emotions, or *surface act,* the worse off you're likely to be. Too great an incongruity between how you really feel and how you pretend to be becomes such a chore that it leads to burnout and all sorts of related negative consequences at work, both for you and for your organization, in part because it's just so friggin' exhausting.

Needless to say, as anyone who's had a bad day at work knows, what happens at work can also seep into your personal life. If you've spent the day pretending to be thrilled your colleague got the big project you thought was yours, or looking alert in a pointless three-hour meeting that kept you from getting your actual work done, you're liable to come home spitting nails. At the very least, you'll have that much less energy for your personal life. You might want to hit the gym or enjoy a relaxed dinner, but you're so depleted from your day's Oscar-worthy performance, and so disconnected from your core self, that you can't muster the resources to do it.

You might assume that people in the hotel industry spend a lot of time in surface-acting hell. ("Yes, sir. We apologize that your dinner arrived three minutes late, sir." "Certainly, ma'am. We would be delighted to bring you a fluffier robe.") And in fact, one research study sought out hotel employees to measure the effects of suppressing feelings on the job and marital conflict at home. Not surprisingly, they found that the spouses of those hoteliers who surface-acted the most hoped that their mates would find a different job as a way of rescuing their domestic lives.

But actually, the ease—and genuineness—with which hotel employees are able to exude hospitality and caring depends to a large degree on the values they bring to the work. If someone is in the business just because she fell into it, or because she wanted to live in Madrid or the Maldives, she might be carrying too heavy an allostatic load, buckling under the stress of constant surface acting. If, however, she is walking her why, in that she truly loves delighting guests and seeing to it that they enjoy themselves during their stay, then she's probably not surface acting at all.

To make decisions that match up with the way you want to live, and to have the work and the career you want to pursue, you have to be in touch with the things that matter to you so that you can use them as signposts. Sometimes we get so "busy" we forget to listen to the heartbeat of our why. Without the navigational aid of knowing what truly matters to you, it's far too easy to spend hours, maybe even years, shuffling papers, surfing the Web, reading pointless emails, yakking in the coffee room, and feeling monstrously unfulfilled. It's by walking your why at work—taking actions in line with what matters to you—that you become more engaged and are able to perform at the peak of your abilities.

For many people, such as with those hotel workers who don't have to fake it, a big part of the "why" of work is the human connection. In an Israeli study, radiologists who were shown photos of the patients whose scans they were reading not only felt more empathetic toward their subjects but also took the time to write longer reports. Because of these changes, they also made 46 percent more accurate diagnoses. Not only that, they all agreed afterward that they liked working with the photos attached to their case files far more than working without the photos.

TAKE THIS JOB AND TWEAK IT

In a perfect world, we'd all have a job in which we are constantly in a state of flow, with the weight evenly distributed on our teeter-totter between challenge and competence, all the while saving humanity, lunching with glamorous people, and making zillions of dollars to boot.

In the real world, jobs like that are hard to come by, and even if such a job awaits, and we're focused on it like a death ray, we'd still likely have to start a few rungs farther down the ladder. If you're busy figuring things out—like my younger self, when I worked in technical writing—you also might have to experiment with different pursuits before deciding what ladder it is you really want to try to climb.

So, what do you do when you know your dream job is somewhere up there at the top of the ladder, or out there on the far horizon, but for any number of predictable reasons—money, timing, location, economy—you still need to keep the job you've got? You show up to what you're feeling ("I'm bored"), you step out and create distance from your hooks ("I can't do better than this"), you examine what is important to you and your want-to motivations ("That said, my coworkers are great"), and then you start tweaking your situation: You take actions that are workable and that will serve you for the long term by bringing you closer to a vital, engaged life.

Tweaking your job, also known as *job crafting,* involves looking creatively at your work circumstances and finding ways to reconfigure your situation to make it more engaging and fulfilling. Employees who try job crafting often end up more satisfied with their work lives, achieve higher levels of performance in their organizations, and report greater personal resilience.

The first step to job crafting is to pay attention to what activities—either at work or outside your job—engage you the most. Maybe you're not in a management position at the office, but you love coaching your son's Little League games on the weekends. Can you start an office mentoring program in which you provide advice to younger workers or institute a Take Your Child to Work Day within your company? Or perhaps you've noticed that, even though you're in the sales department, you're constantly coming up with marketing ideas—some of which have actually been received and implemented by other divisions of the company. Could you ask to sit in on the marketing department's weekly strategy meetings? Could you offer to provide your sales perspective to help with the process? There's an old military basic training saying, "Never volunteer"— the idea being that if a recruit raises a hand when a superior says "I need a volunteer," he or she will be stuck doing something unpleasant, like cleaning toilets. (Of course the corollary to this is that if you don't volunteer, you're likely to be "voluntold.") When it comes to civilian career building, though, volunteering is an excellent way to change the boundaries of your job.

You can also practice job crafting by changing the nature or extent of your interactions with other people. Maybe you have recent immigrants on the shop floor. So go talk to them. Maybe set up an English as a Second Language program. Maybe get their cultural perspective on your company's current product line and use that perspective to diversify the company's offerings.

You can also change how you see what you do through job crafting. Maybe you recently got a big promotion, but now, instead of doing the work you love, you're stuck doing managerial housekeeping. Are you just another bureaucrat now? Well, that depends on what you see as important. If you value being a teacher and mentor, a leader helping people fulfill their potential and improve their lives, then you can find plenty of creativity in managing people.

Jean had the kind of menial job that no one ever fantasizes about as a kid—she worked on an assembly line at a medical equipment plant. Her job was to operate a miniature hole punch that poked tiny openings in the slender tubes that cancer specialists use to deliver drugs directly to tumors. If a hole was only partially punched, the plastic flap left behind could prevent the cancer medication from being properly delivered, or, even worse, it might break off inside the patient, causing harm.

Every working day for twenty-eight years, Jean spent eight hours punching hole after hole in narrow plastic tubing. And for those same twenty-eight years, Jean kept a jar next to her workspace in which she placed each discarded flap. She knew that every one of these tiny bits was not just a piece of plastic; it was a potential life saved. This jar helped Jean find meaning in what otherwise might have been the world's most profoundly dull work. She only had to look over at her jar to understand the importance of what she did. It was her version of those patient photos attached to the radiologists' case files.

Job crafting, of course, has its limits. You can't just stop doing the task you were hired to do while you experiment with different career options. And it's possible your company won't have the resources to help you implement your lofty ideas no matter how great they are. That's why it's important to be open about the process. To get buy-in for your job-crafting ideas, you have to focus on ways to achieve what you want and also create value for the organization. You have to build trust with others as well, especially your supervisor, and then direct your efforts toward the people who are most likely to ac-

commodate you. Your manager may even be able to help you identify opportunities for redistributing tasks in complementary ways.
After all, your dreaded assignment may be your coworker's dream
opportunity, or vice versa.

No amount of crafting will allow you to create the perfect job (as
if such a thing existed anyway) when you're starting from a position
that's totally wrong for you. Job crafting was never going to make me
happy, for instance, as a technical writer, no matter how much I
tweaked my situation. Which is why, yet again, it is so important to
show up to all your emotions and learn from the negatives as well as
the positives. By being emotionally agile, we can use the wrong job to
gain the perspective, skills, and connections necessary to get to the
right job. In the meantime, we can use emotional agility to make
the most, every day, of the job we have now. That's how we ensure
that we're not just making a living, but also truly living.

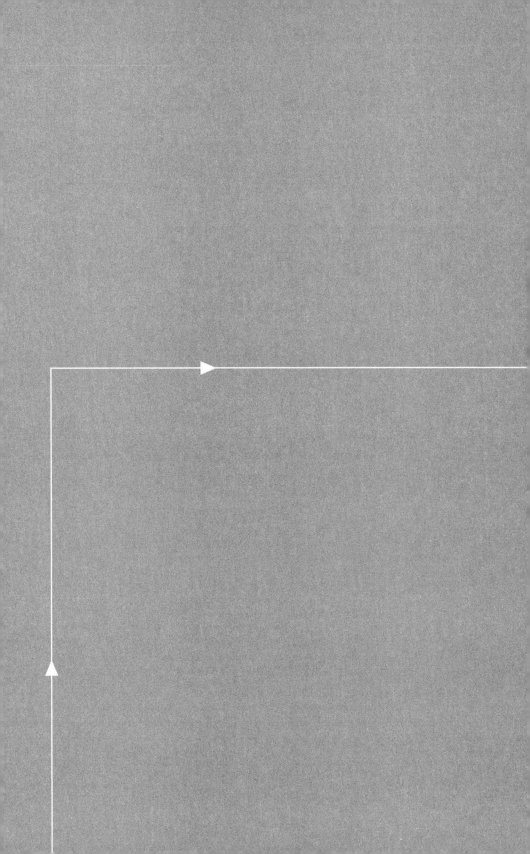

HOOKED

SHOWING UP

STEPPING OUT

WALKING YOUR WHY

MOVING ON

THRIVING

CHAPTER 10

RAISING EMOTIONALLY AGILE CHILDREN

Today's parents are probably the most knowledgeable and conscientious in the history of the planet. Maybe that's because we have fewer children than previous generations did. Perhaps the trend is reinforced by the same connoisseur's impulse that has popularized handcrafted beers and locally sourced and oh so thoroughly provenanced vegetables.

Whatever the reason, as capitalism has gone global and the world has become far more competitive, we no longer believe that our children's success can be left to chance. In an economy in which the top 1 percent can afford luxury beyond belief, the bottom 20 percent can barely afford to eat, and those in the middle have to scramble like crabs in a barrel, modern parents have taken a more curatorial approach toward childhood, with each very deliberate decision directed toward getting their offspring into the best college they can, and ultimately into the kind of career that might possibly allow their kids to have a decent life.

At the same time, our collective focus on self-esteem has expanded. It's a well-meaning reaction to colder, more authoritarian parenting styles of the past, which had plenty of psychologically damaging side effects. But in our attempts to raise our children to be more capable and confident, we're now hyper-attuned to shielding them from any adverse experiences that we worry may shatter their psyches. In a misinterpretation of Dweck's "acknowledge the effort not the result" theories, children are often rewarded for simply trying—receiving an A for effort or a medal just for showing up.

Unfortunately, these efforts underestimate a child's ability to learn and grow from experience, and can have a host of unintended consequences, often the exact opposite of what we had hoped to achieve. For one thing, a focus on achievement promotes a very narrowly defined concept of success—i.e., getting a certain kind of job that, presumably, will allow the child to earn a certain level of income. But that narrow focus on specific preordained paths to achievement is even more dubious because it assumes a static world, when, according to projections, 65 percent of today's elementary-school-age kids may end up doing work that hasn't even been invented yet, and there's ample evidence of that trend already. The top ten jobs in the country in 2010 didn't exist in 2004, and the pace of innovation has only increased since then.

To make matters worse, there's a growing cohort of kids on today's college campuses who did everything right in high school, aced the SAT, got into a fancy university, and find the academic work a breeze, but are completely baffled by life. They have no clue how to deal with a roommate who's a slob, or a romantic interest who just isn't that into them, or, for that matter, with their micromanaging "helicopter" parents who show up for unplanned visits ("Surprise!") and continually check in to see how things are going.

In her book *How to Raise an Adult*, Julie Lythcott-Haims, a former associate vice provost at Stanford University, calls these young people "existentially impotent." She cites studies showing that they often have rates of depression and anxiety comparable to those of incarcerated juveniles, and that they're less open to new ideas and take less satisfaction in life.

Another unintended consequence of overparenting is that kids can grow up thinking that their parents' love is conditional on their behaving a certain way. This leads to *contingent self-esteem,* the belief that their worth must be earned. Contingent self-esteem can manifest itself in the young woman who has always been praised for her appearance and goes on to develop an eating disorder. But it can also be visible in the overachieving student who studies hard, earns top grades, becomes class president—and maybe gets into a top school—but who falls apart when she underperforms on an exam. Or the athlete who trains every day and becomes star quarterback but then shuts down when he flubs a key play in the championship game.

Even parents who would never go so far as to hover or micromanage still want their children to live healthy, productive, successful lives—which makes it hard for any parent, especially when the road gets a bit bumpy, not to intervene and push a child down the path they see as best.

No matter how hard you try to ensure that your kids are successful, happy, and safe, though, you can be sure that temptations will arise and that change is inevitable. You can't predict—and neither can they—a fender bender, a botched math test, the party at which everyone is guzzling beer, or the honor-student buddy who suddenly develops an interest in shoplifting. Nor can you ensure that enrolling a child in Mandarin Chinese lessons or whisking your kid off to coding class will guarantee him or her acceptance into the college of their choice, or into a stable and fulfilling job down the line.

In our increasingly competitive and unpredictable age, one of the best things parents can do to help their children thrive is to teach them the skills described in this book. Emotional agility is like a vaccine that helps inoculate kids against being overwhelmed by the moments of unpleasantness that life no doubt has in store for them. It won't give kids complete immunity, but it will help them develop the flexibility and resilience they need to flourish, even during hard times.

TAKING THE PLUNGE

The summer my son, Noah, was five years old, he and I were steady customers at the town pool. Invariably he would run into friends there, and they would spend the afternoons splashing and playing and engaging in all the usual hot-weather fun that makes the time fly by. But there was one activity that, at least for Noah, made time stand still. Whenever he considered jumping off the high diving board, he froze. All his pals were doing it, and he desperately wanted to join in, but he was too scared to try. He would watch them and remain rooted to the spot, overwhelmed by a fear that was greater than his desire to participate in something he could clearly see was really fun.

We all have these moments in which we think we might want to try something new but just can't get past our fear. For kids, however, facing nerve-wracking experiences is especially challenging be-cause they have a limited history of actually making such leaps (in Noah's case both figuratively and literally). They haven't had time to build up a store of reinforcing outcomes—"I've done this kind of thing before, and it hasn't killed me"—so they're easily hooked by the autopilot response that holds them back, and they get stuck.

Life is full of diving boards and other precipices, but, as we've seen throughout this discussion of emotional agility, making the leap is *not* about ignoring, fixing, fighting, or controlling fear—or anything else you might be experiencing. Rather, it's about accepting and noticing all your emotions and thoughts, viewing even the most powerful of them with compassion and curiosity, and then choosing courage over comfort in order to do whatever you've determined is most important to you. Courage, once again, is not the absence of fear. Courage is fear walking—or in Noah's case, fear diving.

Of course, a child's fear often stirs up a parent's own fear of fear. We're afraid of what our children's reluctance to embrace an experience will mean for their development (or, god forbid, what it reflects about our own parenting skills). We worry about what this reluctance might cost our sons and daughters. We want our children to thrive, and since we can so often see the way forward for them, we try to push them in that direction, assuming that, by doing so, our children will realize that whatever they were reluctant about really wasn't so bad. But as we know by now, emotional agility is not about doing things because you feel you *should* or because someone else wants you to. Rather, it's about being able to make your own intentional choices about how to behave. And that goes for kids too.

When Noah was stuck—literally and metaphorically—on the edge of that diving board, I could have imposed my will on him, telling him what I already knew: If he went ahead and jumped, he'd be fine, and happier for it. Or I could have tried to minimize his genuine worries by telling him, "Don't be silly. Look at how much fun your friends are having. Do you want to miss out on that!?"

Instead, I was able to start a conversation with Noah that we continued later at home. After he acknowledged that he was scared, we talked about how he might feel if he did jump (thrilled and proud); how he might feel if he didn't jump (relieved on some level but disappointed in himself); and critically, how he could go ahead in spite of his fears and jump anyway, because it was important to him.

That is, I first encouraged him to show up to his fear: Evolution has made us wary of heights for a reason, and there's no shame in needing time to adjust to the counterintuitive notion that a one-meter leap into four meters of chlorinated water is a reasonable thing to do.

Simply acknowledging what he was feeling changed Noah's relationship with his fear, allowing him to then step out—to create a dispassionate distance between the emotion and what he wanted to accomplish. This meant distancing himself from both the physical effects of his fear—the cortisol surge, the accelerated heart rate, and the hyperventilation—and from any self-doubting narratives that might have already hooked him at his tender age.

From there we examined his why, or the reasons he genuinely wanted to jump off the high dive: fun, thrills, camaraderie. Along the way, I tried to assure him that the choice to jump or not to jump was entirely *his*. In spite of any peer pressure he might have been subjected to, the high dive was certainly not a have-to, but it could be a want-to.

Noah and I turned the focus away from the outcome—whether success (*splash!*) or a knee-trembling climb back down the ladder—and toward the process: a skill that he wanted to learn and which could be broken down into small steps. Day one: Climb to the top of the ladder. Day two: Walk out to the edge of the board. Day three: Geronimo!

But the next day, soon after we arrived at the pool, Noah simply took a flying leap—no trepidation, no trembling, no baby steps. And then he did it again and again, with endless variations—the Can Opener, the Cannonball—turning the teeter-totter principle into the high-dive principle as he thoroughly enjoyed himself while pushing the limits of his comfort zone all afternoon.

As he'd predicted during our conversation, he was immensely proud of himself—something I could see each time he waved down at me, grinning happily. Talking through his fear hadn't made him any less afraid, nor had examining his "why" changed his motivation. He'd always *wanted* to jump, but until he'd unhooked from the "I can't do it" narrative, he hadn't been able to fully engage with the strong, intrinsic desire that had been there all along.

Of course, the biggest lesson Noah learned wasn't about diving or not diving. In acknowledging yet distancing himself from his emotions and connecting with his why, he learned how to unhook and keep going despite his fear.

When we guide our children through these basic steps toward emotional agility, we give them a lifelong tool. Every time they take a leap—not of recklessness or blind faith, but of eyes-wide-open volition in spite of fear—they practice fear walking, a skill that will help them face many other, much more significant emotional challenges later in life.

LEADING BY EXAMPLE

When I ask parents what their biggest wish is for their children, most say, "I just want them to be happy." To be truly happy, though, one must know simply how to "be," and by that I mean to be effectively with oneself—centered, kind, curious, and not fragile—in a changing world. We all know that love and structure help prepare a child for caring relationships and a successful career, but emotional agility offers a skill set that can translate love and structure into lifelong well-being. For parents, emotional agility provides a skill set for helping their child learn to thrive.

Many of the studies that document the value of helping kids learn the skills to show up, step out, walk their why, and move on have been carried out over long-enough periods of time to trace the development of resilience, morality, willpower, health, psychological stability, and relationship success well into adulthood. Happily, some of these conclusions have started to make their way into popular culture. A notable example is the animated movie *Inside Out,* which explores a girl's varied and changing emotions and shows how even the difficult emotions, like sadness, play an important role in shaping who we are.

For parents, the most effective way to teach your children emotional agility is by practicing it yourself. This can be hard to pull off when your daughter is shrieking "I hate you!" at the top of her lungs, or when your son comes home sobbing after a bad day at school. But these times actually offer you an even more valuable opportunity to model emotional agility. You model critical skills when you step out of your own emotions and respond calmly and compassionately, seeking to understand why your child feels the way he does, instead of rushing to respond to your own feelings.

I have a PhD in this stuff, but trust me, I have been known not only to let my emotions get the better of me but also to make the story *about* me. When Noah was an infant, I took him to the doctor for his first round of vaccinations. There Noah was, in his calm cocoon of existence and at peace with the world, but the moment the first needle stuck him, he started screaming. To a new mother like me, his look of stark outrage seemed to say, "I trusted you! How could you do this to me?" I wanted to comfort him and rushed to say exactly what most parents do in these moments: "It's okay! It's okay!"

Noah continued to wail, and the nurse continued to do her job, but as she did, she turned to me and said something I'll never forget: "No, it's not okay. But it *will* be okay."

She was absolutely right. How foolish of me to tell a person, even a baby who had just been brought into a cold room and handed over to a strange woman who was now poking him with needles and terrifying him, that this was all *okay*! I was dismissing Noah's very clear and immediate, albeit pre-verbal, feelings, denying the very painful reality of his experience. In essence, I was telling him to bottle it!

By the time my husband, Anthony, came home, Noah was well over his anti-vax protest. I, on the other hand, had been trashing myself for hours: I'd spent years studying emotions. I should have known better! Then again, all my geek-work aside, I was a new mom, and this was the first time I'd ever seen my child in such distress and, however ineptly, I'd simply wanted to comfort him.

As soon as Anthony stepped through the door, I told him the whole story.

"Can you believe . . . Noah was crying, and I said, 'It's okay. It's okay!'"

Anthony, who is a very practical doctor type, but also *very* funny, looked at me as I ranted. For a moment he remained completely silent, but then an amused smile came over his face, and he responded, "It's okay, Sue. It's okay."

SEEING YOU, SEEING ME

By being emotionally agile yourself, you will help your children learn the same skills. However, there are other, more proactive steps you can take.

Remember *display rules* from Chapter 3? These are the lessons we teach our kids about what is and is not an appropriate emotional response to any given situation. In extreme cases, a display rule might manifest itself through a directive like "Buck up! Big boys don't cry," which signals to a child that uncomfortable emotions are signs of weakness and to be avoided.

In less obvious cases, we might try to dismiss a child's frustration or sadness: "Oh, he's just tired," or "She's hungry," or "It's a phase." Other times we sugarcoat their distress, "Oh honey, you know you don't really feel that way," or "It's okay. It's okay." (Yes—guilty as charged!) Even when these messages come from a place of love, they can still be counterproductive.

We can also fall into the trap of trying to fix whatever's wrong. Our child comes home from school and says, "No one will play with me," and we might rush in with, "Don't worry, I'll play with you," or we immediately set about contacting the parents of the "mean girls" to set up playdates or smooth things over. These are perfectly natural and understandable ways we try to remedy a loved one's unhappiness. However, while responding in these ways may solve the immediate problem, it deprives the child of the critically important opportunity to sit with her difficult feelings—to show up, step out, and learn from those sometimes heartbreaking real-world situations. They also inadvertently signal to the child "I don't trust your ability to problem-solve." On the other hand, when you take the time to let your child acknowledge her feelings and reassure her that these emotions are normal and healthy, you go a long way in helping your child develop the tools she will need to grow into a productive, emotionally agile adult.

The largest of the ethnic groups in South Africa, the Zulu, greet each other by saying, "Sawubona," which literally translates as "I see you." What is being implied is that by seeing you, I actually bring you into existence. I love this sentiment because it perfectly encapsulates the first step, and one of the most critical, of teaching emotional agility. By simply letting our children know that we see them in full, clearly and without judgment, we signal that we accept and validate their emotional experience. As an added bonus, we actually help them calm down when we do this because children often exhibit a reduction in emotional intensity when a parent is emotionally present. So despite our urge to fix things, to make everything better as quickly as possible, we're better off simply pausing and listening, showing our children by example how to create that space between stimulus and response.

When a child feels fully seen and acknowledged by those around him, it's hard for him not to feel loved and secure. I'm sure we've all watched toddlers on the playground run off to explore something new, only to look back to make sure that their caregivers are still there, all the while trusting that they will be. It is this sense of security—what psychologists call *secure attachment*—that is at the heart of any child's ability to go forth bravely into the great wide world. Secure attachment is the stabilizer of a child's emotional life right on into middle school and adolescence, and on to the formation of his or her adult relationships.

A child's sense of secure attachment—this idea that *I, in all my glory, as well as all my stinkiness and imperfection, am loved and accepted*—allows him not only to take risks in the world but also to take risks with his own emotions. Knowing he will not be invalidated, rejected, punished, or shamed for feeling whatever he feels, he can test out sadness, happiness, or anger and figure out how to manage or respond to each of these emotions in turn.

A child who feels free to experience the full range of emotions without fear of punishment, or the need for self-censorship, learns some key lessons:

Emotions pass. They are transient. There is nothing in mental experience that *demands* an action.

Emotions are not scary. No matter how big or bad any particular feeling seems in the moment, I am bigger than it is.

Emotions are teachers. They contain information that can help me figure out what matters to me—and to others.

To be clear, while raising emotionally agile children requires that you acknowledge and accept their feelings without rebuke, it does *not* mean you need to tolerate tantrums or irrational behavior. You can let kids know their feelings are real, and just as important as anyone else's—"I see you're really annoyed with your baby sister. And yes, I understand that, right now, you want to give her away"— without suggesting every feeling should be acted on. This is where the stepping out comes in. By helping your child learn to label the emotion, gain perspective, and put distance between the impulse and the action, you're reinforcing the idea that, while they don't need to restrain their feelings, they do sometimes need to restrain their behavior.

Again, this kind of compassionate yet ever so slightly detached response can be challenging when your toddler is lying facedown in the supermarket aisle, screaming and kicking, or when your teenager just climbed out of her bedroom window and disappeared on the back of a motorcycle with that Petersen kid. But for both parent and child, it's the showing-up part that lays the foundation for the stepping out—the unhooking that keeps our toughest emotions from getting the better of us.

HOW TO THINK, NOT WHAT TO THINK

I recently asked my mom if she remembered the story I told earlier about the time I tried to run away from home and ended up walking around the block for hours on end. She laughed—of course she remembered. Then she told me something I hadn't known: While I'd circled the block for all that time, she'd actually been following me, just half a block behind. I was only five, after all, and there was no way she was going to let me wander the dangerous streets by myself.

To her immense credit, my mother didn't try to minimize my upset (which might have taught me to bottle), nor did she try to make everything right by placating me. Instead, she allowed me to live with what I was feeling and even let me exercise my own free will, however misguided it was. All the while, though, she maintained her (invisible) tether of protection and attachment by making sure I was safe, and she was ready to intervene in case of a threat. In other words, she kept me physically safe but gave me the gift of emotional autonomy.

Autonomy is a bedrock element of lifelong thriving and is critical to children's moral development. Autonomy means self-governance, or rule by the self, and in psychological terms, an autonomous person lives according to the choices he or she makes. But autonomy is different from mere independence. A teenager's cry of "You're not my boss! I'll stay out all night if I want to!" sounds very independent, but a behavior is not autonomous if it is driven by peer pressure, bad habits, compulsions, or chaotic emotions. Truly autonomous actions are those you fully own and endorse with your deepest self, without coercion from either the outside or your own unchecked impulses. The teenager who always comes home when she's told to because she's afraid of being punished, or because she feels guilty about being disloyal to her parents, isn't acting autonomously any more than the teenager who violates his curfew as an act of rebellion. Instead, the teen who acts with autonomy, in this example, might be home on time because that's the rule—and it's one she believes is perfectly valid and reasonable.

Here's how we can encourage autonomy in a child:

- Honor him for who he actually is (e.g., someone who loves drawing) rather than who you wish him to be (e.g., someone who loves wrestling).
- Give her a true choice wherever possible—which is not the same as not setting limits, or not establishing expectations, or indulging her every whim.
- Provide a rationale for the decisions you make when no choice is possible. "Because I said so!" is not an autonomy-supportive rationale for why your preschooler has to hold your hand when crossing the street. "Because you are small and drivers may not be able to see you, but they can see me" is.
- Minimize external rewards, such as stickers, toys, or cash, for doing things like peeing in the potty instead of a diaper, or doing homework, or getting good grades.

The last two items on this list are especially key in helping children find the "want-to" motivations discussed in Chapter 7. Children raised in a barter-or-bribe economy, just like those raised in a command-and-control environment, don't develop the strong autonomous self that can create distance between real desires and preprogrammed responses—and it makes no difference whether the responses are rebellious or compliant. And people taught to act in the expectation of extrinsic rewards turn out to be less happy, less successful, and have less satisfying relationships than those who are internally motivated.

Encouraging autonomy also helps kids to develop—a "why" to

walk—a set of values that is their own, separate from rewards and requirements. This is especially important as children are faced— and they surely will be—with more ambiguous choices (such as whether or not to take a creative risk) for which there is no certain payoff. The same is true for situations in which there are no pre-defined rules ("You never said I *couldn't* borrow your car to drive to Tijuana"). Only when kids are properly guided toward learning and trusting their own values can they discover their whys and want-to motivations—the ones that lead to genuine thriving.

All this said, there are times when a child will encounter an im-mediate danger. Obviously, in those moments, your desire to en-courage their autonomy will take a backseat to commonsense interventions. When I "ran away" at age five, my mother could see that I wasn't trying to cross the street and that I wouldn't get too far, so she was willing to give me some latitude. If I'd decided to leave home for good at thirteen, I'm sure she would have taken a much stronger stand against my desire to go free-range.

RAISING CHILDREN WHO CARE

Parenting with emotional agility is not just about expressing empa-thy for your child in the moment; it's about modeling empathetic behavior regularly so your children can learn to do the same. You might not see any reason why the first day at a new school should be scary, but you can acknowledge that your child sees it that way. By doing so, you both provide her with security and encourage her nat-ural instinct toward taking other people's feelings into account. Why might the "tough kids" be trying to act so tough? Who else might be feeling lonely and out of place?

This is the process that produces kids who, as they mature, notice the classmate who's been left out, the shy exchange student struggling with a language barrier, the cashier having a bad day, the elderly grocery shopper who needs help with a bag. Later on, they're likely to become attuned to even larger issues of justice and inclusion in the local community and society as a whole. But empathy and perspective taking cannot be instilled by fiat.

In a study at Cornell University, researchers introduced three- and four-year-olds to a "sad" puppet named Doggie. The children were then handed a prized resource: a star sticker. One group of children was presented with the tough choice of giving their sticker to Doggie or keeping it for themselves. A second group had an easier choice: to either give the sticker to Doggie or hand it back to the researcher. The third group was simply told that they *had* to share their stickers with Doggie. Later, when the children were introduced to another "sad" puppet named Ellie, they were each given three stickers—and the option of sharing as many as they wanted. The kids who'd earlier been in the first group—and given the choice to share the sticker with Doggie or keep it for themselves—gave more stickers to Ellie than did those from either of the other two groups. In other words, the children who'd been given a free choice all along were more generous than those who'd been coerced.

Forcing your son to invite a lonely classmate to his birthday party or threatening to punish your daughter if she doesn't apologize for an insensitive comment on the playground may get you a quick result and a temporary feeling of relief. But only by letting your children act autonomously, encouraging them to dig deep to discover their genuine want-to motivations, can you help them unlock their own potential for empathy.

This also applies to such ethical basics as truth-telling. In a study of pairs of one thirteen-year-old and one parent, the teenagers were asked about their parents' treatment of them over the past few months. There was a direct connection between how much the parent tried to control his or her teen's behavior and thoughts and how well the teen understood the value of telling the truth. Kids were more likely to understand the benefits of telling the truth and the costs of lying if they agreed with these statements: "When my parent asked me to do something, he/she explained why he/she wanted me to do it," "My parent gave me many opportunities to make my own decisions about what I do," and "My parent was open to my thoughts and feelings even when they were different from his/hers." On the other hand, those teens who reported a belief in the *high costs* of telling the truth agreed with the statements "My parent made me feel guilty for anything and everything," "My parent refused to accept that I could want to simply have fun without trying to be the best," and "When I refused to do something, my parent threatened to take away certain privileges in order to make me do it."

The virtues of promoting autonomy can also be viewed from a purely practical perspective: You won't always be there with your adult child, holding his or her hand every step of the way and helping him or her navigate every ethical quandary and choice—at least I hope not! Nor will you be there to help your kids step out and unhook every time they're confronted with a powerful emotion or an impulsive thought. When you're a child or even a teenager, you're usually pardoned for foolish, ill-considered stunts. But while a sixteen-year-old will probably be forgiven for letting the air out of the principal's tires (once), a twenty-six-year-old who does the same thing to the boss's SUV isn't likely to be treated as charitably.

When I was about eight years old, I stole a small amount of money from my parents. I still remember the amount: It was two South African rand, which in today's money is the equivalent of about three dollars. My parents figured out what I'd done after I came home with a stash of candy—and an obviously phony story that a very generous friend had bought it for me.

My parents took me for a drive—just the three of us: Mom and Dad in the front and me in the backseat—and had a very serious conversation with me. They spoke of how disappointed they were with my behavior and told me that stealing and lying were not things we did in our family. Then they helped me figure out how I could make it right, including paying them back and apologizing to the friend that I'd pulled into the mess.

It was evident that they took the matter very seriously, but they were also very careful not to shame me in front of my siblings. And they didn't yell or use scare tactics. Instead, they were clear, calm, and, I think, conscious of what they wanted to achieve. By helping me understand the emotional impact on them and on my friend, and not simply lecturing me about how what I'd done was wrong, they allowed me to gain some perspective on my actions rather than adopting a defensive stance (a behavior that often leads to more lying). They stated expectations rather than doling out a punishment. As a result, I felt guilty but not ashamed—a critical difference, as we discussed in Chapter 4—and motivated to solve the problem. And if they'd forced me to deliver one of those "sorry, not sorry"-style apologies, they might have heard the words they wanted to hear, but they wouldn't have given me the opportunity to examine and process the feelings that had motivated my behavior in the first place.

The truth was that I felt isolated at school, and this loneliness was amplified whenever the gaggle of girls I most liked headed off together at recess to buy candy—which I didn't often have the money to do. Because my parents helped me face this discomfort, I was able to have a conversation with them not only about taking ownership of my behavior but also about the strategies I might use to get to know some of my classmates better, and to feel more a part of the fun—without stealing. I also learned how to have a difficult discussion that yields a productive end, which is no small thing.

Had my parents simply punished me, none of that growth would have happened. Even worse, I might have started to think of myself as a child who steals, or my parents might have done the same. By steering clear of this possibility, my parents kept the incident in its rightful place—as something that had happened once and an opportunity to learn. They met me where I was, not where they wanted me to be, and that made all the difference.

EMOTIONAL COACHING

As we've already established, raising emotionally agile children begins in helping them show up to all their feelings, including the difficult ones. While so much of showing up is about "going to" the emotion ("How are you feeling?"), there is also that important element of emotional agility that is about moving on, or "going through" ("What are some options for dealing with this?"). This is when emotional agility meets the search for practical steps to deal with the situation, whatever it may be.

Moving on is best achieved by encouraging your children to brainstorm. When you support them to find solutions on their own—solutions that are meaningful to them—they develop the autonomy that will help them navigate their world, as well as the sense of responsibility that comes with it.

And here we come back to the idea of tiny tweaks: small changes that help your child take on challenges and move toward what is important. The key focus here is on the *process*—being open to experimentation, to giving things a try, and discovering what might be learned—rather than some ideal, pass-or-fail outcome. If your child is worried about making friends at her new school, she isn't likely to hit it off with everyone at once, so you might ask her, "Where are good places to start connecting with people?" For the adolescent navigating the often-harsh world of teenage social media—with its inevitable arguments and name-calling—you might ask, "What are some strategies you could use to manage people you disagree with?"

A while back, a colleague of mine—let's call him Jon—played in a father-son golf tournament with his son, who was six years old. The adults played against the adults, and the kids played against the kids, but about halfway through the course, Jon came across his son, Keith, weeping. Jon gave Keith a hug and gently asked why the tears, but it was clear that no amount of cuddling and conversation on that green would get them to the heart of the matter in time to finish the tournament.

So Jon suggested that it was okay for Keith to cry if he needed to. But he also asked if it was possible for Keith to cry *and* play golf at the same time. He promised his son that if he could get through the nine holes, they would fully explore whatever was upsetting him as soon as the tournament was over. Keith agreed, and father and son split up again and played through to the end on their respective teams. Keith even did well enough to win a trophy.

With a less savvy dad, this easily could have become a story about bottling—burying the difficult emotions and white-knuckling it through the game. (Remember Tom Hanks in *A League of Their Own* yelling, "There's no crying in baseball"?) Often when we demand that weepy or angry kids behave in more socially acceptable ways, we inadvertently send them the message that their feelings don't matter to us.

But Jon took a small, compassionate pause to acknowledge and accept—to show up to—his son's distress. This was enough to help

Keith step out and mindfully and compassionately be with his emotions while still doing what he needed to do that moment: finish the golf game.

When they later had time for a conversation, Jon discovered that his son had been upset because he'd lost a golf ball. In Keith's six-year-old mind, balls were expensive, so the fairly minor incident had ballooned into a full-blown panic.

Jon tells me that now, many years later, he still reminds his son that it's possible to cry and play at the same time. In fact, that kind of self-compassionate "playing through" may be the essence of emotional agility.

THAT'S ALL

Malala. Until 2009, most people had never heard the name. But the Nobel Prize–winning Pakistani teenager has since become a universal symbol for bravery and strength of character. At age eleven, Malala Yousafzai began writing a pseudonymous blog for the BBC about her life in northwest Pakistan—where the Islamic militant Taliban, which controlled the region, forbade most girls from going to school. In her blog, Malala spoke about the importance of education for girls.

After a *New York Times* reporter made a documentary about her life in 2010, Malala received recognition worldwide—and within her own country, death threats. In 2012, the Taliban sent a gunman to kill her as she rode home on the school bus. When the assassin climbed onto the bus and threatened to kill every girl on it, Malala, who was fifteen, didn't hesitate to identify herself as the one he was looking for. He fired three times. One bullet struck her in the head.

Malala's father, Ziauddin, is an education activist himself, and

Malala's parents had raised their daughter, by example, to stand up for what she believed in. As their daughter lay unconscious, in critical condition, Malala's agonized father wondered if he'd done the right thing in encouraging her activism. Her parents' only consolation was knowing that their daughter's "why" was so important to her that she was willing to look directly into the face of death.

As Malala recovered from her wounds, her mother and father discovered that their courage in how they had raised their daughter was to their benefit as well. "She consoled us," her father said in a speech shortly before Malala won the Nobel Peace Prize in 2014, its youngest-ever recipient at the age of seventeen. "We learned from her how to be resilient in the most difficult times." And lest you think his story does not apply to your own child, he added, "She is like any girl. She quarrels with her brothers; she cries when her homework is incomplete."

Ziauddin's real message, though, was one every parent can take to heart: "What has made Malala so special and so bold and so poised? Don't ask me what I did. Ask me what I did not do. I did not clip her wings, and that's all."

CHAPTER 11

CONCLUSION: BECOMING REAL

The children's classic *The Velveteen Rabbit* tells the tale of a stuffed animal's quest to discover what it means to be "real." When the story opens, the Rabbit is having a hard time fitting in with his owner's other toys. The little boy to whom the Rabbit belongs lost interest in him shortly after receiving him, and the other toys, many of which have modern, mechanical parts that make them seem and act real, intimidate the Rabbit. After all, he is made of cloth and sawdust and hardly looks like a real bunny at all.

The Rabbit eventually finds a friend in the wise old Skin Horse, who has lived in the nursery for longer than any of the other toys. "What is REAL?" the Rabbit asks the Skin Horse one day. "Does it mean having things that buzz inside you and a stick-out handle?"

"Real isn't how you are made," says the Skin Horse. "It's a thing that happens to you. When a child loves you for a long, long time, not just to play with, but REALLY loves you, then you become Real."

"Does it hurt?" the Rabbit asks.

Yes, the Horse concedes, but when you're real, you don't really mind being hurt so much. Being real, he says, "doesn't happen often to people who break easily, or have sharp edges, or who have to be carefully kept." Being real requires that you get scuffed up a bit, maybe even become a little shabby.

One night, the little boy can't find his favorite china dog to sleep with, so his nanny grabs the Velveteen Rabbit out of the toy cupboard and tucks him in with the young master. After that, the boy becomes inseparably attached to the Rabbit, hugging him tightly in bed, covering the Rabbit's pink nose with kisses, and taking him everywhere. The boy even brings him to play in the garden, and once accidentally leaves him outside all night. Through it all, the Rabbit becomes increasingly grimy and threadbare. Eventually, the pink gets rubbed off his nose.

At one point, the nanny tries to take the now-filthy toy away, and the boy protests that the Rabbit has to stay, insisting that he's REAL. Which is, of course, music to the Rabbit's satiny but now shopworn ears.

Eventually, thanks to magical intervention by the nursery Fairy, the Velveteen Rabbit actually does become a real, living creature and hops off into the forest. Before, the Rabbit was real to the boy, but now, the Fairy says, he will "be Real to everyone."

Those of us in the "real" world may not be able to tap ourselves with a magic wand and instantly transform ourselves into the people we most long to be. But if we practice emotional agility, we don't need magic. Because emotional agility allows us to be our authentic selves for everyone, every day.

Emotional agility is the absence of pretense and performance, which gives your actions greater power because they emanate from your core values and core strength, something solid and genuine and *real.*

We reach that level of REAL, that level of emotional agility, not through magic, but through a series of tiny steps in everyday moments over the course of a lifetime. Here's how you can start this journey today:

Appoint yourself the agent of your own life and take ownership of your own development, career, creative spirit, work, and connections.

Accept your full self—rubbed-off nose, shabby ears, "good" and "bad" emotions, the whole package—with compassion, courage, and curiosity.

Welcome your inner experiences, breathe into them, and learn their contours without racing for the exit.

Embrace an evolving identity and release narratives that no longer serve you.

Let go of unrealistic dead people's goals by accepting that being alive means sometimes getting hurt, failing, being stressed, and making mistakes.

Free yourself from pursuing perfection so you can enjoy the process of loving and living.

Open yourself up to the love that will come with hurt and the hurt that will come with love; and to the success that will come with failure and the failure that will come with success.

Abandon the idea of being fearless, and instead walk directly into your fears, with your values as your guide, toward what matters to you. Courage is not an absence of fear; courage is fear walking.

Choose courage over comfort by vitally engaging with new opportunities to learn and grow, rather than passively resigning yourself to your circumstances.

Recognize that life's beauty is inseparable from its fragility. We're young, until we're not. We're healthy, until we're not. We're with those we love, until we're not.

Learn how to hear the heartbeat of your own why.

And finally, remember to "dance if you can."

► ACKNOWLEDGMENTS

As it takes a village to raise a child, so a global village is needed to publish a book. More people than I can possibly name here shaped *Emotional Agility* with their support, vision, perspectives, generosity, and love.

Before there was a book, there was an article, and before there was an article, there were ideas and research. I have had the privilege of knowing and learning from some of the most inspirational psychologists and behavioral scientists on the planet. Henry Jackson, your belief in me spurred my research on emotions and their impact on everyday life. Peter Salovey, I can think of no person more innovative, kind, and generous. Your, Jack Mayer's, and David Caruso's thinking has shaped a generation of researchers and practitioners. Martin Seligman, Ed Diener, Mihaly Csikszentmihalyi—your vision of a forum where new and experienced researchers could come together and learn from one another was seminal to many careers, including my own. Marc Brackett, Alia Crum, Robert Biswas-Diener, Michael Steger, Sonja Lyubomirsky, Todd Kashdan, Ilona Boniwell, Adam Grant, Dorie Clark, Richard Boyatzis, Nick Craig, Andreas Bernhardt, Konstantin Korotov, Gordon Spence, Anthony Grant, Ellen Langer, Amy Edmondson, Whitney Johnson, Gretchen Rubin, and my many other colleagues: Your insights have informed this book, and I am deeply grateful for your generosity and your work.

My thinking has been profoundly influenced by research arising from the Association for Contextual Behavioral Science and by the rich discussions on the Acceptance and Commitment for Professionals list, especially the contributions of Steven Hayes, Russ Harris, Joseph Ciarrochi, John Forsyth, Donna Read, Rachel Collis, Kelly Wilson, Hank Robb, Maarten Aalberse, Kevin Polk, Lisa Coyne, Daniel Moran, Amy Murrell, and Louise Hayes. This forum sets the benchmark for openness to learning, curiosity, and sharing, along with a refreshing level of humility.

Ruth Ann Harnisch, words are not enough to convey my gratitude for your support and encouragement. You and Bill Harnisch are a remarkable force for good in the world. Were it not for the two of you and for the pioneering work of the Harnisch Foundation, including the beloved Linda Ballew, Jennifer Raymond, Lindsey Taylor Wood, and all of your visionary colleagues, there would be no Institute of Coaching and the field would not have seen the development it has. To Scott Rauch, Philip Levendusky, Shelly Greenfield, Lori Etringer, and the many others at McLean Hospital and Harvard University who do such important work, thank you for your support in bringing the institute to life. To my institute co-founders, Carol Kauffman and Margaret Moore—it has been a wonderful journey, and I could not imagine two better friends to have made it with. To my fabulous colleagues Jeff Hull, Irina Todorova, Chip Carter, Laurel Doggett, Sue Brennick, Ellen Shub, and Stephenie Girard—my life is immeasurably richer for knowing you.

Alison Beard and Katherine Bell—you believed in the ideas behind *Emotional Agility* and were a key part of the group that shaped the seminal article in the *Harvard Business Review*. It has been wonderful getting to know you over the years, along with the rest of the HBR team, including Courtney Cashman, Ania Wieckowski, Amy Gallo, Melinda Merino, and Sarah Green Carmichael. You strive so diligently and successfully to bring fresh and important ideas to the business world. Thank you.

Without the amazing Brooke Carey at Penguin Avery, this book would not exist. Brooke championed *Emotional Agility* from proposal to the book you hold. Her guidance and judgment were impeccable during every part of the journey. Brooke, you have my profound and lasting appreciation. I am especially grateful to Megan Newman and Caroline Sutton for believing in and supporting this work; to the publicity and marketing team, including Lindsay Gordon, Anne Kosmoski, Farin Schlussel, and Casey Maloney; and to the remarkable copyeditor, Maureen Klier. You have nurtured this book in so many ways. It has been an honor and privilege to work with a team as professional, encouraging, and fun. My gratitude, too, to the wonderful people at Penguin Life: Joel Rickett, Julia Murday, Emma Brown, Emily Robertson, Richard Lennon, and Davina Russell. Bill Patrick—this book would not be what it is without your remarkable intellect, humor, and ability to articulate the difficult. I have learned much from you. Melanie Rehak and Lauren Lipton, I am so appreciative of your contributions and editorial insights.

Christy Fletcher, agent extraordinaire, how do I thank you? Let me count the ways: humor, encouragement, attention to detail, intellect, astonishing acumen, friendship, and so much more. You, the brilliant Sylvie Greenberg, Hillary Black, and the rest of Fletcher & Company are a one-in-a-million team. Any author who has the privilege of working with you can count himself or herself very lucky indeed.

At Evidence Based Psychology, I have had the pleasure of working with an outstanding group of professionals. Without the organization, help, flexibility, and skills of Kimbette Fenol, this book would never have been written. Jennifer Lee, Amanda Conley, Christina Congleton, Karen Monteiro, and Jenni Whalen, I am grateful to have shared this journey with you. To those firm friends and clients who have shared an interest in my work and writing, knowing you has been a remarkable experience. Writing these acknowledgments has made me realize there are so many of you, I could not possibly list all your names here. Karen Hochrein, Michael Liley, Jim Grant, Fabian Dattner, David Ryan, Mike Cullen, Sara Fielden, Tracey Gavegan, Helen Lea, Libby Bell, Sam Fouad, Nicole Blunck, Tim Youle, Jennifer Hamilton, Matt Zema, Graham Barkus, Mike Mister, Leona Murphy, Andy Cornish, Alison Ledger, Stephen Johnston, Juraj Ondrejkovic, and my many other clients and colleagues who have shared with me—thank you for enriching my life with your friendship and my thinking with your insights.

Every child and emerging adolescent needs those adults, in addition to their parents, who love, guide, and mentor them. Meg Fargher is the teacher described in *Emotional Agility*. Meg, you showed me that even in death, there is learning and light. Shalom Farber, you were there for me in so many ways with a helping hand and sound advice. I love and miss you. Glynis Ross-Munro, you saw possibility in me where I had not. The three of you positively impacted me in more ways than can be described. Thank you.

I am me because of the many friends and family members who have loved and been there throughout my life. My best friendship with the extraordinary Yael Farber started when I was just three years old. Aly—our shared journey is one of hands held tight. Thank you. To the kind and generous Laura Bortz, you have been a friend for over four decades and have a special place in my heart. Charlotte and Moshe Samir, Sam Sussman, Liezel David, Alex Whyte, and Richard and Robyn Samir, I am so grateful we are family. Lisa Farber and Jose Segal, Heather Farber, Tanya Farber, Sharon and Gary Aaron, Joelle Tomb and Chris Zakak, Jillian Frank, Bronwyn Fryer, Charbel El Hage, Janet Campbell, Bill and Maureen Thompson, Trula and Koos Human: thank you for the memories, support and laughter.

To my mother, Veronica; my late father, Sidney; my sister, Madeleine; and my brother, Christopher, the lessons in this book are ones you have taught: compassion, perseverance, the value of all emotions, and of walking your why. I am grateful beyond measure.

Anthony Samir, my darling husband, you are my life partner, best friend, coach, and confidant. Noah and Sophie—I am enfolded in your love, encouragement, and acceptance. I am so extraordinarily lucky you chose me to be your mother. The joy and beauty in my world comes from the three of you. Thank you to each of you. I carry your heart with me. (I carry it in my heart.)

► NOTES

CHAPTER 1—RIGIDITY TO AGILITY

5 *"Between stimulus and response"* . . . Frankl, V. E. (1984). *Man's search for meaning: An introduction to logotherapy.* New York: Simon & Schuster.

5 *It also draws on diverse disciplines in psychology* . . . Emotional agility is influenced by research across social, organizational, and clinical psychology. It is especially indebted to the field of ACT (known either as Acceptance and Commitment Therapy or Acceptance and Commitment Training), which was developed by Steven Hayes, a professor and the chair of psychology at the University of Nevada, and his colleagues, and is supported by a generous community of researchers and practitioners in the Association for Contextual Behavioral Science.

Flexibility is a hallmark of health and well-being. A large and growing body of research demonstrates that *lower* levels of the skills underpinning emotional agility predict a *poorer* rate of success and well-being, that *higher* levels are critical to psychological health and thriving, and also that emotional agility can be learned. For excellent overviews, see Kashdan, T., & Rottenberg, J. (2010). Psychological flexibility as a fundamental aspect of health. *Clinical Psychology Review,* 30(7), 865–878; Biglan, A., Flay, B., Embry, D., & Sandler, I. (2012). The critical role of nurturing environments for promoting human well-being. *American Psychologist,* 67(4), 257–271; Bond, F. W., Hayes, S. C., & Barnes-Holmes, D. (2006). Psychological flexibility, ACT, and organizational behavior. *Journal of Organizational Behavior Management,* 26(1–2), 25–54; Lloyd, J., Bond, F. W., & Flaxman, P. E. (2013). The value of psychological flexibility: Examining psychological mechanisms underpinning a cognitive behavioral therapy intervention for burnout. *Work and Stress,* 27(2), 181–199; A-Tjak, J., Davis, M., Morina, N., Powers, M., Smits, J., & Emmelkamp, P. (2015). A meta-analysis of the efficacy of acceptance and commitment therapy for clinically relevant mental and physical health problems. *Psychotherapy and Psychosomatics,* 84(1), 30–36; Aldao, A., Sheppes, G., & Gross, J. (2015). Emotion regulation flexibility. *Cognitive Therapy and Research,* 39(3), 263–278.

7 *One recent study found* . . . Strayer, D., Crouch, D., & Drews, F. (2006). A comparison of the cell phone driver and the drunk driver. *Human Factors,* 48(2), 381–391.

7 *Other studies show that low-grade daily stress* . . . Epel, E., Blackburn, E., Lin, J., Dhabhar, F., Adler, N., Morrow, J., & Cawthon, R. (2004). Accelerated telomere shortening in response to life stress. *Proceedings of the National Academy of Sciences,* 101(49), 17312–17315.

10 *Not long ago I published . . .* David, S., & Congleton, C. (2013, November). Emotional agility. How effective leaders manage their negative thoughts and feelings. *Harvard Business Review,* 125–128.

12 *learning to see yourself as the chessboard . . .* This metaphor is credited to Hayes, S. C., Strosahl, K. D., & Wilson, K. G. (1999). *Acceptance and commitment therapy: An experiential approach to behavior change.* New York: Guilford Press.

13 *I call these small decision moments* choice points . . . This concept is used in David, S. (2009, September). *Strengthening the inner dialogue* workshop facilitated for Ernst & Young.

13 *Sarah Blakely, the founder of Spanx shapewear . . .* Caprino, K. (2012, May 23). 10 lessons I learned from Sarah Blakely that you won't hear in business school. *Forbes.*

CHAPTER 2—HOOKED

20 *most of us speak around sixteen thousand words . . .* Mehl, M., Vazire, S., Ramirez-Esparza, N., Slatcher, R., & Pennebaker, J. (2007). Are women really more talkative than men? *Science,* 317(5834), 82. This sweet study recorded participants' natural language use over a number of days to assess gender differences in talkativeness. Their conclusion: "The widespread and highly publicized stereotype about female talkativeness is unfounded."

22 *And here's a clue to why this progression . . .* This "Mary had a little lamb" example is credited to Steven Hayes.

24 *Suppose for a moment you're taking a class . . .* The German psychologist Wolfgang Köhler originally demonstrated consistent shape-sound mapping. He found that the nonsense word "maluma" was the label given to a round shape and "takete" to an angular one. Ramachandran, V. S., & Hubbard, E. M. (2001). Synaesthesia—a window into perception, thought and language. *Journal of Consciousness Studies,* 8(12), 3–34.

24 *Even two-year-olds . . .* Maurer, D., Pathman, T., & Mondloch, C. J. (2006). The shape of boubas: Sound-shape correspondence in toddlers and adults. *Developmental Science,* 9(3), 316–322.

24 *This association of a certain shape with a certain sound . . .* After damage to his angular gyrus, patient SJ, a former physician, continued to speak English fluently and even to correctly diagnose illness on the basis of symptom lists. But when Ramachandran's team tested him on the meanings of twenty proverbs, the physician got every one wrong. He was locked in a world of literal meanings and couldn't fathom deeper metaphorical connections. Pressed, for instance, to explain "All that glitters is not gold," he said that one should be very cautious when buying jewelry.

Synesthesia, a curious phenomenon that affects 1 to 2 percent of the population, may be an example of hyperconnective cross wiring. It's a demonstration of bouba kiki at its extreme. People with synesthesia are otherwise normal but perceive certain stimuli in both normative and unexpected ways. For example, a number might be perceived as both a number and a color ("5" may be red and "6" purple); a sound may evoke a color (C-sharp is blue) or flavor (the letter "A" might evoke the taste of semi-ripe bananas). Francis Galton first documented the condition in 1880. It tends to run in families and is more common in creative people. See Ramachandran, V. S., & Hubbard, E. M. (2001). Synaesthesia—a window into perception, thought and language. *Journal of*

Consciousness Studies, 8(12), 3–34. Ramachandran, V. S., & Hubbard, E. M. (2003). Hearing colors, tasting shapes. *Scientific American,* 288(5), 52–59.

    The proposed role of the angular gyrus in understanding metaphor has been contested by Krish Sathian and his team at the Emory University. Research is ongoing. Simon, K., Stilla, R., & Sathian, K. (2011). Metaphorically feeling: Comprehending textural metaphors activates somatosensory cortex. *Brain and Language,* 120(3), 416–421.

28   *The poet John Milton summed it up in the seventeenth century . . .* Milton, J. (2009). *Paradise lost.* New York: Penguin Classics (original work published in 1667).

29   *as the philosopher Alfred Korzybski . . .* Korzybski, A. (1933). A non-Aristotelian system and its necessity for rigor in mathematics and physics. *Science and Sanity,* 747–761. This paper was first presented at a meeting of the American Association for the Advancement of Science on December 28, 1931.

30   *Heuristics range from reasonable prohibitions . . .* The upside and downside of heuristics as they relate to flexibility are nicely described in Kashdan, T., & Rottenberg, J. (2010). Psychological flexibility as a fundamental aspect of health. *Clinical Psychology Review,* 30, 865–878. Also see Ambady, N., & Rosenthal, R. (1992). Thin slices of expressive behavior as predictors of interpersonal consequences: A meta-analysis. *Psychological Bulletin,* 111(2), 256–274.

31   *In* Thinking Fast and Slow, *the psychologist Daniel Kahneman . . .* Kahneman, D. (2003). A perspective on judgment and choice: Mapping bounded rationality. *American Psychologist,* 58(9), 697–720.

32   *He describes these kinds of gut responses . . .* Gigerenzer, G. (2011). Heuristic decision making. *Annual Review of Psychology,* 62, 107–139.

32   *But System 1 gut responses have a dark side . . .* Kashdan, T., & Rottenberg, J. (2010). Psychological flexibility as a fundamental aspect of health. *Clinical Psychology Review,* 30(7), 865–878.

32   *In the lab, researchers have had participants watch short videos . . .* These studies describe "change blindness," which denotes difficulties in noticing large changes to visual scenes, or "inattentional blindness," a failure to notice unexpected inclusions in visual scenes. Both effects capture a profound mismatch between what we think we see and what is actually in front of us. These findings are not limited to our visual field. Similar mismatches have been documented, for example, in what we hear or, more accurately, do not hear. Simons, D., & Rensink, R. (2005). Change blindness: Past, present, and future. *Trends in Cognitive Sciences,* 9(1), 16–20; Jensen, M., Yao, R., Street, W., & Simons, D. (2011). Change blindness and inattentional blindness. *Wiley Interdisciplinary Reviews: Cognitive Science,* 2(5), 529–546; Levin, D. T., & Simons, D. J. (1997). Failure to detect changes to attended objects in motion pictures. *Psychonomic Bulletin and Review,* 4, 501–506.

33   *The same researchers behind those experiments did another study . . .* Simons, D. J., & Levin, D. T. (1998). Failure to detect changes to people in real-world interaction. *Psychonomic Bulletin and Review,* 5(4), 644–649.

33   *A tragic, real-life example of this phenomenon took place in Boston . . .* Chabris, C., Weinberger, A., Fontaine, M., & Simons, D. (2011). You do not talk about Fight Club if you do not notice Fight Club: Inattentional blindness for a simulated real-world assault. *i-Perception,* 2(2), 150–153.

34   *psychology professionals were asked to watch an interview . . .* Langer, E., & Abelson, R. (1974). A patient by any other name . . . : Clinician group difference in labeling bias. *Journal of Consulting and Clinical Psychology,* 42(1), 4–9.

35   *People frequently die in fires . . .* Grice, A. (2009). *Fire risk: Fire safety law and its practical application.* London: Thorogood Publishing.

CHAPTER 3—TRYING TO UNHOOK

43 *there are seven basic emotions . . .* Emotions researchers actively debate the number of core emotions, with from six to fifteen commonly cited. By any of these accounts, the so-called "negative" emotions outnumber those labeled as "positive." This "basic" emotions perspective is grounded in the theory that an irreducible number of key emotions are shared across cultures and species and have universal triggers (Ekman, 1999). This perspective can be contrasted with a "constructivist" one (Barrett, 2015), which suggests that emotions do not have definable boundaries between them but, rather, that we actively construct our emotional experience based on the context. Ekman, P. (1999). Basic emotions. In T. Dalgleish & T. Power (Eds.), *The handbook of cognition and emotion* (pp. 45–60). New York: John Wiley & Sons; Clark-Polner, E., Wager, T. D., Satpute, A. B., & Barrett, L. F. (2016). Neural fingerprinting: Meta-analysis, variation, and the search for brain-based essences in the science of emotion. In L. F. Barrett, M. Lewis, & J. M. Haviland-Jones (Eds.). *The handbook of emotion* (4th ed.). New York: Guilford Press; Barrett, L. F. (2014). Ten common misconceptions about the psychological construction of emotion. In L. F. Barrett & J. A. Russell (Eds.), *The psychological construction of emotion* (pp. 45–79). New York: Guilford Press.

46 *men are more likely to bottle than women are . . .* John, O. P., & Eng, J. (2013). Three approaches to individual differences in measuring affect regulation: Conceptualizations, measures, and findings. In J. Gross (Ed.), *Handbook of emotion regulation* (pp. 321–344). New York: Guilford Press. Also see Gross, J., & John, O. P. (2003). Individual difference in two emotion regulation processes: Implications for affect, relationships, and well-being. *Journal of Personality and Social Psychology, 23*(2), 348–362. Two quick caveats are in order: First, although gender differences research demonstrates that men have a greater tendency than women to bottle their emotions, this should not be equated with "all men are bottlers" or "no women are bottlers." The same caveat applies to women and brooding. Second, some people flip between bottling and brooding and vice versa. They might, for example, brood for a while, become concerned with how much they are thinking about the issue, and then try to bury their feelings.

46 *Today, you can see a parody of these stereotypical communication styles . . .* https://www.youtube.com/watch?v=-4EDhdAHrOg.

47 *trying* not *to do something takes a surprising amount of mental bandwidth . . .* Waxer, P. H. (1977). Nonverbal cues for anxiety: An examination of emotional leakage. *Journal of Abnormal Psychology, 86*(3), 306–314.

47 *In a ridiculously simple but very famous study . . .* Wegner, D. M., Schneider, D. J., Carter, S., & White, T. (1987). Paradoxical effects of thought suppression. *Journal of Personality and Social Psychology, 53*(1), 5–13. Also see Wegner, D. M. (2011). Setting free the bears: Escape from thought suppression. *American Psychologist, 66*(8), 671-680.

48 *Bottling is usually done with the best intentions . . .* Litvin, E. B., Kovacs, M. A., et al. (2012). Responding to tobacco craving: Experimental test of acceptance versus suppression. *Psychology of Addictive Behaviors, 26*(4), 830–837.

48 *researchers found that bottling increases . . .* Butler, E. A., Egloff, B., Wilhelm, F. W., Smith, N. C., Erickson, E. A., & Gross, J. J. (2003). The social consequences of expressive suppression. *Emotion, 3*(1), 48–67.

49 *brooders are more likely to be women . . .* Johnson, D., & Whisman, M. (2013).

Gender differences in rumination: A meta-analysis. *Personality and Individual Differences,* 55(4), 367–374.

49 *psychologist Brad Bushman did a study . . .* Bushman, B. (2002). Does venting anger feed or extinguish the flame? Catharsis, rumination, distraction, anger, and aggressive responding. *Personality and Social Psychology Bulletin,* 28(6), 724–731. In this study, the brooders fared the worst when compared with bottlers and a control group. The brooders were angriest and most aggressive. Next came the bottlers, who were still angry but not aggressive. Those in the control group, who were trying neither to bottle nor trying to brood, fared the best.

50 *We might think that these venting sessions . . .* Rose, A., Schwartz-Mette, R., Glick, G. C., Smith, R. L., & Luebbe, A. M. (2014). An observational study of co-rumination in adolescent friendships. *Developmental Psychology,* 50(9), 2199–2209.

51 *brooder's self-focus leaves no room for anyone else's needs . . .* Nolen-Hoeksema, S., & Davis, C. G. (1999). "Thanks for sharing that": Ruminators and their social support networks. *Journal of Personality and Social Psychology,* 77(4), 801–814.

51 Type 1 *and* Type 2 *thoughts . . .* Wells, A. (2009). *Metacognitive therapy for anxiety and depression.* New York: Guilford Press.

51 *It's like quicksand . . .* This metaphor is credited to Steven Hayes. Hayes, S., & Smith, S. (2005). *Get out of your mind and into your life: The new acceptance and commitment therapy.* Oakland, CA: New Harbinger Publications.

52 *Whatever we may think we're accomplishing by bottling or brooding . . .* Aldao, A., & Nolen-Hoeksema, S. (2012). When are adaptive strategies most predictive of psychopathology? *Journal of Abnormal Psychology,* 121(1), 276–281. Also see Mauss, I., Evers, C., Wilhelm, F., & Gross, J. (2006). How to bite your tongue without blowing your top: Implicit evaluation of emotion regulation predicts affective responding to anger provocation. *Personality and Social Psychology Bulletin,* 32(5), 589–602.

52 *But when I hold the books tight to my body . . .* This metaphor has been adapted from Zettle, R. (2007). *ACT for depression: A clinician's guide to using acceptance and commitment therapy in treating depression.* Oakland, CA: New Harbinger Publications.

52 *Openness and enthusiasm are replaced by rules . . .* Nolen-Hoeksema, S., Wisco, B., & Lyubomirsky, S. (2008). Rethinking rumination. *Perspectives on Psychological Science,* 3(5), 400–424.

53 *The unwritten rule book about emotions . . .* For more on the development of emotional display rules, see Zeman, J., & Garber, J. (1996). Display rules for anger, sadness, and pain: It depends on who is watching. *Child Development,* 67(3), 957–973. For a more general discussion on display rules, see Paul Ekman's work.

53 *We learn these rules from our caregivers . . .* Reese, E., Haden, C., & Fivush, R. (1996). Mothers, fathers, daughters, sons: Gender differences in reminiscing. *Research on Language and Social Interaction,* 29(1), 27–56; Root, A., & Rubin, K. (2010). Gender and parents' reactions to children's emotion during the preschool years. *New Directions for Child and Adolescent Development,* 128, 51–64.

54 *two researchers at the University of California, Berkeley . . .* Harker, L., & Keltner, D. (2001). Expressions of positive emotion in women's college yearbook pictures and their relationship to personality and life outcomes across adulthood. *Journal of Personality and Social Psychology,* 80(1), 112–124; Ekman, P., Davidson, R., & Friesen, W. (1990). The Duchenne smile: Emotional expression and brain physiology, II. *Journal of Personality and Social Psychology,* 58(2), 342–353.

55 *They help build vital social . . .* Lyubomirsky, S., Sheldon, K. M., & Schkade, D. (2005). Pursuing happiness: The architecture of sustainable change. *Review of*

General Psychology, 9, 111–131; Seligman, M.E.P., & Csikszentmihalyi, M. (Eds.) (2000). Positive psychology (special issue). *American Psychologist,* 55(1), 5–14; Fredrickson, B. L. (1998). What good are positive emotions? *Review of General Psychology,* 2(3), 300–319; Tugade, M., Fredrickson, B. L., & Barrett, L. F. (2004). Psychological resilience and positive emotional granularity: Examining the benefits of positive emotions on coping and health. *Journal of Personality,* 72(6), 1161–1190.

55   *research shows it's possible not only to be too happy* . . . Gruber, J., Mauss, I., & Tamir, M. (2011). A dark side of happiness? How, when, and why happiness is not always good. *Perspectives on Psychological Science,* 6(3), 222–233.

56   *An excess of freewheeling giddiness* . . . Gruber, J., Mauss, I., & Tamir, M. (2011). A dark side of happiness? How, when, and why happiness is not always good. *Perspectives on Psychological Science,* 6(3), 222–233.

56   *highly positive people can be less creative* . . . Davis, M. A. (2008). Understanding the relationship between mood and creativity: A meta-analysis. *Organizational Behavior and Human Decision Processes,* 108(1), 25–38.

56   *The happy more often place disproportionate emphasis* . . . Gruber, J., Mauss, I., & Tamir, M. (2011). A dark side of happiness? How, when, and why happiness is not always good. *Perspectives on Psychological Science,* 6(3), 222–233. For an excellent discussion on the dark side of positive emotion, also see Gruber, J., & Moskowitz, J. (2014). *Positive emotion: Integrating the light sides and dark sides.* New York: Oxford University Press

57   *negative emotions encourage slower, more systematic cognitive processing* . . . Forgas, J. (2013). Don't worry, be sad! On the cognitive, motivational, and interpersonal benefits of negative mood. *Current Directions in Psychological Science,* 22(3), 225–232; Young, M., Tiedens, L., Jung, H., & Tsai, M. (2011). Mad enough to see the other side: Anger and the search for disconfirming information. *Cognition and Emotion,* 25(1), 10–21.

58   *In one study, participants were given a fake newspaper article* . . . Mauss, I. B., Tamir, M., Anderson, C. L., & Savino, N. S. (2011). Can seeking happiness make people unhappy? Paradoxical effects of valuing happiness. *Emotion,* 11(4), 807-815.

58   *participants were asked to listen to Stravinsky's* Rite of Spring . . . Schooler, J. W., Ariely, D., & Loewenstein, G. (2003). The pursuit and assessment of happiness may be self-defeating. In I. Brocas & J. D. Carrillo (Eds.), *The psychology of economic decisions, 1: Rationality and well-being* (pp. 41–70). New York: Oxford University Press.

58   *The aggressive pursuit of happiness is also isolating* . . .Mauss, I., Savino, N., Anderson, C., Weisbuch, M., Tamir, M., & Laudenslager, M. (2012). The pursuit of happiness can be lonely. *Emotion,* 12(5), 908–912.

58   *To be happy within a given culture depends* . . . Gruber, J., Mauss, I., & Tamir, M. (2011). A dark side of happiness? How, when, and why happiness is not always good. *Perspectives on Psychological Science,* 6(3), 222–233.

59   *Good News About Bad Moods* . . . Moods are generally defined as emotions that last for an extended period; they are not fleeting.

59   *Help us form arguments* . . . Forgas, J. (2007). When sad is better than happy: Negative affect can improve the quality and effectiveness of persuasive messages and social influence strategies. *Journal of Experimental Social Psychology,* 43(4), 513–528.

59   *One study found that shoppers remembered* . . . Forgas, J. P., Goldenberg, L., & Unkelbach, C. (2009). Can bad weather improve your memory? A field study of

mood effects on memory in a real-life setting. *Journal of Experimental Social Psychology*, 45(1), 254–257.

59 *On academic tests, an individual in a more somber mood . . .* Forgas, J. (2013). Don't worry, be sad! On the cognitive, motivational, and interpersonal benefits of negative mood. *Current Directions in Psychological Science*, 22(3), 225–232.

60 *People in less exuberant moments . . .* Forgas, J. (2013). Don't worry, be sad! On the cognitive, motivational, and interpersonal benefits of negative mood. *Current Directions in Psychological Science*, 22(3), 225–232.

60 *Those in negative moods pay more attention to fairness . . .* Forgas, J. (2013). Don't worry, be sad! On the cognitive, motivational, and interpersonal benefits of negative mood. *Current Directions in Psychological Science*, 22(3), 225–232.

60 *In a study of people with strong political opinions . . .* Young, M., Tiedens, L., Jung, H., & Tsai, M. (2011). Mad enough to see the other side: Anger and the search for disconfirming information. *Cognition and Emotion*, 25(1), 10–21.

61 *One study showed that students who expressed benign envy . . .* Ven, N., Zeelenberg, M., & Pieters, R. (2011). Why envy outperforms admiration. *Personality and Social Psychology Bulletin*, 37(6), 784–795.

61 *Embarrassment and guilt can serve important social functions . . .* Stearns, D., & Parrott, W. (2012). When feeling bad makes you look good: Guilt, shame, and person perception. *Cognition and Emotion*, 26, 407–430.

62 *Suppress the sadness under a veil . . .* Hackenbracht, J., & Tamir, M. (2010). Preferences for sadness when eliciting help: Instrumental motives in sadness regulation. *Motivation and Emotion*, 34(3), 306–315.

CHAPTER 4—SHOWING UP

65 *In that 1949 classic, Campbell explored the idea . . .* Campbell, J. (2008). *The hero with a thousand faces* (3rd ed.). Novato, CA: New World Library, 2008.

68 *The Italian Jewish writer Primo Levi . . .* Levi described his experiences in *If This Is a Man* and *The Truce*. When Levi died at sixty-seven after falling from the interior landing of his third-story apartment, authorities quickly described the cause of his death as suicide. However, a rich analysis of Levi's final weeks suggests that an accidental fall, rather than suicide, is more likely. Gambetta, G. (1999, June 1). Primo Levi's last moments, *Boston Review*.

69 *"happy habits" science has currently identified . . .* Self-acceptance could be the key to a happier life, yet it's the happy habit many people practice the least. Research by K. Pine, University of Hertfordshire, March 7, 2014.

69 *According to folklore . . . when a member of a certain tribe . . .* This story may well be apocryphal. It does appear in a collection of essays by the American writer Alice Walker. Walker, A. (2006). *We are the ones we have been waiting for: Inner light in a time of darkness* (pp. 202–204). New York: New Press.

72 *In a study of people going through divorce . . .* Sbarra, D. A., Smith, H. L., & Mehl, M. R. (2012). When leaving your ex, love yourself: Observational ratings of self-compassion predict the course of emotional recovery following marital separation. *Psychological Science*, 23(3), 261–269.

72 *In studies, prison inmates . . .* Tangney, J., Stuewig, J., & Martinez, A. (2014). Two faces of shame: The roles of shame and guilt in predicting recidivism. *Psychological Science*, 25(3), 799–805.

73 *Self-compassion is the antidote to shame . . .* Earlier I described all emotions as having a purpose. What, then, is the purpose of shame? Shame, like guilt, is

considered a "moral" emotion—one that helps to shape our behavior and that of others in society. From an evolutionary perspective, though, shame is thought to have been most adaptive at earlier stages of evolution, as a mechanism for communicating rank and dominance or submission. While it still shapes behavior, it is considered less adaptive than guilt in our current evolutionary period, at a time when humankind is more cognitively, emotionally, and interpersonally complex. Tangney, J. P., & Tracy, J. (2012). Self-conscious emotions. In M. Leary & J. P. Tangney (Eds.), *Handbook of self and identity* (2nd ed.), (pp. 446–478). New York: Guilford Press.

73   *people took part in mock job interviews . . .* Neff, K. D., Kirkpatrick, K., & Rude, S. S. (2007). Self-compassion and its link to adaptive psychological functioning. *Journal of Research in Personality*, 41, 139–154.

74   *people who are more accepting of their own failures . . .* Breines, J., & Chen, S. (2012). Self-compassion increases self-improvement motivation. *Personality and Social Psychology Bulletin*, 38(9), 1133–1143.

75   *It even strengthens your immune system . . .* Pace, T., Negi, L., Adame, D., Cole, S., Sivilli, T., Brown, T., Issa, M., Raison, C. (2009). Effect of compassion meditation on neuroendocrine, innate immune and behavioral responses to psychosocial stress. *Psychoneuroendocrinology*, 34(1), 87–98.

76   *young men and women who had spent the least . . .* The discussion on self-acceptance and social comparisons in this chapter owes a debt to Carson, S., & Langer, E. (2006). Mindfulness and self-acceptance. *Journal of Rational-Emotive and Cognitive-Behavior Therapy*, 24(1), 29–43; White, J., Langer, E., Yariv, L., & Welch, J. (2006). Frequent social comparisons and destructive emotions and behaviors: The dark side of social comparisons. *Journal of Adult Development*, 13(1), 36–44.

79   *someone else's negative evaluation of you is rarely objective . . .* Carson, S., & Langer, E. (2006). Mindfulness and self-acceptance. *Journal of Rational-Emotive and Cognitive-Behavior Therapy*, 24(1), 29–43.

81   *participants who were trying to quit smoking . . .* Bricker, J., Wyszynski, C., Comstock, B., & Heffner, J. (2013). Pilot randomized controlled trial of web-based acceptance and commitment therapy for smoking cessation. *Nicotine and Tobacco Research*, 15(10), 1756–1764.

83   *condition called alexithymia . . .* Lesser, I. M. (1985). Current concepts in psychiatry: Alexithymia. *New England Journal of Medicine*, 312(11), 690–692.

84   *Trouble labeling emotions . . .* Hesse, C., & Floyd, K. (2008). Affectionate experience mediates the affects of alexithymia on mental health and interpersonal relationships. *Journal of Social and Personal Relationships*, 25(5), 793–810.

85   *People who can identify the full spectrum . . .* Barrett, L. F., Gross, J., Christensen, T., & Benvenuto, M. (2001). Knowing what you're feeling and knowing what to do about it: Mapping the relation between emotion differentiation and emotion regulation. *Cognition and Emotion*, 15(6), 713–724; Erbas, Y., Ceulemans, E., Pe, M., Koval, P., & Kuppens, P. (2014). Negative emotion differentiation: Its personality and well-being correlates and a comparison of different assessment methods. *Cognition and Emotion*, 28(7), 1196–1213.

86   *anger can be a sign . . .* Ford, B., & Tamir, M. (2012). When getting angry is smart: Emotional preferences and emotional intelligence. *Emotion*, 12(4), 685–689.

86   *awareness it provides can be channeled . . .* & Ford, B. Tamir, M., When getting angry is smart: Emotional preferences and emotional intelligence. *Emotion*, 12(4), 685–689.

CHAPTER 5—STEPPING OUT

89   *He began to reconnect with his deep love for his wife* . . . Studies show that when
      people write expressively about recent breakups, they are somewhat more likely
      than a control group to reunite with their partners. See Lepore, S. J., & Greenberg,
      M. A. (2002). Mending broken hearts: Effects of expressive writing on mood,
      cognitive processing, social adjustment and health following a relationship
      breakup. *Psychology and Health,* 17(5), 547–560. Pennebaker also studied writing
      through the lens of intact romantic relationships and found that people who wrote
      about their significant others were more likely to still be dating them three months
      later. See Slatcher, R. B., & Pennebaker, J. W. (2006). How do I love thee? Let me
      count the words: The social effects of expressive writing. *Psychological Science,*
      17(8), 660–664. And in case you're curious, James and Ruth Pennebaker are still
      married, and writing is in their blood: He still researches writing, and she is a
      novelist.

89   *he started to see the purpose* . . . Pennebaker, J. (1997). Becoming healthier through
      writing. In *Opening up: The healing power of expressive emotions* (pp. 26–42). New
      York: Guilford Press.

90   *people who wrote about emotionally charged* . . . Burton, C. M., & King, L. A.
      (2008). Effects of (very) brief writing on health: The two-minute miracle. *British
      Journal of Health Psychology,* 13, 9–14.

91   *deeper dive into his work* . . . One of Pennebaker's most impressive works is the
      1997 book, *Opening up: The healing power of expressing emotions.* I met with James
      Pennebaker at the Positive Psychology Conference in Washington, D.C.

91   *intervention Pennebaker had conducted at a Dallas computer company* . . .
      Pennebaker, J. (1997). Becoming healthier through writing. In *Opening up: The
      healing power of expressive emotions* (pp. 26–42). New York: Guilford Press. Also
      see Spera, S. P., Buhrfiend, E. D., & Pennebaker, J. (1994). Expressive writing and
      coping with job loss. *Academy of Management Journal,* 37(3), 722–733.

92   *After many more studies* . . . Pennebaker, J. W., & Evans, J. F. (2014). *Expressive
      writing: Words that heal.* Enumclaw, WA: Idyll Arbor.

92   *writers in these experiments who thrived* . . . Pennebaker, J. W., & Evans, J. F.
      (2014). *Expressive writing: Words that heal.* Enumclaw, WA: Idyll Arbor;
      Pennebaker, J. W., & Chung, C. K. (2011). Expressive writing: Connections to
      physical and mental health. In H. S. Friedman (Ed.), *Oxford handbook of health
      psychology* (pp. 417–437). New York: Oxford University Press.

95   *Take a look at this line drawing* . . . Included with permission by Daniel Kahneman,
      Eugene Higgins Professor of Psychology Emeritus at Princeton University, and
      originally adapted from Bruner, J. S., & Minturn, A. L. (1955). Perceptual
      identification and perceptual organization. *Journal of General Psychology,* 53(2),
      21–28; Kahneman, D. (2003). A perspective on judgment and choice: Mapping
      bounded rationality. *American Psychologist,* 58(9), 697–720.

97   *research in the behavioral and cognitive sciences* . . . Modern thinking on
      mindfulness and associated practices has been deeply influenced by the work of
      Jon Kabat-Zinn, Ellen Langer, and Richard Davidson, to name a few.

97   *Harvard researchers recently performed brain scans* . . . Hölzel, B., Carmody, J.,
      Vangel, M., Congleton, C., Yerramsetti, S., Gard, T., & Lazar, S. (2011).
      Mindfulness practice leads to increases in regional brain gray matter density.
      Psychiatry Research: Neuroimaging, 191(1), 36–43.

97   *By paying attention to what's going on around us* . . . Ricard, M., Lutz, A., & Davidson, R. J. (2014, November). Mind of the meditator. *Scientific American,* 311(5), 38–45; Davis, D., & Hayes, J. (2012). What are the benefits of mindfulness? A practice review of psychotherapy-related research. *Psychotherapy,* 43(7), 198–208.

98   *One of the leaders in mindfulness research* . . . Beard, A. (2014, March). Mindfulness in the age of complexity. *Harvard Business Review.*

99   *When you're mindful of your anger* . . . This lovely article captures the essence of mindfulness in learning and growth: Salzberg, S. (2015, April 5). What does mindfulness really mean anyway? *On Being.*

99   *A series of studies at Harvard* . . . Wilson, T., Reinhard, D., Westgate, E., Gilbert, D., Ellerbeck, N., Hahn, C., et al. (2014). Just think: The challenges of the disengaged mind. *Science,* 345(6192), 75–77.

101 *"green thought in a green shade"* . . . Marvell, A. (2005). The garden. In Andrew Marvell, *The complete poems,* Elizabeth Story Donno (Ed.). New York: Penguin Classics.

102 *I often read my daughter, Sophie, to sleep* . . . Johnson, C. (1955, 2015). *Harold and the purple crayon.* New York: HarperCollins.

104 *Or say a simple word like "milk"* . . . The "milk" exercise, which was first used by the psychologist Edward B. Titchener in 1916, is a staple technique to help people become disentangled from their thoughts and emotions when they are hooked. Titchener, E. B. (1916). *A textbook of psychology.* New York: Macmillan.

106 *"One thing I didn't want to do"* . . . Greenberg, J. (2010). Exiting via the low road. ESPNChicago.com. http://espn.go.com/espn/print?id=5365985.

106 *Research shows that using the third person* . . . Kross, E., Bruehlman-Senecal, E., Park, J., Burson, A., Dougherty, A., Shablack, H., et al. (2014). Self-talk as a regulatory mechanism: How you do it matters. *Journal of Personality and Social Psychology,* 106(2), 304–324.

107 *Techniques for Stepping Out* . . . Techniques 1–4 in this list are adapted from Carson, S., & Langer, E. (2006). Mindfulness and self-acceptance. *Journal of Rational-Emotive and Cognitive-Behavior Therapy,* 24(1), 29–43.

110 *Just saying the words "let go"* . . . This sentiment is beautifully conveyed by Joen Snyder O'Neal, Reflecting on Letting Go, Spring 2001. http://www .oceandharma.org/teachers/Letting_Go.pdf.

111 *"On the return trip home"* . . . Kelley, K. W. (1988). *The home planet.* Reading, MA: Addison-Wesley.

CHAPTER 6—WALKING YOUR WHY

113 *Tom Shadyac gave Jim Carrey his first big role* . . . Oprah.com. (2011, April 4). From multimillionaire to mobile home. http://www.oprah.com/oprahshow /Tom-Shadyac-From-Millionaire-to-Mobile-Home.

113 *"The lifestyle was fine"* . . . https://www.reddit.com/r/IAmA/comments/1dxuqd /im_tom_shadyac_director_of_ace_ventura_nutty.

114 *He also made sure that the choices he made were for himself alone* . . . Oprah.com (2011, April 4). From multimillionaire to mobile home. http://www.oprah.com /oprahshow/Tom-Shadyac-From-Millionaire-to-Mobile-Home.

114 *Asked in another interview whether he was happier* . . . Hassett, S. (2011, January 28). Tom Shadyac wants you to wake up. *Esquire.* http://www.esquire.com /entertainment/interviews/a9309/tom-shadyac-i-am-012811.

114 *He knew he was doing the right thing . . .* Oprah.com (2011, April 4). From multimillionaire to mobile home. http://www.oprah.com/oprahshow /Tom-Shadyac-From-Millionaire-to-Mobile-Home.

116 *certain behaviors really are like colds and flus . . .* Hill, A. L., Rand, D. G., Nowak, M. A., & Christakis, N. A. (2010). Infectious disease modeling of social contagion in networks. *PLOS Computational Biology* 6(11).

116 *One study found that couples are more likely to divorce . . .* Hill, A. L., Rand, D. G., Nowak, M. A., & Christakis, N. A. (2010). Infectious disease modeling of social contagion in networks. *PLOS Computational Biology* 6(11); McDermott, R., Fowler, J. H., & Christakis, A. (2013, December). Breaking up is hard to do, unless everyone else is doing it too: Social network effects on divorce in a longitudinal sample. *Social Forces,* 92(2), 491–519.

116 *A Stanford University marketing professor tracked more than a quarter of a million . . .* Gardete, P. (2015). Social effects in the in-flight marketplace: Characterization and managerial implications. *Journal of Marketing Research,* 52(3), 360–374.

118 *Psychologists asked a group of people in their early twenties . . .* Gelder, J., Hershfield, H., & Nordgren, L. (2013). Vividness of the future self predicts delinquency. *Psychological Science,* 24(6), 974–980.

119 *In another experiment, college-age participants were told . . .* Hershfield, H., Goldstein, D., Sharpe, W., Fox, J., Yeykelis, L., Carstensen, L., & Bailenson, J. (2011). Increasing saving behavior through age-progressed renderings of the future self. *Journal of Marketing Research,* 48, S23–37.

119 *Jeff Kinney is the author of the bestselling kids' series* Diary of a Wimpy Kid . . . Alter, A. (2015, May 22). The bookstore built by Jeff Kinney, the "Wimpy Kid." *New York Times.*

121 *Instead, I see values not as rules that are supposed to govern us . . .* This articulation of values as being qualities of action rather than categories or rules is a hallmark of ACT. For a discussion on this and the key characteristics of values, see, for example, Harris, R. (2008). *The happiness trap: How to stop struggling and start living.* Boston: Trumpeter; Luoma, J. B., Hayes, S. C., & Walser, R. D. (2007). *Learning ACT: An acceptance and commitment therapy skills-training manual for therapists.* Oakland, CA, and Reno, NV: New Harbinger and Context Press; Wilson, K. G., & Murrell, A. R. (2004). Values work in acceptance and commitment therapy: Setting a course for behavioral treatment. In S. C. Hayes, V. M. Follette, & M. Linehan (Eds.), *Mindfulness and acceptance: Expanding the cognitive-behavioral tradition* (pp. 120–151). New York: Guilford Press.

121 *A colleague of mine describes values as "facets on a diamond" . . .* Tim Bowden used this simile in a discussion about values on the ACT professional Listserv discussion (September 12, 2012).

121 *When the author Elizabeth Gilbert was writing her memoir . . .* http://www .elizabethgilbert.com/thoughts-on-writing.

124 *At the age of twenty-four, Sergeant Joseph Darby . . .* Hylton, W. S. (2006, July 31). Prisoner of conscience. *GQ.*

124 *But the more he witnessed, the more he realized that the abuse . . .* Jaffer, J., & Siems, L. (2011, April 27). Honoring those who said no. *New York Times.*

125 *identifying their personal values helped protect a group of minority students . . .* Cohen, G. L., & Sherman, D. K. (2014). The psychology of change: Self-affirmation and social psychological intervention. *Annual Review of Psychology,* 65, 333–371.

126 *female college students enrolled in an introductory physics course . . .* Cohen, G. L., & Sherman, D. K. (2014). The psychology of change: Self-affirmation and social psychological intervention. *Annual Review of Psychology,* 65, 333–371.

126   *subjects of one such study, who affirmed just one core value* . . . Cohen, G. L., & Sherman, D. K. (2014). The psychology of change: Self-affirmation and social psychological intervention. *Annual Review of Psychology,* 65, 333–371.

127   *When Irena Sendler was a seven-year-old* . . . For more information on the remarkable Irena Sendler, see http://lowellmilkencenter.org/irena-sendler-overview.

128   *you will eventually arrive at what I call a* choice point . . . This concept is used in David, S. (2009, September). *Strengthening the inner dialogue,* workshop facilitated for Ernst & Young. For an excellent synopsis of the choice points idea, see this presentation by Russ Harris: https://www.youtube.com /watch?v=tW6vWKVrmLc.

128   *choose moves that are* toward . . . The language of toward and away moves was developed by Kevin Polk, Jerold Hambright, and Mark Webster as part of a broader framework that elegantly illustrates how humans understand and respond to their experiences. Polk, K., & Schoendorff, B. (Eds.). (2014). *The ACT matrix: A new approach to building psychological flexibility across settings and populations.* Oakland, CA: New Harbinger Publications.

129   *"Choices," the philosopher Ruth Chang said* . . . http://www.ted.com/talks/ruth _chang_how_to_make_hard_choices?language=en.

131   *I recall a profound interaction I had with Jane Goodall* . . . Jane Goodall and I had this discussion in September 2007.

132   *A colleague of mine described the dilemma this way* . . . This is paraphrased from a description used by Jonathan Kanter from the University of Washington Center for the Science of Social Connection in an ACT professional Listserv discussion on October 11, 2013.

CHAPTER 7—MOVING ON: THE TINY TWEAKS PRINCIPLE

135   *Cynthia and David were fighting about money* . . . The "Cynthia and David" and "sailing" examples are cited and adapted from the following two articles, respectively: Driver, J., & Gottman, J. (2004). Daily marital interactions and positive affect during marital conflict among newlywed couples. *Family Process,* 43(3) 301–314; Gottman, J., & Driver, J. (2005). Dysfunctional marital conflict and everyday marital interaction. *Journal of Divorce and Remarriage,* 22(3–4), 63–77.

137   *In one follow-up six years later* . . . Smith, E. E. (2014, June 12). Masters of love. *Atlantic.*

138   *But when we aim for tiny tweaks* . . . Karl Weick describes the powerful impact of aiming small in his classic paper on small wins. Weick, K. (1984). Small wins. *Redefining Social Problems,* 39(1), 29–48.

139   *tiny tweak to the mindsets of eighty-four female hotel cleaners* . . . Crum, A. J. (2006, April). Think and grow fit: Unleash the power of the mind body connection. Paper presented at Dr. Tal Ben-Shahar's class Positive Psychology, Harvard University, Cambridge, MA; Crum, A. J., & Langer, E. J. (2007). Mind-set matters: Exercise and the placebo effect. *Psychological Science,* 18(2), 165–171.

141   *People with a fixed mindset* . . . Burnette, J., O'Boyle, E., Vanepps, E., Pollack, J., & Finkel, E. (2013). Mind-sets matter: A meta-analytic review of implicit theories and self-regulation. *Psychological Bulletin,* 139(3), 655–701.

141   *these beliefs can have a profound effect on behavior* . . . Dweck, C. (2008). Can personality be changed? The role of beliefs in personality and change. *Current Directions in Psychological Science,* 17(6), 391–394; Yeager, D., Johnson, R., Spitzer,

B., Trzesniewski, K., Powers, J., & Dweck, C. (2014). The far-reaching effects of believing people can change: Implicit theories of personality shape stress, health, and achievement during adolescence. *Journal of Personality and Social Psychology,* 106(6), 867–884.

141 *one's mindset can be developed and shifted* . . . Paunesku, D., Walton, G., Romero, C., Smith, E., Yeager, D., & Dweck, C. (2015). Mind-set interventions are a scalable treatment for academic underachievement. *Psychological Science,* 26(6), 784–793; Gunderson, E., Gripshover, S., Romero, C., Dweck, C., Goldin-Meadow, S., & Levine, S. (2013). Parent praise to 1- to 3-year-olds predicts children's motivational frameworks 5 years later. *Child Development,* 84(5), 1526–1541.

142 *it is important not to confuse having a growth mindset with simply working harder* . . . http://www.edweek.org/ew/articles/2015/09/23/carol-dweck-revisits-the-growth-mindset.html.

142 *researchers wondered whether they could improve the success rates* . . . Yeager, D., & Dweck, C. (2012). Mindsets that promote resilience: When students believe that personal characteristics can be developed. *Educational Psychologist,* 47(4), 302–314.

143 *Becca Levy from the Yale School of Public Health* . . . This is a fascinating line of research into the impact of age stereotypes on later life. For a good overview of this work, see Levy, B. (2009). Stereotype embodiment: A psychosocial approach to aging. *Psychological Science,* 18(6), 332–336. Also see Levy, B., Slade M. D., & Kasl, S. V. (2002). Longevity increased by positive self-perceptions of aging. *Journal of Personality and Social Psychology,* 83(2), 261–270.

144 *those with negative views on aging* . . . Levy, B. R., Zonderman, A. B., Slade, M. D., & Ferrucci, L. (2009). Age stereotypes held earlier in life predict cardiovascular events in later life. *Psychological Science,* 20(3), 296–298.

144 *people with fixed negative views on aging die* . . . Levy, B., Slade, M., Kunkel, S., & Kasl, S. (2002). Longevity increased by positive self-perceptions of aging. *Journal of Personality and Social Psychology,* 83(2), 261–270.

144 *Studies show that, on average, seniors* . . . For example, Verhaeghen P. (2003, June). Aging and vocabulary scores: A meta-analysis. *Psychology and Aging,* 18(2), 332–339; Fleischman, D. A., Wilson, R. S., Gabrieli, J. D., Bienias, J. L., & Bennett, D. A. (2004, December). A longitudinal study of implicit and explicit memory in old persons. *Psychology & Aging,* 19(4), 617–625; Singer, J., Rexhaj, B., & Baddeley, J. (2007). Older, wiser, and happier? Comparing older adults' and college students' self-defining memories. *Memory,* 15(8), 886–898. Tergesen, A. (2015, October 19). To age well, change how you feel about aging. *Wall Street Journal.*

144 *A few milliseconds before we make a single voluntary move* . . . Rigoni, D., Kuhn, S., Sartori, G., & Brass, M. (2011). Inducing disbelief in free will alters brain correlates of preconscious motor preparation: The brain minds whether we believe in free will or not. *Psychological Science,* 22(5), 613–618.

145 *People who have a growth mindset* . . . Dweck, C. S. (2012). *Mindset: How you can fulfill your potential.* London: Constable and Robinson Limited.

145 *They are less likely to mindlessly conform* . . . Alquist, J., Ainsworth, S., & Baumeister, R. (2013). Determined to conform: Disbelief in free will increases conformity. *Journal of Experimental Social Psychology,* 49(1), 80–86.

145 *In one study, eligible voters were asked* . . . Bryan, C. J., Walton, G. M., Rogers, T., & Dweck, C. S. (2011). Motivating voter turnout by invoking the self. *Proceedings of the National Academy of Sciences,* 108(31), 12653–12656.

149 *Modern neuroimaging tells us* . . . Milyavskaya, M., Inzlicht, M., Hope, N., & Koestner, R. (2015). Saying "no" to temptation: Want-to motivation improves

self-regulation by reducing temptation rather than by increasing self-control. *Journal of Personality and Social Psychology,* 109(4), 677–693.

149 *basic attributes like taste* . . . Sullivan, N., Hutcherson, C., Harris, A., & Rangel, A. (2015, February). Dietary self-control is related to the speed with which attributes of healthfulness and tastiness are processed. *Psychological Science,* 26(2), 122–134.

149 *74 percent of people* said *they would choose fruit* . . . Read, D., & Van Leeuwen, B. (1998). Predicting hunger: The effects of appetite and delay on choice. *Organizational Behavior and Human Decision Processes,* 76(2), 189–205.

150 *We pursue these kinds of goals because* . . . Ryan, R., & Deci, E. (2006). Self-regulation and the problem of human autonomy: Does psychology need choice, self-determination, and will? *Journal of Personality,* 74(6), 1557–1586.

151 *two people with the same goal of losing five pounds* . . . Milyavskaya, M., Inzlicht, M., Hope, N., & Koestner, R. (2015). Saying "no" to temptation: Want-to motivation improves self-regulation by reducing temptation rather than by increasing self-control. *Journal of Personality and Social Psychology,* 109(4), 677–693.

154 *In their bestselling book* Nudge . . . Thaler, R. H., & Sunstein, C. R. (2009). *Nudge: Improving decisions about health, wealth, and happiness.* New York: Penguin Books.

154 *In Germany you must explicitly consent to becoming an organ donor* . . . Johnson, E. J., & Goldstein, D. (2003). Do defaults save lives? *Science,* 302(5649), 1338–1339.

154 *Habit is defined as an externally triggered automatic response* . . . Gardner, B., Lally, P., & Wardle, J. (2012). Making health habitual: The psychology of "habit-formation" and general practice. *British Journal of General Practice,* 62(605), 664–666.

155 *studies of more than nine thousand commuters* . . . Suri, G., Sheppes, G., Leslie, S., & Gross, J. (2014). Stairs or escalator? Using theories of persuasion and motivation to facilitate healthy decision making. *Journal of Experimental Psychology: Applied,* 20(4), 295–302.

156 *Connecting with want-to motivations is key* . . . Gardner, B., & Lally, P. (2012). Does intrinsic motivation strengthen physical activity habit? Modeling relationships between self-determination, past behaviour, and habit strength. *Journal of Behavioral Medicine,* 36(5), 488–497.

156 *Functional magnetic resonance imaging (fMRI) shows* . . . Suri, G., Sheppes, G., Leslie, S., & Gross, J. (2014). Stairs or escalator? Using theories of persuasion and motivation to facilitate healthy decision making. *Journal of Experimental Psychology: Applied,* 20(4), 295–302.

157 *plate that's 10 percent smaller* . . . Van Ittersum, K., & Wansink, B. (2012). Plate size and color suggestibility: The Delboeuf illusion's bias on serving and eating behavior. *Journal of Consumer Research,* 39(2), 215–222.

158 *Anticipate obstacles and prepare for them with "if-then" strategies.* . . . Gollwitzer, P. M. (1999). Implementation intentions: Strong effects of simple plans. *American Psychologist,* 54, 493–503.

159 *Offset a positive vision with thoughts of potential challenges* . . . Gabriele Oettingen has led this fascinating research on the power of mental contrasting. Oettingen, G. (2014, October 24). The problem with positive thinking. *New York Times;* Sevincer, A. T., & Oettingen, G. (2015). Future thought and the self-regulation of energization. In G.H.E. Gendolla, M. Tops, & S. Koole (Eds.), *Handbook of biobehavioral approaches to self-regulation* (pp. 315–329). New York: Springer; Oettingen, G., & Wadden, T. (1991). Expectation, fantasy, and weight loss: Is the impact of positive thinking always positive? *Cognitive Therapy and Research,* 15(2), 167–175.

CHAPTER 8—MOVING ON: THE TEETER-TOTTER PRINCIPLE

165   *We get to that zone of optimal development* . . . The "zone of optimization," in which you are neither overcompetent nor overchallenged but are at the edge of your ability, is to *living a life* what University of Chicago psychologist Mihaly Csikszentmihalyi's "flow" is to *performing a given task*. A person in a state of flow is so absorbed in a particular activity that distractions fade away, and there is no anxiety, just pure enjoyment. For a discussion of flow, I recommend Csikszentmihalyi's *Flow: The psychology of optimal experience* (1990). New York: Harper Perennial Modern Classics.

167   *animal behavior consists of two options* . . . Elliot, A. J. (Ed.). (2008). *Handbook of approach and avoidance motivation.* New York: Taylor and Francis Group.

167   *we show a bias toward the familiar* . . . Litt, A., Reich, T., Maymin, S., & Shiv, B. (2011). Pressure and perverse flights to familiarity. *Psychological Science,* 22(4), 523–531.

168   *participants were given two sets of the same instructions* . . . Song, H., & Schwarz, N. (2008). If it's hard to read, it's hard to do: Processing fluency affects effort prediction and motivation. *Psychological Science,* 19(10), 986–988.

168   *We give more credence to opinions that appear to be widely held* . . . Moons, W., Mackie, D., & Garcia-Marques, T. (2009). The impact of repetition-induced familiarity on agreement with weak and strong arguments. *Journal of Personality and Social Psychology,* 96(1), 32–44.

169   *Imagine you're running late* . . . Litt, A., Reich, T., Maymin, S., & Shiv, B. (2011). Pressure and perverse flights to familiarity. *Psychological Science,* 22(4), 523–531.

169   *When we face known risks* . . . Hsu, M. (2005). Neural systems responding to degrees of uncertainty in human decision-making. *Science,* 310(5754), 1680–1683.

169   *small amount of uncertainty made participants* . . . Gneezy, U., List, J., & Wu, G. (2006). The uncertainty effect: When a risky prospect is valued less than its worst possible outcome. *Quarterly Journal of Economics,* 121(4), 1283–1309.

169   *humans evolved as a social species* . . . Cacioppo, J., & Patrick, W. (2008). *Loneliness: Human nature and the need for social connection.* New York: W. W. Norton and Company.

170   *brain power made us better at judging reliability* . . . Dunbar, R. (2009). The social brain hypothesis and its implications for social evolution. *Annals of Human Biology,* 36(5), 562–572.

171   *people who think poorly of themselves prefer interacting with individuals* . . . Swann, W., & Brooks, M. (2012). Why threats trigger compensatory reactions: The need for coherence and quest for self-verification. *Social Cognition,* 30(6), 758–777.

171   *people with low self-esteem tend to quit their jobs* . . . Schroeder, D. G., Josephs, R. A., & Swann, W. B., Jr. (2006). Foregoing lucrative employment to preserve low self-esteem. Unpublished doctoral dissertation.

172   *mice keep pushing that cocaine lever* . . . Wise, R. A. (2002). Brain reward circuitry: Insights from unsensed incentives. *Behavioral Neuroscience,* 36(2), 229–240.

174   *we're expressing what I call* dead people's goals . . . This idea is adapted from Ogden Lindsley's dead-man test for behavior. Lindsley introduced this rule of thumb in 1965 as a challenge to the metrics that were being used in public schools. He argued that if a dead man could do something (e.g., sit quietly), then it should not be considered a behavior, and that valuable school funds should not be used to

teach children to "play dead." This idea has since found its way into ACT as a litmus test of whether someone is engaging in inflexible, avoidant behaviors. Lindsley, O. (1991). From technical jargon to plain English for application. *Journal of Applied Behavior Analysis, 24*(3), 449–458.

174 *if you do what you've always done* . . . This is attributed variously to Mark Twain, Henry Ford, the motivational speaker Tony Robbins, and the rapper Kendrick Lamar.

175 *Pierre de Fermat was a distinguished judge* . . . Singh, S. (1997). *Fermat's last theorem.* London: Fourth Estate.

175 *Andrew Wiles stumbled on the problem* . . . *Nova* (2000, November 1). Andrew Wiles on solving Fermat. http://www.pbs.org/wgbh/nova/physics/andrew -wiles-fermat.html.

176 *what made an average telegrapher into a great one* . . . Bryan, W., & Harter, N. (1897). Studies in the physiology and psychology of the telegraphic language. *Psychological Review, 4*(1), 27–53.

178 *Malcolm Gladwell popularized the idea* . . . Gladwell, M. (2008). *Outliers: Why some people succeed and some don't.* New York: Little Brown and Company.

178 *The consensus among psychologists and learning specialists* . . . The notion that you'll become an expert with the investment of only ten thousand hours (also known as the "10,000-hour rule") has been widely criticized. For a discussion, see Goleman, D. (2015), *Focus: The hidden driver of excellence.* New York: HarperCollins. Also see Macnamara, B., Hambrick, D., & Oswald, F. (2014). Deliberate practice and performance in music, games, sports, education, and professions: A meta-analysis. *Psychological Science, 25*(8), 1608–1618.

178 *Quality investment requires "effortful learning"* . . . Shors, T. (2014). The adult brain makes new neurons, and effortful learning keeps them alive. *Current Directions in Psychological Science, 23*(5), 311–318.

180 *chronic stress can wreak havoc* . . . Cohen, S., Janicki-Deverts, D., Doyle, W. J., Miller, G. E., Frank, E., Rabin, B. S., & Turner, R. B. (2012, April 2). Chronic stress, glucocorticoid receptor resistance, inflammation, and disease risk. *Proceedings of the National Academy of Sciences, 109*(16), 5995–5999.

181 *Choose What Is Workable* . . . Workability is a key concept in ACT. An action that is workable is leading you closer to the life that you want. Hayes, S. C., Luoma, J. B., Bond, F. W., Masuda, A., & Lillis, J. (2006). Acceptance and commitment therapy: Model, processes, and outcomes. *Behaviour Research and Therapy, 44*(1), 1–25.

182 *Grit embodies—but is not the same as* . . . Duckworth, A., Peterson, C., Matthews, M., & Kelly, D. (2007). Grit: Perseverance and passion for long-term goals. *Journal of Personality and Social Psychology, 92*(6), 1087–1101; Duckworth, A., & Gross, J. (2014). Self-control and grit: Related but separable determinants of success. *Current Directions in Psychological Science, 23*(5), 319–325.

183 *Passion that becomes an obsession* . . . Vallerand, R. (2012). The role of passion in sustainable psychological well-being. *Psychology of Well-Being: Theory, Research and Practice, 2,* 1.

184 *"to go through with his mission"* . . . Arkin, D., & Ortiz, E. (2015, June 19). Dylann Roof "almost didn't go through" with Charleston church shooting. NBC News. http://www.nbcnews.com/storyline/charleston-church-shooting/dylann-roof -almost-didnt-go-through-charleston-church-shooting-n378341.

186 *Stephen J. Dubner compares two things* . . . Dubner, S. J. (2011, September 30). The upside of quitting. http://freakonomics.com/2011/09/30/new-freakonomics -radio-podcast-the-upside-of-quitting.

CHAPTER 9—EMOTIONAL AGILITY AT WORK

197 *humans are biased about their own objectivity* . . . Pronin, E. (2009). The introspection illusion. In Mark P. Zanna (Ed.), *Advances in experimental social psychology,* 41 (pp. 1–67). Burlington, VT: Academic Press.

197 *participants* . . . *were asked to consider a male candidate* . . . *and a female candidate* . . . Uhlmann, E. L., & Cohen, G. L. (2005). Constructed criteria: Redefining merit to justify discrimination. *Psychological Science,* 16(6), 474–480.

198 *Another experiment asked subjects to place bets* . . . Langer, E. (1982). The illusion of control. In D. Kahneman, P. Slovic, and A. Tversky (Eds.), *Judgment under uncertainty: Heuristics and biases.* Cambridge, UK: Cambridge University Press.

198 *In an article for* Harvard Business Review, *I wrote* . . . David, S. (2012, June 25). The biases you don't know you have. *Harvard Business Review.*

198 *known as correspondence bias* . . . This phenomenon, called *correspondence bias* or *fundamental attribution error,* was first described in 1967 by social psychologists Ned Jones and Victor Harris. Jones, E., & Harris, V. (1967). The attribution of attitudes. *Journal of Experimental Social Psychology,* 3(1), 1–24.

199 *Harvard psychologist Daniel Gilbert assigns four root causes* . . . Gilbert, D. T., & Malone, P. S. (1995). The correspondence bias. *Psychological Bulletin,* 117(1), 21–38.

200 *Elaine Bromiley went to the hospital for a minor operation* . . . The case of Elaine Bromiley is well described in Leslie, I. (2014, June 4). How mistakes can save lives: One man's mission to revolutionise the NHS. *New Statesman*; Bromiley, M. The case of Elaine Bromiley. Also see: http://www.chfg.org/wp-content /uploads/2010/11/ElaineBromileyAnonymousReport.pdf

204 *nurses were asked to keep a daily log* . . . Totterdell, P., Kellett, S., Teuchmann, K., & Briner, R. B. (1998). Evidence of mood linkage in work group. *Journal of Personality and Social Psychology,* 74(6), 1504–1515.

204 *Another study suggests that even just* seeing . . . Engert, V., Plessow, F., Miller, R., Kirschbaum, C., & Singer, T. (2014, July). Cortisol increase in empathic stress is modulated by social closeness and observation modality. *Psychoneuroendocrinology,* 45, 192–201.

204 *while stress can be a killer* . . . Keller, A., Litzelman, K., Wisk, L., Maddox, T., Cheng, E., Creswell, P., & Witt, W. (2011). Does the perception that stress affects health matter? The association with health and mortality. *Health Psychology,* 31(5), 677–684.

206 *Just a short train ride south of Vienna* . . . Jahoda, M., Lazarsfeld, P. F., & Zeisel, H. (1974). *Marienthal: The sociography of an unemployed community.* Piscataway, NJ: Transaction Publishers.

207 *retired workers are at risk of accelerated cognitive decline* . . . Rohwedder, S., & Willis, R. J. (2010). Mental retirement. *Journal of Economic Perspectives,* 24(1), 119–38.

209 *one research study sought out hotel employees* . . . Krannitz, M. A., Grandey, A. A., Liu, S., & Almeida, D. A. (2015). Surface acting at work and marital discontent: Anxiety and exhaustion spillover mechanisms. *Journal of Occupational Health Psychology,* 20(3), 314–325.

210 *In an Israeli study, radiologists* . . . Turner, Y. N., & Hadas-Halpern, I. The effects of including a patient's photograph to the radiographic examination. Presented December 3, 2008, as part of the Radiological Society of North America SSM12—ISP: Health Services, Policy, and Research.

211 *Tweaking your job, also known as* job crafting . . . Wrzesniewski, A., Boluglio, N., Dutton, J., & Berg, J. (2012). Job crafting and cultivating positive meaning and identity in work. In A. Bakker (Ed.), *Advances in positive organizational psychology*. London: Emerald.

CHAPTER 10—RAISING EMOTIONALLY AGILE CHILDREN

218 *our collective focus on self-esteem has expanded* . . . Bronson, P. (2007, August 3). How not to talk to your kids. *New York Magazine.*

218 *it assumes a static world, when, according to projections* . . . Davidson, C. N. (2012). *Now you see it: How technology and brain science will transform schools and business for the 21st century.* New York: Penguin.

218 *In her book* How to Raise an Adult . . . Lythcott-Haims, J. (2015). *How to raise an adult.* New York: Henry Holt.

219 *leads to* contingent self-esteem . . . Deci, E. L., & Ryan, R. M. (1995). Human autonomy: The basis for true self-esteem. In M. H. Kernis (Ed.), *Efficacy, agency, and self-esteem* (pp. 31–49). New York: Plenum Press.

224 *studies that document the value of helping kids learn the skills* . . . Snyder, J., Low, S., Bullard, L., Schreperman, L., Wachlarowicz, M., Marvin, C., & Reed, A. (2012). Effective parenting practices: Social interaction learning theory and the role of emotion coaching and mindfulness. In Robert E. Larzelere, Amanda Sheffield Morris, & Amanda W. Harrist (Eds.), *Authoritative parenting: Synthesizing nurturance and discipline for optimal child development.* Washington, D.C.: American Psychological Association; Taylor, Z., Eisenberg, N., Spinrad, T., Eggum, N., & Sulik, M. (2013). The relations of ego-resiliency and emotion socialization to the development of empathy and prosocial behavior across early childhood. *Emotion,* 13(5), 822–831; Katz, L., Maliken, A., & Stettler, N. (2012). Parental meta-emotion philosophy: A review of research and theoretical framework. *Child Development Perspectives,* 6(4), 417–422. Eisenberg, N., Smith, C., & Spinrad, T. L. (2011). Effortful control: Relations with emotion regulation, adjustment, and socialization in childhood. In R. F. Baumeister & K. D. Vohs (Eds.), *Handbook of self-regulation: Research, theory, and applications* (2nd ed.) (pp. 263–283). New York: Guilford Press.

227 *what psychologists call* secure attachment . . . John Bowlby described children's fundamental need to trust their caregivers and to feel seen, accepted, and responded to. He proposed that based on these interactions, children form working models—mental templates—of relationships and the world that have lifelong implications. One of Bowlby's colleagues, developmental psychologist Mary Ainsworth, developed a classification system to describe the quality of a child's relationship with a caregiver. A child who is securely attached has the expectation that he can explore freely and that his caregiver will be responsive and emotionally available when needed. Bowlby, J. (1999). *Attachment* (2nd ed.), *Attachment and Loss* (Vol. 1). New York: Basic Books; Ainsworth, M., Blehar, M., Waters, E., & Wall, S. (1978). *Patterns of attachment.* Hillsdale, NJ: Erlbaum; Ainsworth, M.D.S., & Bowlby, J. (1991). An ethological approach to personality development. *American Psychologist,* 46(4), 331–341.

229 *Autonomy means self-governance* . . . Ryan, R., & Deci, E. (2006). Self-regulation and the problem of human autonomy: Does psychology need choice, self-determination, and will? *Journal of Personality,* 74(6), 1557–1586; Petegem, S., Beyers, W., Vansteenkiste, M., & Soenens, B. (2012). On the association between

adolescent autonomy and psychosocial functioning: Examining decisional independence from a self-determination theory perspective. *Developmental Psychology*, 48(1), 76–88.

230 *people taught to act in the expectation of extrinsic rewards* . . . Kasser, T. (2002). *The high price of materialism*. Cambridge, MA: MIT Press.

232 *researchers introduced three- and four-year-olds to a "sad" puppet* . . . Chernyak, N., & Kushnir, T. (2013). Giving preschoolers choice increases sharing behavior. *Psychological Science*, 24(10), 1971–1979.

232 *teenagers were asked about their parents' treatment* . . . Bureau, J., & Mageau, G. (2014). Parental autonomy support and honesty: The mediating role of identification with the honesty value and perceived costs and benefits of honesty. *Journal of Adolescence*, 37(3), 225–236.

238 *her father said in a speech shortly before Malala won the Nobel Peace Prize* . . . https://www.ted.com/talks/ziauddin_yousafzai_my_daughter_malala?language =en#t-658349.

CHAPTER 11—CONCLUSION: BECOMING REAL

239 *The children's classic* . . . Williams, M. (1991). *The velveteen rabbit* (1st ed. 1922). Garden City, NY: Doubleday.